Cinematic Intermediality

Edinburgh Studies in Film and Intermediality

Series editors: Martine Beugnet and Kriss Ravetto
Founding editor: John Orr

A series of scholarly research intended to challenge and expand on the various approaches to film studies, bringing together film theory and film aesthetics with the emerging intermedial aspects of the field. The volumes combine critical theoretical interventions with a consideration of specific contexts, aesthetic qualities, and a strong sense of the medium's ability to appropriate current technological developments in its practice and form as well as in its distribution.

Advisory board
Duncan Petrie (University of Auckland)
John Caughie (University of Glasgow)
Dina Iordanova (University of St Andrews)
Elizabeth Ezra (University of Stirling)
Gina Marchetti (University of Hong Kong)
Jolyon Mitchell (University of Edinburgh)
Judith Mayne (The Ohio State University)
Dominique Bluher (Harvard University)

Titles in the series include:

Romantics and Modernists in British Cinema
John Orr

Framing Pictures: Film and the Visual Arts
Steven Jacobs

The Sense of Film Narration
Ian Garwood

The Feel-Bad Film
Nikolaj Lübecker

American Independent Cinema: Rites of Passage and the Crisis Image
Anna Backman Rogers

The Incurable-Image: Curating Post-Mexican Film and Media Arts
Tarek Elhaik

Screen Presence: Cinema Culture and the Art of Warhol, Rauschenberg, Hatoum and Gordon
Stephen Monteiro

Indefinite Visions: Cinema and the Attractions of Uncertainty
Martine Beugnet, Allan Cameron and Arild Fetveit (eds)

Screening Statues: Sculpture and Cinema
Steven Jacobs, Susan Felleman, Vito Adriaensens and Lisa Colpaert

Drawn From Life: Issues and Themes in Animated Documentary Cinema
Jonathan Murray and Nea Ehrlich (eds)

Intermedial Dialogues: The French New Wave and the Other Arts
Marion Schmid

The Museum as a Cinematic Space: The Display of Moving Images in Exhibitions
Elisa Mandelli

Theatre Through the Camera Eye: The Poetics of an Intermedial Encounter
Laura Sava

Caught In-Between: Intermediality in Contemporary Eastern Europe and Russian Cinema
Ágnes Pethő

No Power Without an Image: Icons Between Photography and Film
Libby Saxton

Cinematic Intermediality: Theory and Practice
Kim Knowles and Marion Schmid (eds)

edinburghuniversitypress.com/series/esif

Cinematic Intermediality
Theory and Practice

Edited by Kim Knowles and Marion Schmid

EDINBURGH
University Press

Edinburgh University Press is one of the leading university presses in the UK. We publish academic books and journals in our selected subject areas across the humanities and social sciences, combining cutting-edge scholarship with high editorial and production values to produce academic works of lasting importance. For more information visit our website: edinburghuniversitypress.com

© editorial matter and organisation Kim Knowles and Marion Schmid, 2021, 2022
© the chapters their several authors, 2021, 2022

Edinburgh University Press Ltd
The Tun – Holyrood Road
12 (2f) Jackson's Entry
Edinburgh EH8 8PJ

First published in hardback by Edinburgh University Press 2021

Typeset in Garamond MT Pro by
Servis Filmsetting Ltd, Stockport, Cheshire

A CIP record for this book is available from the British Library

ISBN 978 1 4744 4634 1 (hardback)
ISBN 978 1 4744 4635 8 (paperback)
ISBN 978 1 4744 4636 5 (webready PDF)
ISBN 978 1 4744 4637 2 (epub)

The right of the contributors to be identified as authors of this work has been asserted in accordance with the Copyright, Designs and Patents Act 1988 and the Copyright and Related Rights Regulations 2003 (SI No. 2498).

Contents

List of Figures	vii
Acknowledgements	ix
The Contributors	x
Introduction *Kim Knowles and Marion Schmid*	1

Part 1   Mapping the Interzone

1 Film and Performance: Intermedial Intersections   11
   Stephen Barber

2 Carving Cameras: Antonioni's *Lo Sguardo di Michelangelo*   23
   Steven Jacobs

3 The Photo-filmic and the Post-human: Picturesque Landscapes
   at the Peripheries of Global Cinema   38
   Ágnes Pethő

4 Dream Screen: On Cinema and Painting, Blur and Absorption   52
   Martine Beugnet

Part 2   The Intermedial Avant-gardes

5 From the Periphery to the Interstices: Avant-garde Film,
   Medium Specificity and Intermediality, 1970–2015   73
   Christopher Townsend

6 The 'Artist as Filmmaker': Modernisms, Schisms,
   Misunderstandings   88
   Lucy Reynolds

7 The Artwork/Statement as Intermedial Nexus: Paul Sharits's
   N:O:T:H:I:N:G   105
   Barnaby Dicker

Part 3 Technology, Apparatus, Affect

8 Intermediality and the Origins of Cinema   121
Boris Wiseman

9 Cinematography's Blind Spots: Artistic Exploitations of the Film Frame   136
Gabriele Jutz

10 Filming and Feeling between the Arts: Pascale Breton, *Suite armoricaine* and Eugène Green, *Le Fils de Joseph*   150
Marion Schmid

Part 4 Intermedial Creation

11 What Does a Dance Filmmaker See?   167
Adam Roberts

12 Performance, Moving Image, Installation: The Making of *Body of War* and *Faith*   176
Isabel Rocamora

13 Muybridge's Disobedient Horses: *Non-stop Stop-motion*   185
Anna Vasof

14 A Dialogue with Claude Cahun: Between Writing, Photography and Film in *Magic Mirror* and *Confessions to the Mirror*   194
Sarah Pucill

Index   202

Figures

2.1	*Lo Sguardo di Michelangelo* (Michelangelo Antonioni, 2004)	23
2.2	*Lo Sguardo di Michelangelo* (Michelangelo Antonioni, 2004)	28
2.3	*Lo Sguardo di Michelangelo* (Michelangelo Antonioni, 2004)	31
3.1	*Nabat* (Elchin Musaoglu, 2014)	43
3.2	*Timbuktu* (Abderrahmane Sissako, 2014)	45
3.3	*Test* (Alexander Kott, 2014)	46
3.4	*Timbuktu* (Abderrahmane Sissako, 2014)	49
4.1	*Cœur fidèle* (Jean Epstein, 1932)	58
4.2	*Sauve qui peut (la vie)* (Jean-Luc Godard, 1980)	61
4.3	*La Captive* (Chantal Akerman, 2000)	65
7.1	Johannes Vermeer (1632–75), *A Young Woman Standing at a Virginal*	104
8.1	'Mechanical hammer set in motion by two wheels'. Patented 1833 (made in 1922)	130
9.1	*R40 (Précis de décomposition – Masque)* (Éric Rondepierre, 1993–5)	141
9.2	*Und ich blieb stehen. (Thames, London)* (Susanne Miggitsch, 2017)	142
9.3	*Motion Picture (La Sortie des ouvriers de l'usine Lumière à Lyon)* (Peter Tscherkassky, 1984/2008)	144
10.1	*Suite armoricaine* (Pascale Breton, 2016)	154
10.2	*Suite armoricaine* (Pascale Breton, 2016)	155
10.3	*Le Fils de Joseph* (Eugène Green, 2016)	160
11.1	*Hands* (Adam Roberts, 1995)	168
11.2	*blue/yellow* (Adam Roberts, 1995)	173
11.3	*Pieces of the Quiet Dance* (Adam Roberts, 2006)	174
12.1	Isabel Rocamora in 'Attunement', urban performance intervention	177
12.2	*Body of War* (Isabel Rocamora, 2010)	180
12.3	Exhibition view of *Faith* (Isabel Rocamora, 2015)	183
13.1	*Banknotes* (Anna Vasof, 2018)	187
13.2	*Machine* (Anna Vasof, 2015)	189
14.1	*Magic Mirror* (Sarah Pucill, 2013)	198

14.2 *Magic Mirror* (Sarah Pucill, 2013) 199
14.3 *Confessions to the Mirror* (Sarah Pucill, 2016) 200

Acknowledgements

This book grew out of both friendship and a shared intellectual interest in the fundamentally hybrid nature of cinematic expression. We were both working on projects that explored aspects of cinematic intermediality and felt the need to expand this outwards and connect with other scholars in the field. The Arts and Humanities Research Council (AHRC) provided generous support through their Research Networking Scheme, which allowed us to bring together an international group of researchers whose work approaches intermediality from diverse perspectives. Through four thought-provoking workshops and associated public events, we interrogated different facets of intermediality, paying special attention to intermedial practice in the avant-garde and its legacy in the mainstream, the role of technology in the hybridisation of art forms and media archaeology. We wish to thank everyone who took part in and facilitated those workshops, particularly the host universities: the Department of Theatre, Film and Television at Aberystwyth University, the Department of European Languages and Cultures at the University of Edinburgh, Corpus Christi College, University of Cambridge, and the Department of Media Theory at the University of Applied Arts Vienna. Thank you also to our project partners, with whom we collaborated on the public events: Aberystwyth Arts Centre, LUX Centre for Moving Image and Filmhouse Cinema in Edinburgh. Special thanks to Sarah Pucill, Adam Roberts, Isabel Rocamora, Gebhard Sengmüller, Tanya Syed and Anna Vasof for their vibrant contributions to the screenings and artist talks. We are grateful to Gillian Leslie and Richard Strachan at Edinburgh University Press and the anonymous peer reviewer for supporting us through the publication process.

The Contributors

Stephen Barber is Professor of Art History at Kingston University's Kingston School of Art, and a Fellow of the Freie Universität Berlin. His recent monographs include *The Projectionists: Eadweard Muybridge and the Future Projections of the Moving Image* (2020), *Film's Ghosts: Tatsumi Hijikata's Butoh and the Transmutation of 1960s Japan* (2019) and *Berlin Bodies: Anatomising the Streets of the City* (2018). He is currently working on a new book about film and wastelands.

Martine Beugnet is Professor at the Université de Paris, affiliated to the Laboratoire de Recherche sur les Cultures Anglophones (LARCA) and Centre National de la Recherche Scientifique (CNRS). Her books include *Claire Denis* (2004), *Proust at the Movies* (2005, with Marion Schmid), *Cinema and Sensation: French Film and the Art of Transgression* (2012) and *L'Attrait du flou* (2017), on the history and aesthetics of blur. She co-edited the volume of collected essays *Indefinite Visions: Cinema and the Attractions of Uncertainty* with Allan Cameron and Arild Fetveit (2017). Her new monograph, *Le Cinéma et ses doubles: L'Image de film à l'ère du foundfootage numérisé et des écrans de poche* is forthcoming.

Barnaby Dicker is a Visiting Research Fellow at King's College, London, and sits on the editorial board of *Animation: An Interdisciplinary Journal*. His research revolves around conceptual and material innovations in and through graphic technologies and arts, including cinematography and photography, with particular emphasis on avant-garde practices. This has led to work on topics such as animation, proto-cinematography, experimental film, graphic reproduction technologies, comic strips, paleoart and the historiography of aesthetic theories and practices of abstraction.

Steven Jacobs is an art historian specialised in the interactions between film, the visual arts and architecture. His publications include *The Wrong House: The Architecture of Alfred Hitchcock* (2007), *Framing Pictures: Film and the Visual Arts* (2011), *The Dark Galleries: A Museum Guide to Painted Portraits in Film Noir* (2013), *Screening Statues: Cinema and Sculpture* (2017), *The City Symphony*

Phenomenon: Cinema, Art, and Urban Modernity Between the Wars (2018) and *Art in the Cinema: The Mid-Century Art Documentary* (2020). He teaches at Ghent University and the University of Antwerp, Belgium.

Gabriele Jutz is Professor of Film and Media Studies at the University of Applied Arts Vienna and Head of the Department. She has published numerous articles on the history, theory and aesthetics of film – in particular on the cinematic avant-garde, expanded cinema, experimental film sound, art and the moving image and experimental animation. Her books include *Cinéma brut. Eine alternative Genealogie der Filmavantgarde* (2010); *RESET THE APPARATUS! A Survey of the Photographic and the Filmic in Contemporary Art* (co-editors Edgar Lissel and Nina Jukić, 2019); and *Animating Truth(s): The Films of Maria Lassnig and Their Context* (2019).

Kim Knowles lectures in Alternative and Experimental Film at Aberystwyth University in Wales and curates the Black Box experimental strand at the Edinburgh International Film Festival. She has published widely on historical and contemporary forms of avant-garde film, as well as intersections with poetry, photography, architecture and dance. She is the author of two books – *A Cinematic Artist: The Films of Man Ray* (2012) and *Experimental Film and Photochemical Practices* (2020). She co-edits the Palgrave Series in Experimental Film and Artists' Moving Image with Jonathan Walley.

Ágnes Pethő is Professor of Film Studies at the Sapientia Hungarian University of Transylvania in Cluj-Napoca (Romania). She has published extensively on cinematic intermediality, the relationship between film and the visual arts, and on the aesthetic of the *tableau vivant*. She is the author of *Cinema and Intermediality: The Passion for the In-Between* (2011). Her edited books include *Words and Images on the Screen: Language, Literature, Moving Pictures* (2008), *Film in the Post-Media Age* (2012), *The Cinema of Sensations* (2015) and *Caught In-Between: Intermediality in Contemporary Eastern European and Russian Cinema* (2020).

Sarah Pucill has, for three decades, been making 16 mm experimental films that have been shown and won awards at festivals and in museums, galleries and cinemas internationally. Both her recent films, *Confessions to the Mirror* (68 min, 2016) and *Magic Mirror* (75 min, 2013), screened at international venues, including Tate Modern, London Film Festival, Alchemy Moving Image Festival, Institute of Contemporary Arts (ICA), National Portrait Gallery and White Cube Bermondsey, and were staged in museum galleries, including Cobra Museum Gallery, Netherlands (2021), an installation at Ottawa Art

Gallery, Canada (2020), and Nunnery Gallery, London. She lives in London and is a Reader at the University of Westminster.

Lucy Reynolds has lectured and published extensively. Her research focuses on questions of the moving image, feminism, political space and collective practice. She co-ordinates the PhD programme for the Centre for Research in Education, Art and Media (CREAM) at the University of Westminster. As an artist, her ongoing sound work *A Feminist Chorus* has been heard at the Glasgow International Festival, the Wysing Arts Centre, the Showroom and the Grand Action cinema, Paris. She is editor of the anthology *Women Artists, Feminism and the Moving Image*, and co-editor of the *Moving Image Review and Art Journal* (MIRAJ).

Adam Roberts has made prize-winning films, notably with dancers Jonathan Burrows and Sylvie Guillem. He co-founded the film collective *À Nos Amours* with Joanna Hogg to curate overlooked or important moving image work that might not easily find an audience. A retrospective of films by Chantal Akerman and an exhibition of her installation work resulted between 2013 and 2015. A book, *The Chantal Akerman Retrospective Handbook*, was published in 2019. Adam Roberts has recently published *Lamentation. In the Stuart Croft Archive* (2020) and is working on a new film.

Isabel Rocamora is an artist-filmmaker and scholar. Her multi-awarded moving image and performance works have been curated in museums, galleries and festivals worldwide, including the Victoria and Albert Museum, London; CCC Palazzo Strozzi, Florence; National Museum of Photography, Copenhagen; Herzliya Museum of Contemporary Art, Israel; Austrian Cultural Forum, New York; and Koffler Gallery, Toronto. Her AHRC-funded PhD thesis (Edinburgh University, 2019) examines the existential impact of aesthetic experimentation in modernist and contemporary cinema in dialogue with Martin Heidegger's phenomenology and metaphysics. Isabel has taught film extensively, including at the University of Edinburgh. She is a Visiting Scholar at Pompeu Fabra University.

Marion Schmid is Professor of French Literature and Film at the University of Edinburgh. She has published extensively on the interactions between literature, film and the visual arts and on modern French literature. Her books include *Processes of Literary Creation: Flaubert and Proust* (1998), *Proust at the Movies* (2005, with Martine Beugnet), *Proust dans la décadence* (2008), *Chantal Akerman* (2010), *Intermedial Dialogues: The French New Wave and the Other Arts* (2019) and the co-edited collection of essays *Chantal Akerman: Afterlives* (2019, with Emma Wilson). She co-edits the Peter Lang series *European Connections: Studies in Comparative Literature, Intermediality and Aesthetics* with Hugues Azérad.

Christopher Townsend is Professor of the history of avant-garde film in the Department of Media Arts, Royal Holloway, University of London. Recent publications have concentrated on the avant-garde's use and imagination of media from the 1910s to the 1930s, including studies of Francis Picabia, Fernand Léger and Duncan Grant. He is presently completing a book on the relationship of the POOL Group of modernist filmmakers and critics to the mainstream media industry. He is a Senior Research Fellow of the Henry Moore Institute, and recipient of the H.D. Fellowship in American Literature from the Beinecke Library, Yale University, 2019.

Anna Vasof is an architect and media artist. Born in 1985, she studied architecture at the University of Thessaly (2010) in Greece and transmedia art (2014) at the University of Applied Arts in Vienna. Since 2004, her videos and short movies have been presented in several festivals, some of them winning distinctions. She is currently working on her PhD thesis about an animation technique that she is developing with the title *Non Stop Stop Motion*, and at the same time working on designing and building innovative mechanisms for producing critical and narrative videos, actions and installations.

Boris Wiseman is a Visiting Associate Professor at the University of Copenhagen and Director of the Fondation Deutsch de la Meurthe, Cité Internationale Universitaire de Paris. He has written about French anthropology, as viewed in its relationship to contemporary philosophy, especially aesthetic thought, and to French literature in general. Past publications include *Lévi-Strauss, Anthropology and Aesthetics* (2007). He is currently finalising a monograph on Degas and cinema. He has coordinated an eye-tracking experiment at the Sainsbury's Centre for Visual Arts on dancers' embodied viewing of sculpture (see *The Senses and Society*, vol. 14 (3), 2019) and has an abiding interest in methods of interdisciplinary collaboration.

Introduction
Kim Knowles and Marion Schmid

Since at least the turn of the millennium, notions of film as a medium and cinema as an institution have undergone significant transformation. The shift from film to digital media, now a familiar historical narrative, has given rise to a moving image culture no longer bound to traditional sites of encounter and modes of address but taking on fluid identities in new contexts. Circulating widely in the wake of the digital revolution, the 'death of cinema' discourse describes the latest in a series of 'deaths', that, as André Gaudreault and Philippe Marion argue, have come to define a modern medium in a continual state of flux and transformation. Nonetheless, '[w]hat has incontestably changed today', in their view, 'is that cinema no longer has exclusive claim on our heart and is having a lot of trouble getting over the fact.'[1] In an era of media convergence, the association of the seventh art with what Raymond Bellour refers to as 'the lived, more or less collective experience of a film projected in a cinema, in the dark, according to an unalterably precise screening procedure' is now only one of the many ways that audiences see, feel and think the moving image.[2] The wealth of scholarly attention paid in recent years to redefining the contours of film as an art form and recasting the theoretical paradigms employed to understand it point to a form of self-searching that has several historical parallels. For D. N. Rodowick, 'there has never been a general consensus concerning the answer to the question "What is cinema?" And for this reason the evolving thought on cinema in the twentieth century has persisted in a continual state of identity crisis.'[3]

For if 'convergence culture' – to quote the title of the influential book by new media theorist Henry Jenkins – increasingly describes the contemporary media landscape, one could equally argue that the medium of film has always, to some extent, been defined by its intersection with other art forms and technologies.[4] Paradoxically, the search for specificity has frequently folded the other arts into ideas of what constitutes and characterises cinematic expression, from visual music and film poetry to kinetic painting and photography in motion. While the early film theorists of the 1910s and 1920s – Germaine

Dulac, Jean Epstein and Ricciotto Canudo, for example – fought for film to be taken seriously as an art form through analogies with these more established forms of expression, the pioneering works of avant-garde cinema were made primarily by artists working in other media. Man Ray, Fernand Léger, Marcel Duchamp, Hans Richter, Walter Ruttmann, Viking Eggeling and László Moholy-Nagy invigorated film language with formal ideas derived from painting, photography and sculpture, rejecting the reliance on narrative causality and characterisation that had come to dominate an art form in the grasp of commercial concerns. The element of time inherent in the film medium allowed Man Ray to set his photographic compositions in motion and extend his interest in light and shadow, whilst for Richter, Eggeling and Ruttmann it provided the means to explore the temporal evolution and rhythmic relations of simple forms on a flat plane.

The ontology of film, it seems, is intricately bound up with other art forms, and the pursuit of its essence inevitably brings us back to its fundamentally hybrid nature. It is hardly coincidental, then, that the wave of scholarship devoted to redefining film studies in this most intensive period of self-searching should be accompanied by a corresponding 'intermedial turn'. Although reflections on creative cross-fertilisation have been present throughout the history of film – from André Bazin's 1952 article 'For an Impure Cinema: In Defence of Adaptation' to the numerous studies of literary adaptation – intermediality as a term and as a key critical paradigm has gained traction from the late 1990s onwards.[5] In her extensive and thought-provoking study, Ágnes Pethő argues that intermediality has the potential for 'becoming one of the major theoretical issues of contemporary thinking about cinema'.[6] Rather than simply focusing on artistic hybridity as an object of analysis, contemporary scholars have uncovered the radical theoretical implications of its application as a method, opening up, in the process, new ways of understanding cinematic expression in all its hybrid complexity. This is cogently articulated by Lúcia Nagib and Anne Jerslev in the introduction to their collection of essays *Impure Cinema: Intermedial and Intercultural Approaches to Film*:

> By calling impure cinema a method rather than an object, we are proposing not to betray or thwart Bazin's original purpose but, on the contrary, to bring to the fore his dramatic call for a new emancipated criticism, capable of understanding cinema beyond the constraints of the medium's specificity.[7]

But if the concept of 'impure cinema' derives from Bazin, modern theories of cinematic intermediality express an interest in the creative articulation of 'in-betweenness', a concept first developed by Raymond Bellour in a series of essays exploring the intersections between film and other art forms.[8] Riding the edges and in-betweens of different artistic media can be a way of exploring liminal identities and states, eliciting complex affective responses that appeal to the physical body of the spectator. Pethő's *Cinema and Intermediality: The Passion for the In-Between* remains the most detailed theorisation of intermediality from this perspective, offering valuable insights into how artistic overlaps draw out the inherently multi-sensory nature of the film medium. Drawing on the phenomenological tradition, Pethő states: '"Sensing" the intermediality of film is therefore grounded in the (inter)sensuality of cinema itself, in the experience of the viewer being aroused simultaneously on different levels of consciousness and perception.'[9] This approach highlights the difficulty in consciously articulating artistic boundary crossings in the viewing process, arguing that the merging of media calls upon the body to make 'sense' of these often very tangible layers. Pethő's formulation of in-betweenness benefits from its extensive theoretical scope and provides a source of inspiration for a number of chapters in this volume.

Emerging from the International Research Network 'Film and the Other Arts: Intermediality, Creativity, Medium Specificity', funded by the Arts and Humanities Research Council (2015–17), the present collection of essays develops ideas first explored in a series of workshops that brought together researchers from a range of Humanities disciplines (Film and Media Studies, History of Art, Theatre and Performance, Modern Languages), as well as creative practitioners. Fostering dialogue between theory and practice, the network examined the manifold ways in which the moving image is revitalised by artistic crossovers and fusions, with a particular emphasis on the permeability between cinema and the other arts in avant-garde and experimental practice and its legacy in mainstream film. Veering away from the relationship between literature and film, which has tended to dominate discussions of cinematic intermediality, our aim was to explore how intermedial practice, both historical and contemporary, can be understood either outside a narrative context or in relation to works that problematise narrative in some way. Central to this examination was the consideration of process – how and why artists work with specific materials, technologies and aesthetic approaches – as well as a plural interpretation of intermediality as a theory, method and intersensual approach.

Pursuing these reflections, this volume investigates a broad range of films – from cinema's beginnings to the digital era, including both mainstream and experimental practice, world cinema and peripheral cinemas – with a view to offering a more comprehensive understanding of the role of intermediality in moving image creation. Giving voice to both theorists and cinema practitioners, we try to emphasise the material gesture as much as the visual texture, and the chapters shift variously between the haptic image on the screen and the lived experience of making and thinking between one art form and another. From the spaces of creation to the sites of artistic encounter, our attention also turns at times to works made not only for the cinema but also for the gallery space, bringing us back to the problematisation of those once-familiar terms 'film' and 'cinema'. If intermediality involves the consideration of sensuous in-betweens, then the liminal space of the gallery and its itinerant visitor surely open up fertile ground for a reassessment of how the spectator of moving image works can, to return to Pethő, be 'aroused simultaneously on different levels'. Bridging the gap between theory and practice, this collection aims to stimulate debate along some recognisable trajectories, whilst at the same time opening up new pathways for thinking about how intermediality, as both a creative method and an interpretative paradigm, might be explored alongside probing questions of what 'cinema' is, has been and can be.

In light of our aim to develop a more varied critical framework for exploring the relationship between cinema and its sibling arts, the book is organised into four thematic parts. The first, 'Mapping the Interzone', maps out cinema's rich encounters with some of its most influential artistic predecessors: performance, sculpture, painting and photography. Our focus here is on the pathways and fusions between cinema and other non-verbal arts, as well as on the theoretical implications of these inter-artistic exchanges. The collection opens with a programmatic piece by Stephen Barber on the long-standing intermedial relations between moving-image culture and performance. Looking at the ways in which film reframes and refashions the experience of the live performance, Barber argues that the concept of intermediality – traditionally associated with the 1960s and 1970s – can, in fact, be traced back to early cinema's roots in performance culture. Spanning more than a hundred years of film history, from Eadweard Muybridge's experiments in sequential photography to the Berlin-based film pioneers Max and Emil Skladanowsky and contemporary Lebanese visual artist Rabih Mroué, the essay explores cinema's enduring preoccupation with and incorporation of performance. Shifting our attention to the often overlooked intersection between cinema and sculpture, Steven Jacobs turns to Michelangelo Antonioni's short film *Lo Sguardo di Michelangelo* (*Michelangelo Eye to Eye*, 2004) as a poignant example of filmmakers' endeavours to give visibility to an art which, in all respects, seems diametrically opposed to their own. Reflecting on the differences between the two arts, Jacob foregrounds the ways in which the mobile, immaterial medium of film evokes, but also reconfigures and remediates, the static, tactile materiality of sculpture.

In her essay on the interpenetration between the 'photographic' and the 'cinematic', on the other hand, Ágnes Pethő looks at the photo-filmic qualities inherent in three films at the periphery of world cinema: Abderrahmane

Sissako's *Timbuktu*, Alexander Kott's *Test* and Elchin Musaoglu's *Nabat* (all made in 2014). For Pethő, the recurrent tableau shots, as well as the incorporation of genuine photographs, in these films offer an 'adequate form to unfold a kind of post-human landscape', allowing them to address urgent questions of human violence, destruction and vulnerability. Martine Beugnet, in a wide-reaching essay that takes us from French Impressionist filmmaker and theorist Jean Epstein to our digital era, identifies low definition and blur as intermedial figurations that tend to 'draw the cinema image towards painterly forms'. Connecting the concept of absorption – first developed in the context of painting – to the moving image, she examines the effect of blur on human representation, notably its soliciting of a more empathetic spectatorial involvement and its negotiation of intimacy and distance.

From the intermedial experiments of the historical avant-garde to Fluxus, Pop Art or Structural Film, the avant-garde has been a particularly fertile breeding ground for media encounters. Our second part, 'The Intermedial Avant-gardes', shines a spotlight on the 1960s and 1970s as a moment of heightened intensity for intermedial thought and practice, where questions of medium, method and creativity were being reconsidered and revitalised. In a historiographical piece examining the period from the 1970s to the present day, Christopher Townsend identifies two major tendencies in the study of the avant-garde. Whereas the first extensive scholarly scrutiny of the cinematic avant-garde originated in the visual arts and was conducted by practising filmmakers, he demonstrates, it gradually migrated into the discipline of literary studies. Cautioning against the use of intermediality as 'a tool of academic recuperation and reification', Townsend outlines the benefits and pitfalls of both approaches. Homing in on film artist Annabel Nicolson's seminal 1972 article 'Artist as Filmmaker', Lucy Reynolds pinpoints striking commonalities in the use of the film medium between two movements in 1970s Britain that held themselves apart: conceptual artists and artist filmmakers. With reference to Nicolson's 'film actions' and the film installations of David Dye, as well as to their conceptual counterparts such as Dan Graham and John Hilliard, she redraws the map of the 'wider cultural networks, allegiances and art communities in London and internationally during the early 1970s'. Taking us to the other side of the Atlantic and into structural filmmaking, Barnaby Dicker illuminates the intermedial practice of visual artist Paul Sharits, whose 1968 flicker film *N:O:T:H:I:N:G* and its corresponding 'Notes', published in *Film Culture* the following year, establish a dialogue with Johannes Vermeer's *A Young Woman Standing at a Virginal*. By means of connecting the theoretical notion of 'differential specificity' to the nexus between artwork and statement inherent in *N:O:T:H:I:N:G*, the essay unravels Sharit's 'theoretically and emotionally driven' stop-frame meditation on one of the most iconic paintings by the Dutch master.

To what extent was the invention of cinema the result of technological innovations or, rather, should we understand its emergence as an inherently intermedial phenomenon? How does intermediality alter the filmic apparatus, *dispositif* and conditions of spectatorship? And what role can cinema's sister arts play in the non-verbal expression of affect and thought? These are the guiding questions our contributors have asked themselves in Part 3, 'Technology, Apparatus, Affect'. For Boris Wiseman, the origins of cinema are intimately – indeed, inseparably – linked to intermediality. Whether it be in early camera obscuras, Carlo Ponti's *Megaletoscopio*, designed to view albumin photographs, or the 'speaking photographs' of Georges Demeny's *Phonoscope*, Wiseman argues, 'cinema emerges, here and there, in different forms, including accidental, in-between media'. His remarks on the 'oddly in-between state – neither moving nor entirely still' of moving images before the invention of cinema resonate in Gabriele Jutz's chapter on the aesthetic potential of the film frame as an interstitial entity between photography and cinematography. If Jutz acknowledges the inherently intermedial character of visual practices predating the birth of cinema, her focus here is on the installations and filmic and photographic works of four contemporary visual artists: Gebhard Sengmüller, Peter Tscherkassky, Susanne Miggitsch and Eric Rondepierre. Broadening the discussion to 'migrations' between film and several other arts, including literature, painting and theatre, Marion Schmid identifies intermedial strategies at work in two recent French films revolving around questions of personal growth and transmission, Pascale Breton's *Suite armoricaine* and Eugène Green's *Le Fils de Joseph* [*The Son of Joseph*]. With special reference to Proust, Georges de La Tour and Caravaggio, she argues for the significance of the other arts in the two films as a way of 'making "sensible" central human concerns without recourse to language'.

The final part of the book, 'Intermedial Creation', gives voice to four award-winning moving image artists, who draw on and reconfigure cinema's sister arts in their filmic practice. We are delighted to showcase a selection of their works at the crossroads between film, dance, performance and photography, and to offer them a platform to reflect on their creative practice. The section opens with an essay by London-based filmmaker, writer and curator Adam Roberts, who has made a series of films with dancers and choreographers, including Sylvie Guillem and Jonathan Burrows. Meditating on the intimate relationship between the filmmaker and the dancers in movement, Roberts evokes his 'pursuit of the curve or stretch or reach of the body', his 'search of its capacities or its potential', which the filmmaker captures in filmic frames. The expressiveness and fragility of the human body are equally central to the creative practice of British–Spanish artist filmmaker Isabel Rocamora, who pursues her own roots in performance in her films and installations shaped by 'human gesture, place, temporality and presence'. Rocamora foregrounds the humanist concerns behind her films *Body of War* (2010) and *Faith* (2015), two works that draw on the performative nature of combat or ritual to interrogate questions of trauma, human transgression and alterity. In an altogether different register, teeming with irony and mischief, Vienna-based architect and media artist Anna Vasof takes inspiration from and reframes the pre-cinematic experiments of Eadweard Muybridge – evoked previously in Stephen Barber and Boris Wiseman's essays – in her animation work. At the intersection between video, performance and photography, her ongoing project *Non-stop Stop-motion* 'investigates where we can find the essence of cinematic illusion when we look into everyday life and what happens when we use everyday situations, objects, spaces and actions as cinematographic mechanisms'.

The volume closes with an essay by the British artist Sarah Pucill on her creative responses to Surrealist photographer, sculptor and writer Claude Cahun, an avant-garde artist best known for her gender-bending self-portraits. In her films *Magic Mirror* (2013) and *Confessions to the Mirror* (2016), Pucill re-enacts Cahun's photographs in the form of *tableaux vivants*, creating new connections between the French artist's visual and written work and her own creative practice. Pucill's 'dialogues' with an artist engaged in questions that deeply resonate with her own, yet which were initially pursued in a different medium, sharply throw into relief what has concerned us throughout this volume: the manifold, dazzlingly creative ways in which moving image artists – from the origins of cinema to our digital era – have drawn on the other arts to nourish their imaginaries and enrich their artistic language.

Notes

1. André Gaudreault and Philippe Marion, *The End of Cinema? A Medium in Crisis in the Digital Age* (New York: Columbia University Press, 2015), pp. 14–15.
2. Raymond Bellour, 'The cinema spectator: A special memory', in Gertrude Koch, Volker Pantenberg and Simon Rothöhler (eds), *Screen Dynamics: Mapping the Borders of Cinema* (Vienna: Austrian Film Museum, 2012), p. 9.
3. D. N. Rodowick, 'An elegy for theory', *October*, 122 (Fall 2007), p. 11.
4. Henry Jenkins, *Convergence Culture: Where Old and New Media Collide* (New York and London: New York University Press, 2006).
5. The original title of Bazin's article, 'Pour un cinéma impur: Défense de l'adaptation', has been translated into English as 'In defense of mixed cinema'; André Bazin, 'In defense of mixed cinema', in *What Is Cinema?*, ed. and trans. by Hugh Gray, 2 vols (London: University of California Press, 1967–71), vol. 1, pp. 53–75.

6. Ágnes Pethő, *Cinema and Intermediality: The Passion for the In-Between* (Newcastle: Cambridge Scholars, 2011), p. 1.
7. Lúcia Nagib and Anne Jerslev (eds), *Impure Cinema: Intermedial and Intercultural Approaches to Film* (London and New York: I. B. Tauris, 2014), p. xxi.
8. Raymond Bellour, *L'Entre-images: Photo, cinéma, vidéo* (Paris: La Différence, 1990).
9. Pethő, *Cinema and Intermediality: The Passion for the In-Between*, p. 69.

Part 1

Mapping the Interzone

CHAPTER 1

Film and Performance: Intermedial Intersections
Stephen Barber

This chapter explores the complex intermedial bindings at the intersection of moving image culture and performance. It looks at some of the ways in which distinctive transformations are undergone by film when it comes to form an amalgam with performance. Film may work to overhaul and reframe the experience and the time and space of live performance events, notably via the incorporation of moving image elements into the space of performance and through spectatorial responses to experimental projection approaches and strategies. Such experiments have been prevalent in recent performance art deploying moving image elements, and the chapter uses the example of a recent work by the Berlin-based Lebanese artist Rabih Mroué to investigate this interrelationship of film and performance. The concept of intermediality is often traced from the 1950s or 1960s, but I argue here that it originates with the first moments of moving image culture, notably in the formative work of Eadweard Muybridge in the 1880s and 1890s, and in the first European public projections of film, often undertaken in performance spaces and with subject matters focused upon performances, in 1895. Although intermediality as an entity is often closely associated with experimental and avant-garde practices of moving image culture, it has experienced moments of exceptional crossover into popular public culture, within institutional frameworks such as the Osaka World Exposition of 1970, when projection experiments focused upon performance were viewed by public audiences of many millions of spectators within distinctive architectural environments of projection.

Experimental moving image culture has often been concerned with intermedial intersections, and the devising of ways to traverse – or else construct hybrids of – art and media forms is integral to the origins of moving image projection, as well as to eras of intensive social and political contestations demanding new visual forms, such as the 1960s and the contemporary era. In many ways, digital media intensify and accelerate those processes of the amalgamation of apparently disparate art forms, rather than overturning or annulling them. The tenacity with which moving image culture has probed performance's manifestations indicates the exceptional persistence that film has demonstrated as a medium illuminating other art forms. The intersection of film and performance could be seen as a distinctive entity in its own right, with very particular, combative dynamics and an accompanying set of demands for its spectators.

Critical and theoretical frameworks and approaches may operate in a range of ways, as exemplified by several recent or influential publications. Approaches may operate by looking specifically at a particular urban or national framework in which experimental film and performance intersected, generating notable corporeal and sensorial spectatorial effects from their experimental conjunction, as in Peter Eckersall's monograph *Performativity and Event in 1960s Japan: City, Body, Memory* (Palgrave, 2013), with its focus on Japanese arts and the cities of Tokyo and Osaka. Studies may also examine international and art-historical contexts to look at how the intersection of experimental film and performance will often result in distinctive and often contradictory material residues (in the forms, for example, of archives of deteriorating film reels and the tangible detritus of performance in its artefacts), exemplified by the essays in Paul Schimmel's collection *Out of Actions: Between Performance and the Object* (Thames & Hudson, 1998), especially Kristine Stiles's essay 'Uncorrupted Joy: International Art Actions'. Many recent studies of Expanded Cinema concepts incorporate close examinations of the conjoined intentions of filmmakers and performance artists in moving performatively beyond the habitual parameters of cinematic projection; *Expanded Cinema: Art, Performance and Film*, edited by A. L. Rees, David Curtis, Duncan White and Steven Ball (Tate, 2011), for example, gives a comprehensive and nuanced account of such approaches. Studies may also focus on analysing the divergent dimensions of time and space in the intersection of film and performance, as in my study *Performance Projections* (Reaktion, 2014).

Such critical and theoretical approaches could well be almost infinite in their amplitude, and take many different configurations in each particular investigation, since they necessarily focus upon multiple areas of conjunction and intersection, and of interstices and interzones, between media. Such sites of film's contacts with other arts will invariably shift and mutate, according to the ways in which their space and time are perceived, and in accordance with the endurance across film's history of such intersections and their persistence or abrupt vanishing. The parameters and survival of film itself have been increasingly uncertain in the last decades, at least since the prevalence of digital image-making from the 1990s, with film's centenary in 1995–6 and its aftermath marked in books such as Paulo Cherchi Usai's *The Death of Cinema: History, Cultural Memory and the Digital Dark Age* (BFI, 2001); as such, film's standing in relation to performance, in particular, has been a pivotal marker of its enduring capacity to undertake such traversals of art forms, as well as of its potential increasing fragility or endangeredness.

Film itself originated in a traversal of art forms, in its development (at least partially) from sequential photography, guided especially by Eadweard Muybridge's experiments in the USA and Europe in the 1880s and 1890s. Muybridge not only invented many of the technological and projection-based contexts for that movement of film beyond sequential photography, but also closely bound moving image culture to performance, both through his work's content in performative gestural (and often repetitive) movements and in his own work as a live performer, standing directly alongside his projection screen in auditoria to deliver his own vocal and gestural analysis of his work. Muybridge undertook widescale performance tours of his moving image experiments, presenting them to public and arts club audiences in cities throughout Central Europe in 1891, and also commissioned the construction of the first auditorium designed explicitly for the screening of moving image sequences – many of them with performative contents – to public audiences, with his Zoopraxographical Hall at the Chicago World's Columbian Exposition of 1893. Such moments of seminal interconnection between film and performance, at the volatile instant of moving image culture's development from sequential photography, form parallels in illuminating ways with film's contemporary disappearance into the engulfing dimensions of digital image culture.

The intersection of film and performance is especially at stake in the dimensions of time (including that of time's repetitions) and in space (notably, space as a fissured and transformational entity), and these two dimensions are worth looking at closely in order to gauge film's intermedial capacities and its openness to intersections with other art forms. Film and performance are often perceived as an unequal pairing in which film must work primarily to document performance, rather than the other way round; in that sense, film must serve to secure the time of performance, by manoeuvring its own time to coincide with that of performance, with the aim of holding performance's ephemeral time in such a way that it can be perceived in the future, through film's ostensible solidity in grounding duration. If a performance has not been filmed (as in many instances in the 1960s, when film cartridges or reels remained relatively expensive, or when it simply did not occur to participants that a filmic record needed to be made), contemporary researchers will ask: why was it not filmed? And the performance is then reduced to the status of subjection to participants' and audience members' memories. But it could be useful also to reverse that pairing and to explore the ways in which performative dimensions (beyond those of acting) work to sustain film's capacity for experimentation in such areas as rapid editing, filmmakers' interventions in the screening space (such as those of Lettrist cinema of the early 1950s, among others) and expanded cinema.

The time of filmed performance may be immediate or take on a durational quality that becomes an integral element of the spectator's experience. For example, a filmic document of a performance may last for only a split second in duration, as with the film of the 1971 performance by the artist Chris Burden, *Shoot*, in which the artist is shot and wounded in an art gallery space. Alternatively, a filmic document may unfold over several hours, as with Andy Warhol's films. A filmic document may be shot in extreme proximity to the performers' bodies, as, for example, with the 1960s films by Kurt Kren of the performance events of the Viennese Aktionists (films in which Kren also often appeared as a performer), thereby accentuating an element of 'corporeal time', or it may be documented from a distance, or even from overhead, as with the filmed performance undertaken by the American artist Robert Smithson on the completion in 1970 of his work *Spiral Jetty*, in which he performatively ran at speed around the entire course of the spiral in the Utah Great Salt Lake, while his action was filmed from above by a cinematographer in a circling helicopter. In that era, Smithson imaginatively conceived of cinemas, to be built in caves, in which *only* films of performances would be projected, possessing a kind of primordial time. In all of those examples of filmed performance, or of performatively accentuated film, the dimension of documentation is closely linked to the sense of immediacy, corporeality, intimacy, movement or gesture which is ostensibly salvaged by film from the performance before it expires, caught at exactly the moment before it would otherwise vanish. Over the past three decades or so, as filmed documentation of performance has been elevated in stature through its prominence in art-museum retrospectives of performance art, film has attained a new archival status, with the aim that lost or marginal performances may be revivified through film's intervention in their survival, and thereby transmitted to spectators who were not present within the (often small) audiences for seminal performance art events.

But it may be a misconception that film can be depended upon to document performances and hold them safe for archival consultation in a future time. In her 2006 book *Death 24x a Second: Stillness and the Moving Image*, the film theorist Laura Mulvey emphasises the quality of mortality that film (as well as photography) always carries, and which infiltrates everything it comes into contact with:

> Looking back, the life span of film and photography as the predominant media of their era has been comparatively short, bounded by a defined beginning, the fixing of the indexical image, and end, the perfect imitation of the indexical image by digital technology.[1]

For Mulvey, film inhabits an interzone of stillness in its documentational dimension, with its dynamic movement arrested. Film archives can themselves decay and disintegrate (as has often happened with those of World's Fairs or Expositions), either via neglect or through film's various material fragilities, which also extend to those of digitised film documents of performances. Many prominent filmmakers of performance, such as Kurt Kren and Takahiko Iimura, have envisaged the purpose of their work as being the inverse to that of documenting performance, instead conceiving of the process as one in which film generates something entirely new by momentarily passing through performance's gestures. It could be argued that performance, rather than film, is actually the medium that holds a more tangible durational dimension through its corporeal emphasis, and that the respective times of film and performance could even be antithetical or contrary ones, soldered only for an instant in their amalgamation by film's contact.

In terms of space as the site of film's interconnection with performance, film always possesses the potential to transform performance's site, as in its spatial reframing for the future of live events and their locations. The spatial simultaneity of film and performance converges only at the moment of cinema's origins, in the 1890s and 1900s, when the spaces assigned to performing arts and to the projection of films were often identical ones, as with many of the first projection venues for film, adapted from former performance venues (often used at the same time and within the span of the same encompassing programme of events, for screenings and performances). Some of the most illuminating spaces in which to explore the many conjunctions of film and performance are in the forms of auditoria architecturally conceived as environments for spectators to experience film and performance with as great a degree of spatial and temporal coincidence as possible, as with the many 'film-theatres' of the Broadway avenue of Los Angeles, designed by architects such as S. Charles Lee in the 1920s and 1930s. Such spaces of interposed film and performance have often now fallen into obsolescence, and what remains of them are distinctive urban sites in which conjunctions of film and performance can often be resuscitated, as, for example, in the contemporary use of such abandoned auditoria in Los Angeles for experimental transdisciplinary arts events.

The most demanding environments for the filming of performance have frequently been those of open-air urban spaces, especially those in states of transformation, with challenging conditions for the filmic rendering and seizing of performing bodies, rather than those located in indoor, static venues. In exploring temporal and spatial approaches to the intersection of film and performance, it is often the case that the imposing volatility of distinctive urban environments, as contexts for the filming of performing bodies, generates the defining framework for intermedial and conceptual investigation.

As two examples for analysing the intricate conjunction of film and performance, and the particular spatial and temporal dynamics which that intersection generates, this chapter will now explore moments from the beginnings of film, in the 1890s work (primarily concerned with performance) of the Skladanowsky brothers in Berlin, and from its most recent manifestations, in the interfacing of film, digital media and performance, in the work of Rabih Mroué. In both cases, the status of the 'experimental' is at the forefront of that intermedial innovation.

The Berlin-based innovators of filmmaking and spatial moving image projection, Max and Emil Skladanowsky – largely forgotten in the contemporary context, in part because of the extreme brevity of their involvement with film – emerged from a background in performance; they had been conjurors and magicians before they became filmmakers and film projectionists. In every dimension of their filmmaking and film exhibition work, performance comprised an intimate, adjacent or interconnected presence.

Although celluloid film became commercially available in Europe in 1893, it took a further two years before the Skladanowsky brothers in Berlin and the Lumière brothers in France had honed their projection equipment to the point of being ready to arrange public projection events. Max and Emil Skladanowsky showed their own films in November 1895 at the Wintergarten ballroom of the Central Hotel in Berlin, several weeks before the Lumière brothers' projections in Paris in the following month. Crucially, the films they projected in Berlin were all films of performances, projected in a performance venue and shown spatially directly alongside acts of performance, as a 15-minute-long component within a performance-based programme. In the following year, 1896, they abandoned their filmmaking of performance, and instead attempted to attract new audiences by making films of urban space; but an essential intimacy and complicity between film and the performing arts extends right from film's origins in 1895 and is formulated from the start as being an experimental conjunction, in both its technological and its aesthetic dimensions.

Film's relationship to performance, at the beginnings of moving image culture, possesses a very distinctive sense of experimentation, along with the desire, above all, to define and position film, in its emergence, in relation to the other arts, and to performance in particular. In many ways, celluloid-based film began with the compulsion to record performance. That preoccupation in 1895 with recording moving image sequences of performance possessed many precedents, but Muybridge's experiments across moving image and performance media, in the preceding years, formed an especially crucial inspiration. Muybridge's many projection tours in Europe and the USA – on which he showed his moving image sequences recorded on glass discs, projected with his specially designed projector, the 'Zoopraxiscope' – had included several lecture–performances in Berlin. Muybridge's image-captured performances took the form of dances, actions and gestures which he had choreographed and recorded himself, during his 1880s multi-camera work undertaken at the University of Pennsylvania in Philadelphia and other sites. The Skladanowsky brothers attended Muybridge's projection event in 1891 in Berlin at the Urania hall: a venue established for the demonstration of technological and cultural innovations. Between 1891 and 1895, Muybridge's work in glass disc-based moving image projection came to an abrupt end, in part because his own technologies became obsolete; he switched his attention to compiling an immense scrapbook devoted to his experiments, which took up the final decade of his life. During those same years of 1891–5, the Skladanowsky brothers developed ideas towards their own projection experiments, and celluloid's introduction (as an experimental medium) allowed them the opportunity to envisage large-scale public moving image events.

A pivotal element of film's relationship to performance, in the mid-1890s, was that film projection was often undertaken by figures who had previously been involved in other arts, and then brought their experience of those arts – performance, above all – to new developments in film. The Skladanowsky brothers' extensive prior training in conjuring and magic-lantern work, and their ability to improvise solutions to technical impasses, gave them the capacity to adapt their technological knowledge flexibly to moving image work. They decided to reinvent themselves as filmmakers (at a moment when that status remained undefined), oriented both to the technological challenges of experimental work and also to the potential financial gains to be made from projecting their experiments to large-scale public audiences in adaptable auditoria. During the summer of 1895, in open-air conditions with maximum natural illumination, they filmed many of the performers (acrobats, dancers, wrestlers) then passing through Berlin on tours; each film lasted several seconds and would be elongated by being projected in repetition as a loop.

One of the principal reasons why the Skladanowsky brothers chose in 1895 to film performances, rather than another subject matter, relates to their expected audience; in the mid-1890s, Berlin had extraordinarily avid popular and artistic audiences for all kinds of innovative, novel performers, who arrived in Berlin from every part of the world and performed across many different types of venue. The Skladanowsky brothers' films were of the performers who were attracting most attention in Berlin at the moment of filming. A further four months or so passed before their films were projected, by which time those celebrated performers had physically moved on from Berlin to other tours, with the result that their presence in the Skladanowsky brothers' films, on their projection, accentuated the aura of absence or spectrality that was highlighted by audiences and reviewers.

After undertaking test screenings in a local café, the Skladanowsky brothers were able to secure an engagement from the Central Hotel to show their films there; at that time, the hotel's ballroom was one of the most prominent performance venues in Berlin. They were contracted to project their films on most evenings of November 1895, starting on the first of the month; the projections were scheduled as the final part of a three-hour programme which would otherwise consist solely of live performances of one kind or another. That positioning of film projection as a final element of the evening serves to highlight its experimental character, as well as the sense of anticipation generated towards it. Live performance lapsed, and film began, with nothing beyond it. The audience at the Wintergarten ballroom was partly composed of the Central Hotel's guests, from many countries, deeply engaged with new forms of popular entertainment. By contrast, Muybridge's glass disc projections in Berlin, four years earlier, had been for a local audience largely of anatomists, scholars and inventors.

The spatial configuration of the ballroom involved several stages, with the audience mainly seated around circular tables in front of each stage. As such, it differed in audience positioning from the more familiar configuration which film projection adopted in subsequent years, with parallel rows of seating. By the time the Skladanowsky brothers' films were projected, at the evening's end, on to a screen placed on a side stage, the audience had already been watching live performances for two and three-quarter hours. As a result, that audience must have perceived the films as being subject to distinctive separations in time and space from their witnessing of performance. Some of the audience members would have recognised the filmed performances as showing those same figures they had had the opportunity to witness in a live performance context, in that same venue or another in Berlin, around four months earlier. They would also perhaps have perceived the films as a strange or aberrant residue of the live performances they had just been watching for the previous two hours or so, with the live performances now, in a sense, visually transmuted into a startling and unprecedented medium.

In order to be able to film performances – and to project them publicly – it had been necessary for the Skladanowsky brothers to invent and manually construct their own film cameras and film projectors, in the same way that other inventors and innovators of film in that era (such as Louis Le Prince in Leeds, the Lumière brothers in Lyon and William Dickson in New Jersey) had done in the preceding years, with greater or lesser degrees of success.

Although innovators in moving image culture often stole ideas from competitors, especially if they were able to observe public experiments in projection, the particular dilemma of that era was always that of projecting celluloid film to a high standard at which the spectator's eye could recognise human movement. The Skladanowsky brothers had to invent entirely their own projector, which they called the 'Bioskop', using two separate reels of celluloid that were fed alternately through the projector's twin gates; they used a strategy of projecting their films from behind the screen. For all innovators, projection posed great dangers, of both conflagration and malfunction; in many ways, projection itself was (and is) a performative act, that required intense concentration and needed to be achieved without any technological malfunction, in order to maintain the spectacle of film and of the performances it held.

In 1893, two years before their first public projections at the Central Hotel's ballroom, the Skladanowsky brothers shot an experimental test film, in direct sunlight on the roof of a building in Berlin's Prenzlauerberg district, with the Berlin cityscape in the background. By that time, they had built a film camera and had some newly available celluloid film, but had not yet devised their Bioskop projector. One brother filmed the other brother performing a kind of clumsy dance, lifting his arms and legs into the air. The intimacy and near-simultaneity of the oscillating status of filmmaker and performer is tangible in that film. As it transpired, the film was too rudimentary to be shown as part of the professional projections of 1895; for many years it was believed lost, and appeared to belong to a distinctive subcategory of the lost films of performance, in which a performance has been filmed, but the footage has been either destroyed, forgotten about or simply discarded. However, in this case, a few original frames of the film reappeared in the 2010s in the local museum archives of Berlin's Prenzlauerberg district.[2]

In choosing, at the first moment of moving image culture, to film performances, the Skladanowsky brothers drew on their own experiences, as performers themselves and also as entrepreneurs of performance. The proprietors of the Central Hotel hired them for an engagement of two months, with the first month consisting of the film projections, and the second month taking the form of the Skladanowsky brothers' staging of a spectacular live performance in which the events of a sea battle involving great tanks of water were shown to the audience; in that sense, their role as filmmakers was a fragile and ephemeral one, soon returned to the domain of performance. The successful projection of filmed performance in November 1895 proved to be a one-off phenomenon for the Skladanowsky brothers, since the demands of audiences for film moved so rapidly in the following months that they almost immediately had to find another subject matter. They were also rapidly surpassed by their competitors, such as the Lumière brothers. In choosing subsequently to film the subject matter of urban space, in 1896 and the first months of 1897, they capitalised on the opportunities for mobility provided by their short-lived moving image projection tours to cities such as Copenhagen, and within Germany itself, especially to the port city of Stettin, where they shot a city film in densely crowded urban space one afternoon, developed it immediately, and then projected it to their audience (at a Stettin concert hall) on the evening of the same day. But their career abruptly ended when the Skladanowsky brothers fell out over a family inheritance in the spring of 1897, and their films of performance were very rarely seen until they were reassembled for a centenary screening at the Berlin Film Festival in 1995.

To close this chapter, I will move from the origins of moving image culture, in its intersections with performance, to the contemporary moment to examine the work of the internationally renowned Lebanese, Berlin-based filmmaker and performance artist, Rabih Mroué. Mroué's work – mostly exhibited in art-museum contexts, and often holding a live element in his accompanying lecture–performances alongside a screen – is exceptional in its sustained, in-depth exploration of the interzone between film and performance, within the contexts of engulfing, accelerating technological transmutations and also of intensive social turmoil, especially that of the recent civil war in Syria. In particular, Mroué's work *The Pixellated Revolution* (2012–) analyses the very dangerous filming – via iPhones, by protesting citizens in Syria – of government army snipers trained to shoot and kill immediately whoever they saw wielding a film camera or a handheld moving image device in urban space.

Mroué's work, like that of the Skladanowsky brothers, emerged directly from previous work in performance, and demonstrates how performative dynamics are transmitted and projected into the domain of moving image culture; he was already a renowned actor and performance artist in Lebanon before turning the focus of his work to the intersections between film and performance, and that work maintains a close sense of the historical role of filmmaking in the documentation of performance. Many of Mroué's performative works, undertaken in the auditoria of art museums which are simultaneously exhibiting his artworks interrogating film's connections to performance, consist of him simply sitting at a table with an iMac, alongside a large projection screen, vocally analysing the moving image sequences he is projecting, in the form of what he calls a 'performance–lecture'. His status as a film-analysing performer resonates strongly with the lecture–performances undertaken in 1891–3 by Muybridge, positioned directly alongside his own projection screen, vocally analysing his glass disc sequences, though using a wooden pointer rather than an iMac.

Mroué often works with found footage (as in experimental or avant-garde filmmaking practices), in the form of iPhone sequences recorded by protestors in Syrian cities shortly before they were shot by government snipers. In works such as *The Pixellated Revolution*, such found footage appears to have been amalgamated into Mroué's own work, in which the dual status of 'filmmaker' and 'performer' is presented as a near-identical, simultaneous one, that cannot any longer be fully disentangled in the cross-media imperatives of contemporary visual culture. His work fluidly transits a range of media and investigates the uncertain or volatile spaces between them, especially in relation to moments of social chaos and technologically focused conflict. As well as his background in performance, Mroué's history is that of a combatant; he fought as a very young teenager in the Lebanese civil war in the early 1980s, in which members of his family were killed or injured, and he relates those experiences (such as that of the ocularly focused sniper) to the ongoing civil war in Syria. *The Pixellated Revolution* concerns a particular era in the Syrian civil war, now already several years in the past, during which Mroué collected numerous sequences from YouTube and other websites: films which existed on the internet for a certain time and then, in most cases, abruptly disappeared. In a number of those films, the person filming the sniper with an iPhone (with the aim of amassing documentation for future trials, or as historical evidence) continues to track that figure for an extended duration, but then, invariably, the sniper notices that he is being filmed, and a direct eye-to-eye confrontation ensues between the filmer and the sniper. As Mroué emphasises in his vocal commentary: 'The Syrian protestors are filming their own deaths.'[3] For Mroué, the protestors appear still to possess a split second opportunity to drop their iPhones and escape from the sniper's line of fire, but they do not, either because of the compulsion to keep on filming, or else because of the performative tension which freezes the moment. The protesters hesitate for that split second, and are then shot and fall to the ground, dropping their iPhones which continue to film; they are then heard crying out that they have been wounded or are dying.

The status of the moving image sequences which Mroué archived for *The Pixellated Revolution* lecture–performances could never be verified with absolute certainty; although many thousands of protesters in Syrian cities are known to have been killed by government snipers, Mroué notes in his commentary that it is impossible to determine that the sequences posted on YouTube and other sites are definitely authentic documents. Like all found footage, and filmic documents in general, there always exists the outside possibility that the materials are fabricated and have been 'performed'. To explore that possibility, Mroué made a coda to *The Pixellated Revolution* in the form of a short film, entitled *Shooting Images*, consisting precisely of such a performative recreation or re-enactment, filmed on the rooftops of Beirut. This recreated sequence emphasises film's potential malleability or duplicity in relation to the corporeal realities of performance and reveals the complex dynamics enduringly at work at the intersection between film and performance, especially in the current era of technological upheaval.

Mroué's work has a contemporary focus, but it also exhibits in-depth, research-based preoccupations with the history and prehistory of film and its performative dimensions, notably in its focus upon the 1880s experiments of the French scientist Étienne-Jules Marey, to construct a so-called 'photographic gun' which would record moving image sequences of the flights of birds, as well as on the 1870s optographic experiments of the German scientist Wilhelm Kühne that investigated the possibility of discovering, on the retina of a murdered person's eye, an image of the killer's face (in Mroué's work, a face which resonates with those of the Syrian snipers). His work also engages directly with the history of performance art, especially from the 1960s, with its preoccupations with the duplicitous nature of image sequences, and the reversal or overturning of power formations.

In conclusion, Mroué's work demonstrates how vitally ongoing the exploration of the interzone between film and performance remains in the work of contemporary artists, often informed by an exhaustive knowledge of how that intersection has endured – transforming but always retaining key preoccupations – since the first celluloid moving image experiments and projections of the 1890s. That exploration of the intersecting, intermedial domains of film and performance holds the potential to illuminate and provide valuable insights for matters of urgent current importance, such as civil strife, the surveillance of urban space and the contested status of the human body and eye in contemporary culture.

Notes

1. Laura Mulvey, *Death 24x a Second: Stillness and the Moving Image* (London: Reaktion Books, 2006), p. 31.
2. I am very grateful to the curators of the Prenzlauerberg Museum for showing me the surviving frames of the Skladanowsky brothers' 1893 test film, as well as to curators of other moving image archives in Berlin and Potsdam which preserve the Skladanowsky brothers' projectors, cameras and other materials.
3. This account of Rabih Mroué's work is based on several extended conversations with him in Berlin in 2015, as well as on moving image documentation of his lecture–performances provided by Mroué.

CHAPTER 2

Carving Cameras: Antonioni's Lo Sguardo di Michelangelo
Steven Jacobs

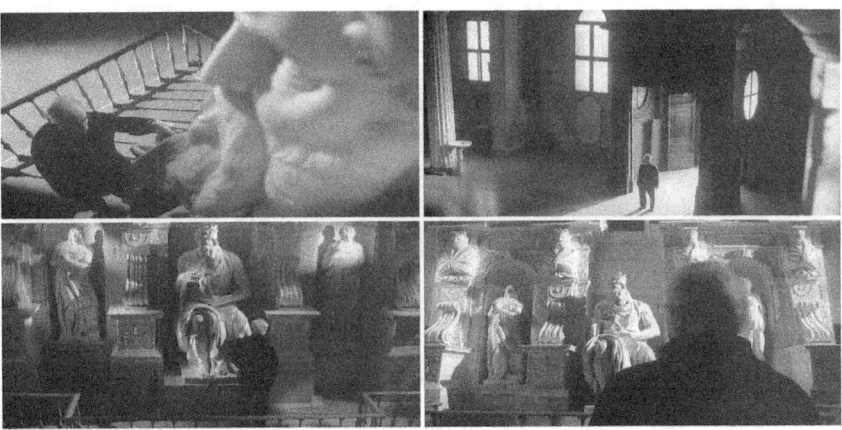

Figure 2.1 *Lo Sguardo di Michelangelo* (Michelangelo Antonioni, 2004).

SCULPTURE VERSUS FILM[1]

Sculpture and film seem to be opposites. Whereas sculpture is an artistic practice that involves not only static but also material, three-dimensional and durable objects, the cinema produces kinetic, immaterial, two-dimensional and volatile images. However, film has also been applauded as a medium perfectly suited to represent sculpture. Sculptures invite movement on the part of the viewer, as shifting positions in space are necessary to see and experience them in the round. By means of editing and camera movements, cinema constructs such mobility, which, in addition, came to be seen as perfectly complementary to sculpture's immobility. Because of its dynamic nature and its integration of multiple perspectives into a single experience, film can make manifest the stability as well as the spatial properties of sculpture. These qualities have made the extensive cinematic visualisation of sculptures highly attractive throughout film history, as demonstrated by widely divergent films such as *Ein Lichtspiel: Schwarz Weiss Grau* (László Moholy-Nagy, 1930), *Die steinernen Wunder von Naumburg* (Curt Oertel and Rudolf Bamberger, 1932), *Visual Variations on Noguchi* (Marie Menken, 1945), *Thorvaldsen* (Carl Theodor Dreyer, 1949) and *L'Enfer de Rodin* (Henri Alekan, 1957), among many others. In recent years too, prominent filmmakers and artists have created important cinematic studies or reveries of sculptural volumes: *Static* (Steve McQueen, 2009), *Concrete & Samples III Carrara* (Aglaia Konrad, 2010), *The Eternal Lesson* (Christoph Girardet, 2012), *Inventory* (Fiona Tan, 2012), *Rotations* (Javier Téllez, 2012–13), *The Beginning: Living Figures Dying* (Clemens von Wedemeyer, 2013), *It for Others* (Duncan Campbell, 2014), *The Night Gallery* (Mark Lewis, 2014) and *The Hidden Conference: A Fractured Play* (Rosa Barba, 2015).[2]

MICHELANGELO'S *MOSES*

Another remarkable recent film dealing with sculpture is *Lo Sguardo di Michelangelo* (2004) by renowned filmmaker Michelangelo Antonioni, whose interest in the visual arts has marked many of his films.[3] Soon after its release, Jonathan Rosenbaum called *Lo Sguardo di Michelangelo* Antonioni's 'most interesting film since *Red Desert* (1964)' and 'one of the first truly durable reflections to date on digital cinema'.[4] This 19-minute-long film opens with an intertitle – the only textual information in the film apart from the credits – stating that 'in 1985, Michelangelo Antonioni suffered a stroke and was confined to a wheelchair. In 2004, through the magic of cinema, he made this visit to San Pietro in Vincoli.' In this church, situated on the Esquiline Hill in Rome, the ninety-two-year-old film director contemplates the famous statue of Moses made by his illustrious namesake, Michelangelo Buonarroti (1475–1564), whose art had been explored by filmmakers earlier. Apart from the curious biopic *The Agony and the Ecstasy* (Carol Reed, 1965), the famous Renaissance sculptor and painter had been the subject of several interesting documentary films such as *Michelangelo* (Carlo Ludovico Ragghianti, 1964) and *Michelangelo: A Self-Portrait* (Robert Snyder, 1989). Noteworthy is Curt Oertel's impressive *Michelangelo: Das Leben eines Titanen* (1938), which tells the story of the dramatic life of Michelangelo simply by showing a succession of locations and artworks, without actors. With the help of sound effects, skillful lighting and impressive (often subjective) camera movements, Oertel turned the contemplation of art into a thrilling cinematic experience. In addition, he succeeded in evoking the plasticity of Michelangelo's sculptures, including his 1513 statue of Moses, and the texture of their marble surfaces. In 1950, the film was recut under the supervision of Robert Flaherty and Robert Snyder, and rereleased as *The Titan*, winning the Academy Award for Best Documentary Feature.

The statue of Moses was initially part of Michelangelo's design of an elaborate monument honouring Giuliano della Rovere, Pope Julius II, who was known as the 'Warrior Pope'. Michelangelo received the commission for the design of the monument in 1505.[5] However, facing numerous difficulties and disappointments, the project pursued the artist for more than forty years – Ascanio Condivi, in his *Vita di Michelagnolo Buonarroti* (1553), describes the history of the Julius monument as 'the Tragedy of the Tomb'.[6] Only in 1512, with the decoration of the Sistine Chapel ceiling complete, could Michelangelo resume work on the mausoleum that would contain about forty sculptures. Between 1512 and 1513, he completed three statues for the project: the *Dying* and *Rebellious Slaves* (now in the Louvre, Paris) and *Moses*, which is retained in the final version. After the death of Julius in 1513, Michelangelo was forced to change the whole design, transforming the freestanding monument into a variant of the traditional wall-tomb, for which he carved *The Genius of Victory* (now in the Palazzo Vecchio in Florence) and four unfinished *Slaves* (in the Accademia in Florence) during the 1520s. Throughout the following years, Michelangelo struggled with the della Rovere family, the descendants of Julius, until a compromise was reached in 1545 and a greatly reduced tomb ended up in the Rovere family church of San Pietro in Vincoli, as opposed to Saint Peter's in the Vatican. The final version of the monument consists of only a few sculptures, most of them being life-sized or even bigger, including the colossal and awe-inspiring *Moses* – a figure increasingly identified with the Pope in Renaissance Rome.[7] Michelangelo presents the prophet as a powerful figure who looks to his left, holding the tablets of the Law under his right arm while he grasps an impressive beard between his hands. In combination with the horn-like protuberances on his head (based on a mistranslation in the Latin Vulgate) the beard gives Moses an inhuman, demonic aspect.

Lo Sguardo di Michelangelo also draws attention to the other statues that are part of the monument, such as the figures of Leah and Rachel situated in the niches on either side of the Old Testament prophet, representing the Active and Contemplative Life (roles Dante assigned to them in the *Purgatorio*). In between these statues are massive volutes surmounted by herms, while the upper part of the monument includes the reclining figure of Pope Julius, flanked by a prophet and a sybil. The considerable changes of scale in the final assemblage of the figures, which was unveiled in the church of San Pietro in Vincoli in 1547, has almost nothing in common with the initial project and the high hopes with which Michelangelo had started. As a result of these major alterations, the massive figure of Moses seems somewhat too big for its new context. According to Linda Murray,

> the pose, with one leg advanced slightly in front of the other, the turn and immense prominence of the head, with its majestic flowing beard, the

exaggeration of the facial expression, would not be so strikingly obvious were the figure seen at the height and distance which were envisaged and allowed for in its conception.[8]

Despite its somewhat unfortunate final display, the *Moses* statue, expressing the *terribilità* of the Old Testament prophet, the artist and his Papal patron, remains impressive. As Murray noted, many interpretations of the figure have been made,

> ranging from Moses's rage at the Jews' idolatry of the Golden calf to the symbolism of antique River Gods, to an anguished spiritual self-portrait, or the confrontation of the Active and Contemplative Life, for which a suitable companion figure [of Saint Paul] is hypothesised.[9]

One of the statue's famous beholders, admirers and interpreters was Sigmund Freud, who visited the statue for the first time in September 1901 and went to see it again on many occasions. 'Every day for three lonely weeks of September 1913,' Freud wrote, 'I stood in the church in front of the statue, studying it, measuring it and drawing it until there dawned on me that understanding which I expressed in my essay.'[10] In this 1914 essay, entitled 'Der Moses des Michelangelo', Freud wrote that 'no piece of statuary has ever made a stronger impression on me than this', and he further associates Michelangelo's rendition of the Prophet with the moment in the biblical narrative when the prophet descends from the mountain the first time, carrying the tablets, and finds the Hebrew people worshipping the Golden Calf, as described in Exodus.[11] But Freud also describes Moses in a complex psychological state. Rage is in his eyes and in every muscle of his body, but the tension in the body and the fondling of his beard also show hesitation. According to Kenneth Gross, Michelangelo's Moses evokes for Freud 'a Hebraic (if not a Freudian) calm, a repose more curiously haunted, more fraught and opaque than the classical calm'.[12] Ready for a moment to leap up in wrath, Michelangelo's Moses is in between two states and Freud precisely draws our attention to 'bodily forms that appear to be moved and restrained, awakened and depressed by forces that are never fully their own'.[13] As a result, the statue of Moses evokes change and movement – an aspect that makes the statue perfect for film.

LIGHT AND EYES

Freud's analysis and detailed descriptions resonate in Michelangelo Antonioni's long, hard look at the sculpture in *Lo Sguardo di Michelangelo*. Despite the digital trickery that made it possible to represent Michelangelo Antonioni walking without a cane, the film is quite simple. Its minimal action consists solely of Antonioni entering the church of San Pietro in Vincoli to look at Michelangelo's *Moses* and some of the other statues of the monument. He also touches the statue and then leaves the church again. Having no dialogue or voice-over commentary, the film is almost silent. We can vaguely hear Antonioni's footsteps among the muffled sounds and muted echoes in the church. Towards the end of the film, a choir quietly sings a Palestrina *Magnificat* while Antonioni walks away from the monument and leaves the church, passing into the light of the Roman streets.

The presence of this light is telling. The first and last shots of this 15-minute film show us the open church doors and sunlight entering the darkened interior, almost like the light beam of a film projector. Light not only is a prerequisite for cinema, this film reminds us; it also makes sculpture visible and even palpable. Light modulates the marble volumes, creating contrasts between the polished surfaces and the dark pools of shadow. In so doing, Antonioni situates himself in a long tradition of filmmakers who have used light and shadow to evoke the plasticity of sculptures, from the opening sequence featuring Ancient Greek statues of Leni Riefenstahl's *Olympia* (1938) to the haunted statuary in Jean Cocteau's *La Belle et la bête* (1946) and the great documentaries on sculpture such as Moholy-Nagy's *Lichtspiel* (1930), Dreyer's *Thorvaldsen* (1949) and Alekan's *L'Enfer de Rodin* (1957). Oertel's *Michelangelo: Das Leben eines Titanen* (1938), too, uses spectacular chiaroscuro effects in order to give volume to many Michelangelo sculptures, including his statue of Moses.

As every museum curator knows, the display of sculpture needs particular care with lighting – it comes fully into its own in the presence of natural, changing daylight. Michelangelo's *Moses* has a special bond with sunlight. This became much clearer after a recent restoration of the entire Tomb of Pope Julius II. According to Antonio Forcellino, the restorer and architect entrusted with cleaning the masterpiece,

> Michelangelo used lead to polish only the parts of the statue that jut out the most – the ones hit by direct sunlight – and left the others with a more rustic finish, using pumice stone and sand. Thus, the sculpture takes on a completely new depth, with a pictorial quality.[14]

These pictorial qualities were already mentioned by Giorgio Vasari in his description of the statue in his *Vite* (1550/1568), where he states that it is 'delicately carved, downy, and soft, and drawn out in such a way that it seems as if the chisel has become a brush'.[15] Furthermore, it became apparent that Moses looks to the side because he is searching for a beam of light streaming through a window that once existed but was later removed. For Michelangelo, the light had a great value as a symbol of the direct relationship between Moses and God.

Light, vision and optics are also emphasised in other ways in *Lo Sguardo di Michelangelo* – literally *Michelangelo's Gaze*, and released in English as *Michelangelo Eye to Eye*. Tellingly, the first shot of the monument shows us the face of Pope Julius, which is then followed by a close-up of his closed eyes. Likewise, the first image of Moses is a close-up of the Prophet's eye, taken from one side with Antonioni out of focus in the background. While Maurizio dell'Orco's camera elaborately explores the sculpture, inserts show us a gazing Antonioni. Respecting classical eye-line matches, Roberto Missiroli's editing even suggests an exchange of glances between the Old Testament figure and the ageing film director. Extreme close-ups of Moses's eyes are followed by a close-up of Antonioni wearing glasses. Subsequently, an over-the-shoulder shot of Antonioni looking at the monument enables us to see the surfaces of marble through his glasses. We literally look at the statue with Antonioni and look through his eyes. His glasses, forcing the cameraman to adjust his focus, are an optical device tallying with a long tradition of contraptions and strategies of looking at sculptures in indirect ways, with the help of mirrors or coloured windows, in flickering torchlight, or with rapidly blinking eyes, as Goethe did in front of the statue of the Laocoön.[16]

Antonioni seems to suggest that looking at Michelangelo's *Moses* directly is difficult, almost impossible. The first shots focusing on the monument do not show us Moses but the statue of Julius and various other details of the upper part of the monument, as if we need to avoid the monumental figure that draws all attention. Only after a few minutes do we see a first glimpse of the Moses figure, an extreme close-up of his eye with the director out of focus in the background. It is as if looking at Moses or looking into his eyes is physically impossible – an effect that was already mentioned by Giorgio

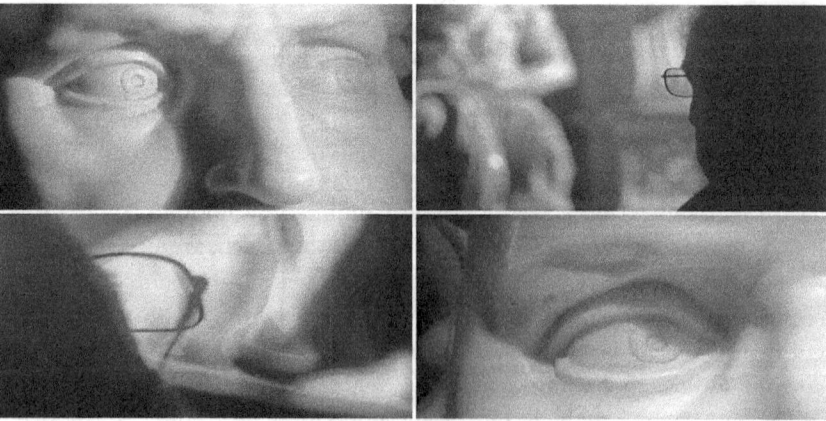

Figure 2.2 *Lo Sguardo di Michelangelo* (Michelangelo Antonioni, 2004).

Vasari, who stated that 'it seems that while you gaze at the statue, you feel the desire to ask for a veil to cover his face, so splendid and radiant does it appear to onlookers'.[17]

HANDS

The emphatic focus on eyes and vision, however, is balanced with an outspoken interest in touch and hands. The film's English title – *Michelangelo Eye to Eye* – is misleading, as Antonioni's exploration of the Renaissance monument could as well be properly labelled *Michelangelo Hand to Hand*. The camera, for instance, focuses on Moses's expressive hands fondling his beard. In addition, the film contains several shots showing Antonioni touching and caressing the marble, which was selected in Carrara by Michelangelo himself. Furthermore, at a certain moment, it looks as if Antonioni's hands are drawing in air, delineating the contours of the sculpture, as if he 'looked' with his hands or as if he 'felt' the statue without touching it.

With this explicit juxtaposition of visual and tactile perception, *Lo Sguardo di Michelangelo* rearticulates some of the discussions central to sculptural theory since the eighteenth century. In his 1778 treatise on sculpture, Johann Gottfried Herder linked the difference between painting and sculpture to the distinction between sight and touch but he also noted that the apprehension of sculpture is not a literally tactile experience but a visual perception that was closely connected to a tactile exploration.[18] Herder also emphasised the kinesthetic apprehension of sculpture since it involved a mobile kind of viewing, which does not seize on the statue as a fixed form but senses its wholeness as it glides over its surfaces. Clearly different from the simultaneity of painterly viewing, the apprehension of a sculptural shape could never be assimilated in a single fixed image or moment.

These ideas marked theories on sculpture throughout the nineteenth century; they were particularly important in the 1890s, at the moment of the film medium's inception. In *Das Problem der Form in der bildenden Kunst* (1893), which would become a key reference for early formalist accounts of sculpture, Adolf von Hildebrand advocated the idea that the apprehension of free-standing sculptures was dependent on a painterly model of formal coherence.[19] Although he recognised a tactile or 'haptic' way of seeing, which differs from a painterly one in which stable forms were dissolved in atmospheric effects, Hildebrand's idea of vision was essentially two-dimensional. Inspired by perception psychology, Hildebrand was convinced that our spatial mapping of the world involves two-dimensional representations. He consequently conceived plastic form not so much as a three-dimensional shape but rather as the two-dimensional view of an object which presented its overall shape with greatest clarity. The apprehension of a piece of sculpture was thus marked by the tension between a clearly defined stable image and a mobile kinesthetic experience of the shifting partial views. Modern sculptors, who had liberated sculpture from their architectural anchoring, had thus to overcome the many variable forms of a sculpture in the round by defining a principal viewpoint from which the sculpture became manifest as a satisfying whole – an issue that was also a major problem for the photography of sculpture, as art historian Heinrich Wölfflin had noted in a series of articles published between 1896 and 1915.[20]

It is noteworthy that Michelangelo's *Moses* is a free-standing sculpture that became part of a linear arrangement of the wall-tomb (in contrast with the original design of the free-standing mausoleum). As a result, Antonioni's camera is not able to move around the sculpture as, for instance, Roberto Rossellini's did in the famous museum scene in *Viaggio in Italia* (1953), in which Ingrid Bergman visits the classical sculptures of the Farnese Collection in the Archaeological Museum of Naples. Nor was it possible to put the massive *Moses* on a rotating pedestal to explore all sides of the statue, as is often done in many key documentaries on sculpture, such as the short films by Hans Cürlis in the 1920s and Dreyer's film on Thorvaldsen, or even in feature films involving statues such as in the sequence featuring Ancient Greek gods in Jean-Luc Godard's *Le Mépris* (1963). In contrast, the camera scans the Moses figure from the front and sides; its slow gliding over the surfaces evokes Antonioni's own tranquil movements, which are also echoed in the slow and steady rhythm of the editing.

Through these camera movements and the shifting camera positions, Antonioni emphasises the sculptural qualities and the solidity of Michelangelo's statue. In so doing, Antonioni makes manifest one of the key qualities originating from the intriguing encounter between cinema and sculpture. On the one hand, film enables us to 'feel' the three-dimensionality, weight and even texture of sculptural volumes. On the other hand, however, film inevitably transforms sculptures into pure optical phenomena. Even the most heavy and solid volumes are turned into floating, airy shapes on the screen. Film disconnects the sculpture from the viewer; it gives to sculpture a kind of imaginative field quite apart from the viewing subject, that is akin to painting. Film transposes the sculpture from its real and physical space to an imaginative realm. What is more, with its possibility of changing or shifting points of view, film even perfectly answers to what Alex Potts defines as a crucial feature of sculptural viewing: the 'interplay between a relatively stable apprehension of the overall shape of a work and an unfixed close viewing of the modulations of form and play of light on the surface'.[21] Filmic explorations of sculpture make this 'haptic' approach possible. *Lo Sguardo di*

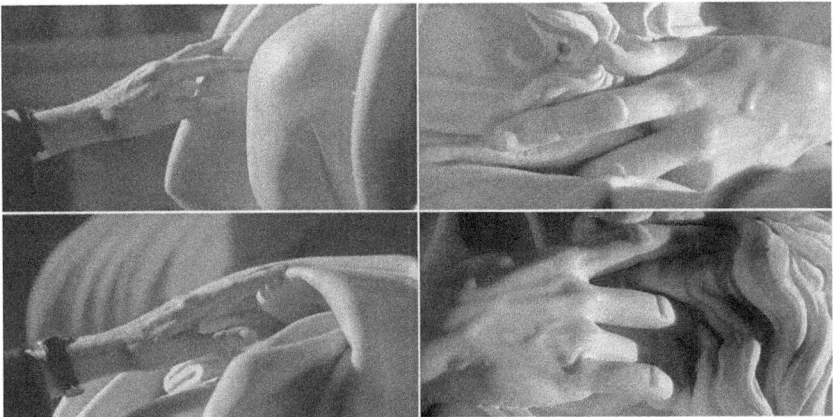

Figure 2.3   *Lo Sguardo di Michelangelo* (Michelangelo Antonioni, 2004).

Michelangelo fully appeals to an intimate, embodied and multi-sensory viewing, recognising haptics and texture as essential components of the film medium, as scholars such as Vivian Sobchack, Laura Marks and Jennifer Barker have demonstrated.[22]

The materiality of the sculpture is further emphasised by focusing on a form of interaction between the statue and a beholder – in this case Antonioni, who finds himself both behind and in front of the camera. By linking the director and the sculpture through editing or by including the sculpture and its beholder in the same shot, Antonioni emphasises the concrete presence of the statue, not only as a marble object but also as a (super)human character. According to William Tucker, 'sculpture, of its nature, is object, in the world, in a way in which painting, music, poetry are not'.[23] This 'reality effect' of sculpture, its materiality in space or its physical existence in the 'real world', is a recurring topic in seminal theoretical texts on sculpture. In contrast to paintings, sculptures are part of the realm in which we are living; they occupy our space. For Tucker, sculptures and their beholders are united because of a sense of gravity, which 'unites sculpture and spectator in a common dependence on and resistance to the pull of the earth'.[24] For filmmakers – perhaps in part so as to overcome the lack of physical co-presence between the film beholder and the sculptural object – this physical confrontation between sculpture and beholder has proven an attractive motif, as can be seen in numerous scenes involving figurative sculpture: the desecration or destruction of statues in *October* (Sergei Eisenstein, 1927) or *City Lights* (Charlie Chaplin, 1931), the touching of a statue's face in the MoMA garden scene in John Cassavetes's *Shadows* (1959), or the erotic encounters between humans and statues in *L'Âge d'or* (Luis Buñuel, 1930), *Le Sang d'un poète* (Jean

Cocteau, 1931), *The Song of Songs* (Rouben Mamoulian, 1933), *One Touch of Venus* (William Seiter, 1948) and *Laura: Les ombres de l'été* (David Hamilton, 1979), among many others. When a sculpture features in a narrative film, it is almost always a figurative statue, as filmmakers tend to present the statue as a substitute for a real person. This dominance of the human figure, however, is inherent in the art of sculpture itself, which does not include still lives or landscapes as the art of painting does. According to Rudolf Arnheim, 'more radically than the other arts, sculpture is monopolised by the subject matter of the human figure'.[25] Precisely because sculpture exists in real space, it gives us a more immediate physical sense of a human presence.

Metamorphosis

In the process of filming, the sculptures undergo a transformation. By means of Antonioni's close-ups, details of the sculpture, such as the hands or the beard of Moses or the folds of his clothes, are transformed into an almost surreal, Mount Rushmore-like landscape. Antonioni's film clearly demonstrates that the medium of film not only represents, reproduces or duplicates artworks, but also that it reconfigures, reimagines and remediates them. Like all interesting films on art, *Lo Sguardo di Michelangelo* transforms or translates the original artwork from one medium to another, creating a new hybrid. Details, which are seen simultaneously by the beholder facing the original, are in a film unfolded in time by means of camera movements and editing techniques. Furthermore, film also frames the artwork in a way selected by the director or cameraman – the statue becomes part of another image. As in other interesting films about sculptures, *Lo Sguardo di Michelangelo* deals in a highly conscious way with its framings, creating new visual balances and tensions within them. Changing the statue into something else, the film perfectly tallies with André Malraux's opinions about the transformative power of photography *vis-à-vis* artworks. According to Malraux, his illustrated art books such as *Le Musée imaginaire* (1947) and the three-part *Le Musée imaginaire de la sculpture mondiale* (1952–4) 'have found in sculpture – which black and white prints reproduce more faithfully than they do paintings – their privileged domain'.[26] In the case of the reproduction of sculptures, Malraux recognises that photography is not a simple transparent medium. He acknowledges that 'the angle from which a work of sculpture is photographed, the focusing, and, above all, skillfully adjusted lighting, may impart violent emphasis to something the sculptor himself merely hinted at'.[27] Photography, consequently, does not represent sculptures but it translates, transforms or 'metamorphosises' them. Malraux advocates that sculpture benefits from photography (more than painting does), not because photography is more faithful to sculpture, but because photography acts more forcefully upon objects that demand to have a point of view imposed on them.²⁸ Photographic reproductions bring sculptures to the two-dimensional space that is the realm of photography and film.

One element of the impact of filming on a piece of sculpture is exemplified in Antonioni's shifting viewpoints, alternating low-angle and high-angle shots, which bring to mind discussions on the ideal viewpoint of the *Moses* sculpture. In 1878, for instance, Anton Springer claimed that the strained state of the figure, the disproportionate limbs, the illogical heaping of drapery over the right knee, and the ignoble face would disappear if the statue were placed on high and seen from below, as Michelangelo originally intended.²⁹ Seen from below, the figure is transformed. The proportions are 'corrected' by the increase in the depth of the lap and the reduction in the length of the torso. What is more, a low-angle view also exchanges the impression of tension and anger, so strong in the level views, for greater composure, dignity and majesty.

Pygmalionism and Death

Film not only transforms the statues; it also makes them move. The cinema mobilises sculptures in many ways. Film not only subjects stable statues to a narrative dynamic or to the passing of time; it also turns them into moving shapes and patterns through montage and camera movements. In addition, the encounter between a sculpture and a film camera makes the confrontation between movement and stasis explicit. Furthermore, the juxtaposition of movement versus stasis also invokes the confrontation between life and death. Film not only mobilises statues; it also animates them, makes them alive. Suggesting visual, psychological and physical forms of interaction between himself and the *Moses* statue, Antonioni acts as a modern Pygmalion, the legendary Cypriot sculptor who created his own perfect female out of ivory. According to Ovid's *Metamorphoses*, the beauty of his virtuous statue was so breathtaking that the sculptor fell in love with his own creation and beseeched Venus to bestow life upon it. The artist's wish was granted and the cold ivory turned to warm flesh at his touch.³⁰ Not surprisingly, the motif of a sculpture coming to life was cherished by many filmmakers, as their medium is based precisely on the animation of the still image. Antonioni, too, presents cinema as a Pygmalean medium. With the help of camera movements, editing and light, it is, first and foremost, the film that animates the static sculptures. Like Pygmalion, Antonioni touches the sculpture. Not coincidentally, he even touches Moses's knee, evoking a popular legend stating that, upon the completion of the Moses sculpture, Michelangelo struck the right knee asking, *Perché non parli?* ('Why aren't you talking?'). There is a scar on the knee thought to be the mark of Michelangelo's hammer.[31] With his gesture, Antonioni not only evokes Michelangelo's own fascination with the myth of the living statue in relation to the *Moses* sculpture; he also situates himself in the tradition of literary Pygmalean fantasies about the *Moses* statue by authors such as Salomon Ludwig Steinheim, Giuseppe Revere and Freud.[32]

In *The Dream of the Living Statue*, Kenneth Gross notes that the idea of a statue coming to life is bound to the opposing thought: that the statue was once something living, 'a creature stilled, emptied of life, turned to stone or bronze or plaster', and that cultural history abounds in fantasies in which living beings are turned into stone, whether through love, grief, terror or jealousy – including such figures as Niobe, Aglauros, Echo and Atlas.[33] Represented on film, static sculptures seem to come alive, but they are always regarded as dead matter when juxtaposed with living beings. The association of sculptures with death is related to their function in the film's narrative, as well as in reality: sculptures often memorialise luminaries or are funerary monuments – something that is also the case in Michelangelo's monument for Pope Julius II in San Pietro in Vincoli. In addition, *Lo Sguardo di Michelangelo* turns and twists the relations between life and death, or movement and stasis, as the muscular and perennially young Moses figure is contrasted with the sculptural features of Antonioni's old and rigid face, almost stagnated due to a stroke. In front of the sculpture, he is hardly moving, evoking the statuesque beauty of the characters in his modernist masterpieces of the 1960s – *L'Avventura* (1960), *La Notte* (1961), *L'Eclisse* (1962), *Il Deserto Rosso* (1964). As the intertitle at the beginning of the film states, it is through the 'magic of movies' that we see the director, who was confined to a wheelchair since the 1980s, visiting the sculpture on foot. Moses's monumentality becomes more powerful through the encounter with the vulnerable body of Antonioni, who is confronting his own mortality at the age of ninety-two. In so doing, the funeral monument of the quintessential 'Renaissance Pope' also becomes a work of commemoration for Michelangelo Antonioni. This is emphasised by the film's soundtrack, which consists only of the muffled sounds of the city streets, vague echoes of footsteps and creaking wooden church furniture reverberating in the church interior. The silence of the statues, their muteness (represented as if we long for them to speak) contributes to their solipsistic inaccessibility and mystery, mirrored by Antonioni's own meditative silence.

Notes

1. This article elaborates on some of the arguments discussed in several chapters in Steven Jacobs, Susan Felleman, Vito Adriaensens and Lisa Colpaert's *Screening*

Statues: Sculpture and Cinema (Edinburgh: Edinburgh University Press, 2017), in which Antonioni's film is only briefly mentioned.
2. See Penelope Curtis, *Sculpture on Screen: The Very Impress of the Object* (Lisbon: Calouste Gulbenkian Museum, 2017).
3. See Dominique Païni (ed.), *Lo Sguardo di Michelangelo: Antonioni e le arti* (exhibition catalogue) (Ferrara: Ferrara Arte, 2013); Steven Jacobs, 'Between EUR and LA: Townscapes in the work of Michelangelo Antonioni', in Ghent Urban Studies Team (eds), *The Urban Condition: Space, Community, and Self in the Contemporary Metropolis* (Rotterdam: 010 Publishers, 1999), pp. 324–42; and Angela Dalle Vacche, 'Michelangelo Antonioni's *Red Desert*: Painting as ventriloquism and color as movement', in *Cinema and Painting: How Art Is Used in Film* (Austin: University of Texas Press, 1996), pp. 43–80.
4. Jonathan Rosenbaum, 'The Gaze of Antonioni', *Rouge* (2004). Available at <http://www.rouge.com.au/4/antonioni.html> (last accessed 4 August 2020).
5. Linda Murray, *Michelangelo* (London: Thames & Hudson, 1980), pp. 54, 97–102 and 164–6. See also Erwin Panofsky, 'The first two projects of Michelangelo's Tomb of Julius II', *The Art Bulletin*, 19–2 (December 1937), pp. 561–79.
6. Ascanio Condivi, 'The life of Michelangelo Buonarroti' (1553), in *Life, Letters, and Poetry* (Oxford: Oxford University Press, 1999), p. 52.
7. Brett Foster, 'Types and shadows: Uses of Moses in the Renaissance', in Jane Beal (ed.), *Illuminating Moses: A History of Reception from Exodus to the Renaissance* (Leiden: Brill, 2014), pp. 353–406, in particular p. 393.
8. Linda Murray, *Michelangelo* (London: Thames & Hudson, 1980), p. 99.
9. Murray, *Michelangelo*, p. 102.
10. Sigmund Freud, 'Letter to Edoardo Weiss' (12 April 1933), in Edoardo Weiss, *Sigmund Freud as a Consultant* (New York: Intercontinental Medical Book Corporation, 1970), p. 74.
11. Sigmund Freud, 'Der Moses des Michelangelo', *Imago*, 3–1 (1914), pp. 15–36. English translation included in Sigmund Freud, *The Standard Edition of the Complete Psychological Works of Sigmund Freud*, vol. XIII, 1913–14 (London: Hogarth Press, 1955), pp. 209–38. This interpretation is contradicted by many other commentators. MacMillan and Swales, for instance, state that the statue depicts the moment when Moses sees God, as described in Exodus 33. See Malcolm MacMillan and Peter Swales, 'Observations from the refuse-heap: Freud, Michelangelo's Moses, and psychoanalysis', *American Imago*, 60–1 (March 2003), pp. 41–104. See also Jerome Oremland, 'Freud and Michelangelo's Moses Statue', *Doppio Sogno: Rivista Internazionale di Psicoterapia e Istituzioni*, 10 (2005). Available at <http://www.doppio-sogno.it/numero10/ing/13.pdf> (last accessed 4 August 2020); Mary Bergstein, 'Freud's "Moses of Michelangelo": Vasari, photography, and art historical practice', *The Art Bulletin*, 88–1 (March 2006), pp. 158–76; and Asher Biemann, *Dreaming of Michelangelo: Jewish Variations on a Modern Theme* (Stanford, CA: Stanford University Press, 2012), p. 57. The figure of Moses continued to fascinate Freud until the very end of his life. One of his last publications was *Der Mann Moses und die monotheistische Religion* (Amsterdam: Albert de Lange, 1939).

12. Kenneth Gross, *The Dream of the Moving Statue* (Pennsylvania: Pennsylvania State University Press, 2006), p. 187.
13. Gross, *The Dream of the Moving Statue*, p. 191.
14. Alessandro Serrano, 'Michelangelo's "Moses" shines once again' (6 February 2017). Available at <http://www.italianways.com/michelangelos-moses-shines-once-again/> (last accessed 4 August 2020).
15. Giorgio Vasari, *The Lives of the Artists* (Oxford: Oxford University Press, 1991), p. 434.
16. Johann Wolfgang von Goethe, 'Observations on the Laocoon', originally published in *Propyläen*, I, 1 (1798) and republished in John Gage (ed.), *Goethe on Art* (Berkeley: University of California Press, 1980), p. 81.
17. Vasari, *The Lives of the Artists*, p. 434.
18. Johann Gottfried Herder, *Plastik: Einige Wahrnehmungen über Form und Gestalt aus Pygmalions bildendem Traume* (Riga and Leipzig: Hartknoch & Breitkopf, 1778). See also Alex Potts, *The Sculptural Imagination: Figurative, Modernist, Minimalist* (New Haven, CT: Yale University Press, 2000), pp. 28–34.
19. Adolf von Hildebrand, *Das Problem der Form in der bildenden Kunst* (Strassburg: Heitz & Mündel, 1893).
20. Heinrich Wölfflin, 'Wie man Skulpturen aufnehmen soll', *Zeitschrift für bildende Kunst*, VII (1896), pp. 224–8; VIII (1897), pp. 294–7; and XXVI (1915), pp. 237–44.
21. Potts, *The Sculptural Imagination*, p. 98.
22. Vivian Sobchack, *The Address of the Eye: A Phenomenology of Film Experience* (Princeton, NJ: Princeton University Press, 1992); Laura U. Marks, *The Skin of Film: Intercultural Cinema, Embodiment, and the Senses* (Durham, NC: Duke University Press, 2000); and Jennifer M. Barker, *The Tactile Eye: Touch and the Cinematic Experience* (Berkeley: University of California Press, 2009).
23. William Tucker, *The Language of Sculpture* (London: Thames & Hudson, 1974), p. 107.
24. Tucker, *The Language of Sculpture*, p. 145.
25. Rudolf Arnheim, 'Sculpture: The nature of a medium', in *To the Rescue of Art: Twenty-Six Essays* (Berkeley: University of California Press, 1992), p. 88.
26. André Malraux, *Psychologie de l'art* (Geneva: Skira, 1947), p. 17. See also André Malraux, *Les Voix du silence* (Paris: Gallimard, 1951); and André Malraux, *Le Musée imaginaire de la sculpture mondiale* (Paris: Gallimard, 1952–4).
27. Malraux, *Psychologie de l'art*, p. 24.
28. See Henri Zerner, 'Malraux and the power of photography', in Geraldine Johnson (ed.), *Sculpture and Photography: Envisioning the Third Dimension* (Cambridge: Cambridge University Press, 1998), pp. 116–30.
29. Anton Springer, *Raffael und Michelangelo* (Leipzig: Szeemann, 1878), p. 241. See Earl E. Rosenthal, 'Michelangelo's Moses, dal di sotto in sù', *The Art Bulletin*, 46–4 (December 1964), pp. 544–50.
30. Victor Stoichita, *The Pygmalion Effect: From Ovid to Hitchcock* (Chicago: University of Chicago Press, 2008).

31. This anecdote can be found in numerous texts on Michelangelo's *Moses*, particularly in tour guides. It is also often mentioned in compilations of legends and anecdotes regarding the lives of famous artists. Similar anecdotes appear in biographies of other famous sculptors such as Donatello. See, for instance, Emil Pirchan, *Künstlerbrevier: Vom Arbeiten, Leben und Lieben der Maler, Bildhauer und Baumeister aus zwei Jahrtausenden in aller Welt* (Vienna: Wilhelm Frick, 1939), pp. 58, 21.
32. See Biemann, *Dreaming of Michelangelo*.
33. Gross, *The Dream of the Moving Statue*, p. 15 and p. 75.

CHAPTER 3

The Photo-filmic and the Post-human: Picturesque Landscapes at the Peripheries of Global Cinema
Ágnes Pethő

The way that the technology and aesthetic of film, photography and painting come together in digital cinema has emerged as perhaps the most intriguing phenomenon of intermediality today. Once these formerly distinct media could also be perceived as modulations of the same image, produced, retouched or displayed on the same digital devices, the discourse on the relationships between photography, film and painting shifted correspondingly from mapping their mutual influences within the history of the arts towards describing their amalgamation, as well as understanding 'the photographic', 'the cinematic' or 'the painterly' as transversal concepts (applicable beyond the divisions of traditional media) in the aesthetic of contemporary arts. The concept of the photo-filmic can be seen as central for this vast new area of research. Despite the contraction of the two words, 'photo' and 'filmic', the term (coined by Alexander Streitberger and Hilde Van Gelder)[1] does not denote the emergence of a new hybrid media from the merger of photography and film in the digital age but may instead refer to various ways of layering structures of film and photography within one image. We can therefore speak of such images as active 'visual events' in which 'heterogenous temporalities, perceptions, uses, and meanings collide and overlap'.[2]

This chapter focuses on the photo-filmic qualities of three films made at what we may consider the periphery of world cinema (Mauritania, Russia, Azerbaijan), yet enjoying a certain degree of visibility within the international arthouse film festival circuit: *Timbuktu*, directed by Abderrahmane Sissako, *Test (Ispytaniye)*, by Alexander Kott, and *Nabat*, by Elchin Musaoglu (all made in 2014). These films offer copious examples of the use of a certain kind of photo-filmic tableau, an image that looks like an individual photograph, framed from a central perspective, with minimal movement and a shot duration long enough to enable contemplation as a single picture. Such images appear in a relative autonomy and do not have a conventional rhetorical effect in the narrative; rather, they strike the viewer primarily as 'photographic'. They foreground the individual photograph's inherent, ambivalent connection to life and death, as well as its close ties with the art of painting through a primary emphasis on the visual construction of a frame. As such, they become the appropriate form to unfold a kind of post-human landscape, a setting for eschatological narratives told in the minimalist mode, for mulling over the clash between elemental, biological existence and powerful forces of society (terrorism, wars and nuclear disaster) that threaten this existence with imminent destruction. On the one hand, their 'politics' of the picturesque, based on an extensive use of landscape tableaux, is consistent with the already established canon of slow cinema, in which deliberate slowness and the photographic display of spaces and objects conveying non-action, immobility and inertia enable an elegiac meditation on the destructive forces of man enacted upon humanity and nature. On the other hand, however, these films also demonstrate the rich affordances of photo-filmic images, through both the way photography is explicitly included in films, and the way that the in-betweenness of photography and film becomes productive either by means of infusing the quality of the 'photographic' into cinema, halting the flow of images by lingering on photographic framing/deframing, or the other way around, through introducing cinematic movement into the still frames.

PICTORIALISING THE WORLD THROUGH THE PHOTOGRAPHIC

Although all three films present specific geographical locations and protagonists in an ethnic and historical context, with stories inspired by real events, they belong to the emerging transnational type of filmmaking[3] that caters to a global audience with simple, fable-like plots. The condensed narratives, underscored by the laconic one-word titles (*Timbuktu*, *Test* and *Nabat*) focus on basic emotions connected to parenthood, love and grief, which emphasise not the here and now but the anywhere and anytime. Furthermore, all of these films perform a movement from particular to universal through pictorial stylisation, as the picturesque tableau shots display both a connection to and a disconnection from a historically localisable profilmic reality. This shift from specific to universal is combined with an unsettling mixture of documentary realism and pictorial detachment, and we see a rigorous control over detail and adherence to structure on the pictorial level, only to be seriously undermined by themes of extreme violence, vulnerability and transience.

In *Timbuktu*, the legendary city named in the title, once famed for its wealth and fabulous collections of ancient manuscripts, is under the occupation of radical Islamists, who impose a cruel and absurd rule which includes banning music and football or stoning young unmarried couples to death. The main characters are a cattle herdsman, his wife and daughter, who live in a tent among the sand dunes outside the city and do not flee, believing that they will somehow escape the danger posed by the jihadists. In the end, however, both he and his wife are shot to death. In the folktale-like Russian film, *Test*, the time is not the present, but August 1959, when Russia performed its first hydrogen bomb test in a supposedly uninhabited region somewhere in remote Kazakhstan. Excluded from the political map of the Soviet Union, this spot is home to a father and teenage daughter living in harmony with nature, looking after their sheep. There is even a love story involving the daughter and the rivalry between two young prospective suitors from the small settlement nearby, but it all comes to an astonishing end with the nuclear explosion, appearing like an eruption of the sun that literally sweeps them away in one magnificent breath.[4] *Nabat* brings us closer to the present in another region of the former USSR, the site of ethnic and territorial conflict between the Armenians and the Azerbaijani over the enclave of Nagorno-Karabakh (which took place from 1988 to 1994, with the border clashes resuming in 2008 and sporadic violent attacks still going on in 2020). The war, which left the land devastated and thousands killed or displaced, is, however, only a distant background to the film, which does not name the conflicting parties. It concentrates instead on the quiet drama of a mother, Nabat, presenting the day-to-day chores of the elderly woman, who refuses to leave her home even after the village has been completely deserted. She stays behind to take care of her sick husband, and affectionately tends the grave of her only son, killed in the war. In the end, after single-handedly burying her husband, she remains and dies all alone, literally fading into the final aerial landscape shot that bookends the film, resonating with a similarly slow sequence at the beginning, in which her figure first appears on the winding footpath to the village (Figure 3.1).

What I would like to highlight, using the example of these films, is the performativity of this type of aestheticism that is achieved through a picturesque quality, through instances in which a sensation of the 'photographic' is inscribed within the 'cinematic'. The most striking example of the three is undoubtedly *Test*, whose director, Alexander Kott (also a photographer), reinforced this moving-picture-book impression by making the film absolutely speechless. What the photographic brings to the cinematic in this case is not the emphasis on an indexical relation to the profilmic reality, but a certain 'disconnect' through the conspicuous mediation of the high-definition image and the careful composition of each frame, which always means, at the same time, the connection between the eye, the lens and the hand: the gesture of moulding the visible into a picture.

This may remind us of the intersection of painting and photography in the idea of the 'picturesque' in its duality, referring both to something pleasing to the eye and to something that looks like a picture in nature. The popular notion, introduced in the eighteenth century by William Gilpin[5] in connection with landscape painting, meant not only 'a peculiar kind of beauty, which is agreeable in a picture',[6] but 'the conjunction of nature picture, eye'.[7] The picturesque meant a 'system of judicious selection and combination [. . .] amounting to a systematic process of aesthetic ordering',[8] or as Gilpin explained, 'nature gives us the material of landscape: woods, rivers, lakes, trees, ground, and mountains: but leaves us to work them up into pictures, as our fancy leads'.[9] The discourse on the picturesque not only sought to advance landscape painting up the hierarchy of established genres in the eighteenth and nineteenth centuries,[10] but led directly to 'painters burning with desire' for the 'conception of photography', according to Geoffrey Batchen,[11] and as such, it could be seen as a kind of 'proto-photographic' thinking.[12] Photography then appropriated it in turn as a strategy of so-called pictorialism, to emancipate itself from a mere technological innovation and to make visible its descent from the traditional aesthetic principles of painting, to highlight, in the words of Peter Galassi, that 'photography was not a bastard left by science on the doorstep of art, but a legitimate child of the Western pictorial tradition'.[13] Or, as Roland Barthes put it, '"Pictorialism" is only an exaggeration of what the Photograph thinks of itself.'[14] The picturesque, in this way, is not just a quality but a gesture shared by painting and photography: a foregrounding of constructedness and aestheticism, of a kind of 'imageness' that has a 'beautifully circular' dynamic, to quote Rosalind Krauss, in which a 'given moment of the perceptual array'[15] always reconnects with established patterns in a picture. Therefore, the 'photographic' permeates the 'cinematic' through the picturesque in the most natural way. What makes it intriguing in the examples of these films is its connection with post-human landscapes.

The opposition of nature and culture is the essence of all depictions of landscape in fine art (whether they are mere backgrounds to human figures, complex allegories, vehicles for ideas or projections of emotions, sublime vistas or domesticated environments, attesting to the power of God or to the power of Man transforming and inhabiting the Earth, or reducing it to mere shapes and colours). In these films the tableau compositions pictorialise nature in all its grandeur, together with the destructive effect of human aggression which blows apart a harmonious coexistence of nature and culture. And while the discourse on post-humanism is most often concerned either with the loss of the human point of view in favour of the machine or with the dehumanising world of technology, these films push to the background contemporary conflicts between humanity and its destructive technologies of war and engage instead a photo-filmic pictorialism in which the tension between movement and stillness, human and non-human, high *techné* in the image quality and old technology (or no technology) in the world portrayed are nested within the revival of the picturesque tradition in an unsettling way.

The tableau compositions in these films, placing their protagonists in their environment in long shots or showing the surrounding landscape from a wide angle, symbolically wrap up their whole world. The careful inclusion in the frames of significant ethnographic and geographic details, architecture, and objects that define a household and way of living alternates with extreme large-scale compositions of elements of nature (earth and sky: mountain ranges in *Nabat*, the desert in *Timbuktu*, the vastness of the steppe in *Test*). The gesture of constructing the image is playfully alluded to in *Test* by showing the young girl's own scrapbook of collages using magazine cut-outs, twigs, dry leaves and cotton wool. The scrapbook that miniaturises the world reiterates the difference in scale between the world of the protagonists and a more universal perspective revealed in 'the larger picture' suggested by the wide landscape shots, alluding to the precarity of their situation. The sheer difference in scale recurring in all three films adds a kind of cultural non-specificity, or even post-human viewpoint, in which it is not man and the universe seen from a metaphysical perspective (as we would see, for example, in the small human figures set against the infinity of nature in a Romantic painting), but only a shift from the way the human eye looks around to what the mechanical gaze of the camera can show. The presence of maps on the walls in *Test* and in *Nabat* are further examples of differences in perspective, and are not only signs of the scientific interest in understanding the world we live in (as we see in the maps and globes included in the famous seventeenth-century Dutch paintings), but indicative perhaps of a failed aspiration of mankind to reduce the whole world to a human scale. There is also an opposition between the fixed structure of the map and the instability of the human condition. As the films show, maps enfold the world within the homes, but homes and people can be easily erased from the 'map' in a larger perspective. The inclusion of people in the wide frames makes them almost invisible, and scenes often stage the disappearance of figures in a landscape, which only echoes the exclusion of the protagonists from the world depicted in the film (the small community is disregarded and wiped out by the nuclear test in Kott's film; the jihadists imprison and execute everyone in *Timbuktu* who does not comply with their regulations; Nabat finds herself in a village that has been completely evacuated, see Figure 3.1).

At the same time, the incongruity between the beauty of the photographic frames and the themes of violence and destruction at the core of the narratives adds an affective charge that ranges from the melancholic to the melodramatic. Melodrama always presents an innocent victim who has to face antagonistic forces that prove to be overwhelming. 'One can speak of melodrama only if

Figure 3.1 Staging the disappearance of figures in a landscape: Elchin Musaoglu's *Nabat* (2014).

the environment represents a force incommensurate with the protagonist's powers.'[16] In classical melodrama, this insurmountable power can be either social, emotional or physical in nature; in modernist melodramas, however, it is not the presence but the absence of something that proves emotionally debilitating. But what happens when, in our so-called 'post-human' times, as Bruno Latour put it, the questions we have to deal with are just 'too big for everybody' and we all live like fish inside a bowl, while there is 'an ocean of catastrophes that [. . .] unfold' around us?[17] In these films the protagonists appear in situations over which they have absolutely no control, where their bare existence is threatened by brutal forces. However, these forces are unusually portrayed: the jihadists appear somewhat childish and even humanely flawed in *Timbuktu*, destruction is enacted by unseen agents and is both majestic and unexpected in the doomsday vision of *Test*, and in the quiet life of *Nabat* the war is present only in distant noises. The films thus seem to retain the palpable imbalance of power, but also effectively remove from the visible frame the real antagonists in the equation. It is never really two sides set against each other; it is the same humankind that inspires admiration and abomination, who may feel a perplexing collective guilt over the violence plaguing the world while being victims at the mercy of uncontrollable forces. The immense cruelty and the absurdity of the destruction appears inscrutable and just as overwhelming as the picturesque beauty of the world surrounding the protagonists (who remain enclosed in their 'fishbowl'). This emphasis on the all-pervasive aestheticism of the images not only provides a puzzling contrast or pictorial 'disconnect' from the disconcerting narrative but also makes such landscapes post-human icons of the world, which have become detached and incomprehensible not because they remind us of some divine power or the lack thereof, but because they pictorialise in the same way, filtered through the impassive lens of the camera, both the human lifeworld and its destruction.[18]

THE PHOTO-FILMIC IN BETWEEN LIFE AND DEATH

In the picture-perfect landscapes, shocking content is rendered in a strikingly glossy style. In *Timbuktu*, following the conflict arising from the killing of the family cow by a fisherman, the infuriated herdsman, Kidane, attacks him and, as they struggle, accidentally shoots the fisherman, whose death will ultimately seal his own fate as well, being caught and sentenced without mercy by the jihadists who have seized power. The fight between the two men ends in a tableau in which, once more, the figures become lost in the landscape, one submerged in the lake, the other wading through the shallow water in an extreme long shot enclosing the whole watery expanse at sundown. The scene is followed by a closer shot of the discovery of the dead body, in which people are reduced to mere shadows reflected in the shimmering surface of the lake, in the warm, golden light of sunset. The scene in which Nabat buries her husband is composed in a similar long shot against the painterly rendering of the setting sun, just like the images of the toxic, radioactive nature in *Test* (for example, the contamination and subsequent passing of the father is rendered in a disturbing visual pun, showing the silhouette of the old man against the horizon, as if literally swallowing the setting sun that appears as a ball of fire). Sites of death are just as photogenic as sites of life, as we see in the idyllic domestic tableaux. This is, however, an unsettling pictoriality that may be categorised as 'pretty', shaping images into 'poster-like tableaux vivants', a style treated with utter disdain by Siegfried Kracauer, as Rosalind Galt reminds us.[19] None the less, as Galt emphasises, 'prettiness can offer its own politics'.[20] By mapping out a world that is rich in sensuous details (textures, ornaments, everyday objects), images may offer an anthropological density in an appeal to global attention. As such, they may appear as a critical strand of art cinema that addresses socio-political (or in these cases, bio-political) issues in a picturesque, trans-cultural form that counters the Eurocentric rejection of the Oriental and decorative, and reconnects with this pictorial tradition. Accordingly, we may notice how some of the attractive tableaux showing the loving togetherness of the family in *Timbuktu* seem to articulate in this way an explicit dialogue with the traditional group compositions that have become a staple for Orientalism in painting (see Figure 3.2).

This gesture of incessant pictorialisation introduces, at the same time, another type of circularity into the picturesque (beside the enclosure of nature

Figure 3.2 Abderrahmane Sissako, *Timbuktu* (2014): tableau compositions in dialogue with the Orientalist tradition in painting.

into a picture, the dissolving of the unique in the multiple and multipliable, discussed by Krauss and quoted earlier), one that not only disconnects, but reconnects the image to the human world through the conspicuous mediation of photographic technology. First of all, the films effectively fuse the complex pictorialist tradition with a style of digital photography already vernacular in the age of Instagram, which is promoted by international photography competitions (and due to which the picturesque has come to signify something pleasing to the eye that looks not like a picture in nature, but like an award-winning photograph). This new digital aesthetic infuses the picturesque with a pronounced post-human quality by relying conspicuously on the affordances of digital technology, of the latest cameras and lenses, and produces, as a marker of artistry, either what Lev Manovich calls a kind of 'super-realism', which shows 'much more detail than a human eye can see from the same point of view',[21] or adds its own viewpoint, independent of the human eye. It also continues, in an extreme form, the legacy of the picturesque in art not only by promoting landscape depictions against other genres but by moving landscape shots (together with cityscapes) to the top of the hierarchy (as a study of award-winning photographs shows[22]). In such pictures a kind of frontal tableau has become a norm in which the camera angle is strictly parallel to the ground, and shows the horizon in a horizontal line or, in the case of the now popular aerial shots of drone photography, the earth is flattened as a drawing, textured by colours and lines.

While none of the films mentioned in this chapter can be reduced entirely to such a popular picturesque style, they are clearly adhering to its conventions in their eye-catching compositions and, to varying degrees, perhaps even consciously addressing its audiences. They contrast an appealingly contemporary form with the destruction of a simple way of life unfolding in a

Figure 3.3 Sites of destruction rendered in a 'poster-like tableau vivant' style in Alexander Kott's *Test* (2014).

closeness with nature and are imbued with an elegiac quality through 'the still frame's association with death' (Figure 3.3).[23]

Photographs or the act of photography appear in the film to substitute more direct forms of destruction with the 'catastrophe', the inevitability of death that Barthes identified in each photograph.[24] In *Nabat*, for example, photographs become the signs of life disappearing from the village. The photographer has lost the only photo of Nabat's son, who died in the war, causing much pain to the old woman, who later desperately rummages through the photographs scattered around the photographer's abandoned house. Death as the absence of the living is even more poignant in the missing photograph amid the pile of unknown people's family pictures, which not only multiply the single photo's connection to death but, as there is no one to see them any more, deny even their similarly inherent possibility of memorialising the dead. Also, an ironic equality is instituted between the displaced villagers' photos and the 'out of place' cut-outs of Marilyn Monroe or Che Guevara pinned to the wall. In a bitter photographic pun at the end of the film, the camera reveals that Nabat has filled in the empty frame intended to hold the photo of her son with the picture of Che.

In one of the most memorable scenes of the Russian film, *Test*, the young suitor of the girl takes photos of her with an old-fashioned camera and returns at night to project the image on to the wall of the girl's house, as if it were a movie. The ghost-like photo-filmic image, distorted by the texture of the decaying wall, not only hints at the convergence of technologies but reminds us, yet again, of photography/film as an imprint of life that doubles as a death mask (in the way Bazin has famously described in 'The Ontology of the Photographic Image'[25]). In the movie it also forebodes the actual demise of the protagonists by possibly reminding us of the shadows of people seared on to the walls by the explosion of the atomic bomb in Hiroshima and Nagasaki. In both these films, photography is a mark of displaced terrors, of unspeakable acts against humanity that remain off screen. While *Timbuktu* features no photographs, there are ubiquitous mobile phones. The jihadists, as avid cinematographers, are also shown in the process of shooting a propaganda video, with a young recruit made to rehearse a speech in a fixed-frame frontal composition captured by a small digital camera. Thus, by the subtle inclusion of photography and film, *Timbuktu* and *Test* allude also to technology as a real bio-power that has irreversibly transformed our lifeworld, viewed in terms of a garden (to quote the title of Ihde's famous work on post-phenomenology[26]). The real power of technology in this case does not lie in the inequality between human and machine but is revealed in its attachment to humans, as an extension of body and mind, related to affect and emotion (for instance, the missing photo acts as real torture for *Nabat*, while the photo-filmic camera enables the courtship of the young man in *Test* and is used as a means for political propaganda in *Timbuktu*).

Last but not least, we should speak of the interaction between the 'photographic' and the 'cinematic' that runs through these films, of the way in which the expressivity of photographic aesthetic absorbed by the still frames is always dependent on their arrangement in a cinematic montage, as well as on the intertwining of stillness with movement. If the 'photographic' can be seen as a 'hint of stillness within movement'[27] that always threatens to bring cinema's technological illusion of life to a halt,[28] the work of the 'cinematic' is the exact opposite: it reanimates the mechanically fragmented whole and infuses the still images with life through the introduction of movement. Therefore, when speaking of the 'photo-filmic', we need to focus our attention on both components at all times. This duality may also recall Bruno Latour's concept of 'iconophilia', which stresses the meshing of stasis and movement, in contrast with 'idolatry', which favours the immovable image. 'The iconoclast dreams of an unmediated access to the truth, of a complete absence of images,' he writes.

> Iconophilia is respect not for the image itself, but for the movement of the image. It is what teaches us that there is nothing to see when [. . .] we focus on the visual itself, instead of the movement, the passage, the transition from one form of image to another.[29]

In the first images of *Test*, for example, we see the face of the father in close-up, sleeping peacefully on what seems to be a cushion made of lambskin; then there is a sudden cut to an aerial wide shot showing him from the position of a drone high above as a tiny figure lying in the back of a truck, only to continue with another extreme close-up of the sheep, revealed to be sleeping just as peacefully as the man, as the slow camera movement reframes their heads side by side. There are several other scenes like this in which the sudden cut or transition from one viewpoint to another, or from a human scale to a non-human one, builds a sequence via a typical photographic deframing and reframing which playfully recontextualises its subject. The photo-filmic performativity in cinema is always predicated on such oscillations perceived in a superimposition, reframing or collage. Most typically, it also emerges through meshing the stasis of the photograph with the sensuous experience of tracing the movement of a single element in the frame as the rush of vitality and intensity, thus materialising it literally as *tableau vivant* (for instance, in the long sequence of water flowing slowly towards the solitary dried-up tree).

In *Timbuktu* we see how the 'photographic' image is enhanced through its enfoldment within a narrative cinematic sequence. There is a scene in which we see how one of the jihadist leaders, who is attracted to the wife of the protagonist, approaches the woman and her daughter when the husband is away. She is washing her hair and the man demands that she cover her head. The woman defies him and he leaves slightly embarrassed, like a teenager who does not really know how to deal with the sudden surge of complex emotions. In the subsequent scene, the jihadist and his young interpreter are riding in a jeep and they come upon a configuration of hills in the desert that resembles the pubic mound of a woman. Frustrated, the man takes out his gun and mows down the tuft of grass popping up between two sand dunes (Figure 3.4). The image harks back to an old tradition in painting, the anthropomorphisation of the landscape that reveals 'an underlying animist, metamorphic thought that considers nature as a unitary living organism'[30] and superimposes the female anatomy over the geomorphic shape, thus transforming the abstract, generic image of the body into a unique and affective photo-filmic body framed in the tableau. It also playfully transposes and reverses the fashionable trope of the photographic bodyscape (the body viewed as a landscape) on to film, displaying an explosive intensity within a single frame unravelled in the moving sequence. A similar, yet more straightforward, transfer takes place in the first images of the film, in which gunmen are shooting at wooden sculptures in the desert and blowing off the women figures' breasts, and in which, again, destruction is symbolically aimed both at the human body and, by extension, at the body of a specific culture.[31] The scene is symptomatic of all three films, in which complex and large-scale political tensions are replaced with elemental human emotions or brute impulses.

At the same time, the sequence is yet another example that reveals that the oscillation between film and photography becomes crucial in establishing an intermedial discourse in which the two major strategies of the photo-filmic described above (that is, photography appearing in film and the

Figure 3.4 The anthropomorphisation of the landscape in *Timbuktu* (2014): hills resembling the pubic mound of a woman.

interpenetration of the 'photographic' and the 'cinematic'[32]) are, at the same time, complementary in reinforcing the photographic quality of the films, and antithetical, inasmuch as they deepen the tension between the latent 'death drive' in photographic stillness[33] and the animistic force integral to moving pictures. There is an impression of media fusion in quasi-autonomous tableau compositions, but this condensed form becomes really saturated as it unravels into a series of sensations discernible in between art and life, abstraction and raw corporeality, and so on. It also makes us understand that the photo-filmic should not be considered as a simple merger of terms denoting the connection of the two media, but should be defined, more than anything else, by a performative quality manifested in the mutual permeability of the 'photographic' and the 'cinematic'.[34] Modulating in between stasis and motion, stability and subversion of stability, and releasing unsettling affects through incongruities in scale and aestheticism, the photo-filmic becomes a figuration that packs together both the vitality and the vulnerability of the world. It also captures situations of powerlessness in powerful images.

We see similar features in some of the films made by more famous auteurs like Abbas Kiarostami, Nuri Bilge Ceylan (both of them fine-art photographers as well), Alexander Sokurov or Jia Zhangke, who also use large-scale landscape tableaux (often combined with ethnographic details and the self-reflexivity of the camera). However, the three films chosen for analysis make more palpable a historical connection between painting, photography and film, while they rely more ostentatiously on the disquieting, paradoxical aspects of an all-pervasive pictorialisation in the digital age. The crisp, poster-perfect images we see in these films align with the much-debated tradition of the picturesque, of the 'good, unifying and reasonable forms proposed for identification' that Lyotard identifies as the opposite of a more subversive type of art.[35] This is an aesthetic that negotiates its visibility on the shifting terrain in between high art and popular culture. It is also a form that relies on the deep imbrication between traditional arts and new media, and one that is continually reloaded with the tensions of intermedial in-betweenness.

Notes

1. Alexander Streitberger and Hilde Van Gelder, 'Photo-filmic images in contemporary visual culture', *Philosophy of Photography*, 1–1 (2010), pp. 48–53.
2. Brianne Cohen and Alexander Streitberger (eds), 'Introduction', in *The Photofilmic: Entangled Images in Contemporary Art and Visual Culture* (Leuven: Leuven University Press, 2016), p. 12.
3. Two of them are also co-productions that involve an international crew. *Timbuktu* is a French–Mauritanian production directed by Abderrahmane Sissako (a filmmaker born in Mauritania but raised in Mali, who learned his trade in Moscow in the footsteps of Andrei Tarkovsky and is now working in France). The Azerbaijani film, *Nabat*, has a famous Iranian actress (Fatemah Motamed-Aria) in the title role and a director with a history of documentary filmmaking in Turkey.
4. The French title of the film is actually *Le Souffle* (*The Breath*).
5. William Gilpin, *Three Essays: On Picturesque Beauty; On Picturesque Travel; and On Sketching Landscape: to which is Added a Poem, On Landscape Painting* (London: R. Blamire, 1792).
6. William Gilpin, *An Essay upon Prints Containing Remarks upon the Principles of Picturesque Beauty, etc.* (London: G. Scott for J. Robson, 1768), p. 2.
7. Geoffrey Batchen, *Burning with Desire: The Conception of Photography* (Cambridge, MA, and London: MIT Press, 1997), p. 75.
8. Batchen, *Burning with Desire*, p. 75.
9. Gilpin, *Three Essays*, p. 159.
10. As in literature, where the epic was considered for centuries the highest form in the fine arts, at least in Europe, so-called history painting, based on narratives from history, religious literature or mythology, was the most prestigious genre.
11. See Batchen, *Burning with Desire*.
12. Batchen, *Burning with Desire*, p. 69.
13. Peter Galassi, *Before Photography: Painting and the Invention of Photography* (New York: Museum of Modern Art, 1981), p. 12.
14. Roland Barthes, *Camera Lucida* (1980) (New York: Hill and Wang, 2010), p. 31.
15. Rosalind Krauss, 'The originality of the avant-garde: A postmodernist repetition', *October*, 18 (Autumn 1981), p. 62.
16. András Bálint Kovács, *Screening Modernism: European Art Cinema, 1950–1980* (Chicago: University of Chicago Press, 2007), p. 89.
17. Bruno Latour, 'Waiting for Gaia. Composing the Common World Through Arts and Politics. A Lecture at the French Institute, London, November 2011', p. 2. Available at <http://www.bruno-latour.fr/sites/default/files/124-GAIA-LONDON-SPEAP_0.pdf> (last accessed 15 September 2019).
18. This kind of cinema has affinity with recent installation art projects dealing with disasters of the Anthropocene, like John Akomfrah's multi-channel video installations, or essay films like Nikolaus Geyrhalter's *Homo Sapiens* (2016), which has moving photographic tableaux filmed in 4K and shows a series of abandoned post-industrial sites reclaimed by nature as traces of the fragility of human existence.

19. Rosalind Galt, *Pretty: Film and the Decorative Image* (New York: Columbia University Press, 2011), p. 120.
20. Galt, *Pretty: Film and the Decorative Image*, p. 17.
21. Lev Manovich, *Instagram and Contemporary Image*, electronic manuscript (2017), p. 61. Available at <http://manovich.net/content/04-projects/152-instagram-and-contemporary-image/instagram_book_manovich_2017.pdf> (last accessed 17 August 2019).
22. See Manovich, *Instagram and Contemporary Image*, pp. 62–3. The second most popular genre of award-winning pictures in the digital age is a variation of landscape photography portraying people, often engaged in some activity, against an 'exotic "national" landscape background' (p. 63), which is a clear descendant of the Orientalist tradition.
23. Laura Mulvey, *Death 24x a Second: Stillness and the Moving Image* (London: Reaktion Books, 2006), p. 70.
24. Barthes, *Camera Lucida*, p. 96.
25. André Bazin, 'The ontology of the photographic image', in *What is Cinema?* (Berkeley: University of California Press, 1967), vol. 1, pp. 9–11.
26. Don Ihde, *Technology and the Lifeworld: From Garden to Earth* (Bloomington: Indiana University Press, 1990).
27. Mulvey, *Death 24x a Second*, p. 67.
28. Mulvey compares it to the mechanics of the 'beautiful automaton', which is wound down 'into its inanimate, uncanny form' (*Death 24x a Second*, p. 70).
29. Bruno Latour, 'How to be iconophilic in art, science and religion', in Peter Galison and Caroline Jones (eds), *Picturing Science, Producing Art* (New York: Routledge, 1998) p. 421.
30. Michel Jeanneret, *Perpetual Motion: Transforming Shapes in the Renaissance from Da Vinci to Montaigne* (Baltimore and London: Johns Hopkins University Press, 2001), p. 259.
31. The scene recalls with some irony the famous essay film of Chris Marker and Alain Resnais, *Statues Also Die* (1963), which condemned the removal of African artworks from their natural cultural context (the place where they are being literally destroyed in the film).
32. I have explored further possibilities of the emergence of the sensation of the photo-filmic in another essay (Ágnes Pethő, 'Figurations of the photofilmic: Stillness versus motion – stillness in motion', in Cohen and Streitberger (eds), *The Photofilmic*, pp. 221–43) that contains several examples from contemporary visual culture and presents two different models for the interaction of the 'photographic' with the 'cinematic' in the films of Béla Tarr and Pedro Costa.
33. See Mulvey, *Death 24x a Second*.
34. This is consistent with the idea that I have emphasised elsewhere that intermediality in general should be regarded as a performative notion (Ágnes Pethő, *Cinema and Intermediality: The Passion for the In-Between*, Newcastle: Cambridge Scholars, 2011, p. 42).
35. Jean-François Lyotard, 'Acinéma', *Wide Angle*, 2 (1978), p. 58.

CHAPTER 4

Dream Screen: On Cinema and Painting, Blur and Absorption

Martine Beugnet

As a film theorist and essayist, Jean Epstein is best known for his advocacy of *photogénie*, a term he invented to describe cinema's incomparable capacity for capturing the world in its endless variability, and expressing its unceasing instability and fluidity.[1] For Epstein, the art of film thrived on this particular aptitude, a predisposition for the manifestation of the fleeting and the indefinite that, he thought, filmmakers should seek and enhance.[2] Shunning the Baudelairian denunciation of photographic-based representation as narrowly mimetic, Epstein thus included film in the long tradition that posits the inseparability of art, imagination and the indefinite.[3]

Produced with the help of defocus or filters, by camera motion, the filming of fast-moving objects, the alteration of the recording speed or the superimposition of frames, blur features prominently amongst the effects of the techniques first developed by the filmmakers of the silent era, who were bent on establishing cinema as an art form. Whether it affects part or the integrality of the image, and plays out as a simple attenuation of contours or as the near fusion of forms, blur appears to contribute naturally to the *photogenic* quality of film.

Yet to consider the effect and meaning of blur in film in relation to Epstein's concept of *photogénie* arguably points to a paradox or ambiguity in his theorising. For, whereas Epstein (a filmmaker who was a master of blurred effects) argued that *photogénie* was medium-specific, as one of the key manifestations of the *photogenic* plasticity of the film image, blur also brings out some of its richest intermedial qualities. In particular, in its attenuation of details and contours, emphasising the whole at the expense of the parts, blur tends to draw the cinema image towards painterly forms. This is not to say that cinema imitates painting, however: even in the pictorialist or 'soft-style' school of filming, the effects of defocus, produced in the duration and variability of a time-based photographic medium, are uniquely cinematic. Distinguished from mere simulation, the kind of stylistic echoes that blur creates between film, photography and painting may therefore qualify as *photogénie*.[4] Indeed, as we will see, the resonances are not unidirectional, and offer a complexity that extends well beyond questions of aesthetic appropriation.

In what follows, I propose to explore some of the ways in which low definition or blur orchestrates the encounter between film and painting. Depending on the technique, film stock, the choice of analogue or digital filming, and the degree of experimentation, such an encounter may take an endless variety of forms. In this instance, I will content myself with looking in particular at the effects of blur on the representation of the human form and, by extension, interrogate the regimes of identification or absorption that are produced when the depiction of the figure eschews visual clarity. For, whether it appears in the hazy, trembling form of 8 mm film, or is caught in the swirling chaos of low-definition, handheld video images, the blurred figure ceases to be a mere assemblage of signifiers to be deciphered by the viewer, becoming instead an experience in sensory perception that requires the spectator to relinquish part of her objective distance to the work.

Created by low or indirect lighting, filters or defocus, the kind of effects I am interested in may be reminiscent of the soft, hazy touch typical of Dutch Renaissance painting; equally, when resulting from the deliberate choice of low definition and the imprint of movement, they appear closer to the Expressionist figuration epitomised by Francis Bacon's work, a style of painting that had initially drawn inspiration from photography and cinema's motion-blur. With reference to films ranging from the silent to the digital era, I will start by looking at the ways in which the softening of contours creates a sense of absorption and elicits an empathetic response from the viewer while, at the same time, at the crossroads between closeness and concealment, the blurring of lines also manifests a tension between intimacy and distance. In turn, I will explore the different kind of absorption offered by the chaotic universes of the cinema of sensation, before discussing the tension between theatricality and absorption in evidence in recent filmmaking. Drawing on Daniel Arasse's study of Vermeer and Michael Fried's classic exegesis on Diderot and painting, as well as Deleuze's writings on silent cinema and on Bacon, I will attempt to outline both theoretical and formal correspondences.

Epstein is not the first to describe or practise cinema as the medium of the elusive and open-ended. From the initial accounts of the first public screenings, to Siegfried Kracauer's observation of the Lumière brothers' predilection for what he coined 'the indeterminate', the capacity of the cinema to manifest the world in its confusion has been singled out repeatedly.[5] Epstein, however, like Germaine Dulac and the other exponents of the first film avant-garde, went further: they did not merely recognise this particular capability of the medium, but promoted experimentation that sought to exploit and enhance it at the recording, as well as the developing, stage. Influential, if less radical than their European avant-gardist counterparts, the advocates of the so-called 'soft-style' elected to adapt some of the 'pictorialist' precepts to film to similar aims.[6]

Hence, in the silent era, filmmakers developed a broad range of techniques destined to emphasise the material and expressive qualities of film, often to the detriment of the 'readability' of its representational content. Part of this experimentation resulted in a declination of blurs, from slight haziness to sheer confusion of lines, and thus a heightening of the plastic quality of the film image reminiscent of painterly techniques: between the soft-style cinematography of Josef von Sternberg and the frenzied camera work of Abel Gance, early cinema offered a broad variety of visual moods capable of emulating the classic *sfumato*, as well as the tormented Turnerian fogginess.[7] The advent of synchronised film sound, however, worked to marginalise such practices: from the 1930s onwards, clear contours and the constancy of figures became the norm, considered necessary to make dialogue and other sounds immediately intelligible, as well as readily assignable to precisely identified sources.[8]

The experimentations of the first avant-garde have nonetheless continued to be a key concern of experimental and art cinema, providing precious alternatives to reductive concepts of film as, first and foremost, a mode of communication. In this persistence of the avant-gardist legacy, blur is not confined, as in mainstream cinema, to the expression of the faulty or amateurish, or to a form of internal montage that serves to guide the gaze towards that part of the image most pertinent to narrative aims.[9] As a natural counterpoint to forms of imaging that favour instantly and fully legible images, in film as in painting, blur fosters an element of mystery and uncertainty, a capacity to elicit curiosity and doubt, and, by extension, to ensure the 'spectator's share'.[10] The enigmatic presentation of the main character, in the opening shot of Marcel L'Herbier's *El Dorado* (1921), is an intriguing reminder of a cinematic form in the making, later curtailed as the more standardised grammar of narrative film became established.

L'Herbier's melodrama begins with a scene at the El Dorado music hall that gives the film its name. The central character, Sibilla, is a cabaret dancer, and she is introduced in the first shot, sitting on stage amongst a line of other dancers waiting to perform. If its presentation of the heroine in her habitual surroundings makes sense in narrative terms, there is nonetheless something strange about this opening shot: whilst the image, including the dancers on either side of Sibilla, is sharp, showing all the detail of their intricate costumes, jewellery and heavily made-up faces, the silhouette of the main protagonist is blurred. To create this effect, unusual at a time when the kind of everyday post-production manipulation we associate with Photoshop was still unthinkable, L'Herbier apparently used a steamed-up filter small enough to cover only part of the lens (the shooting script indicates the presence of a '*cache verre vapeur*').

L'Herbier's decision to fog the silhouette of his main protagonist is soon explicated: if Sibilla appears blurred, it is because she is not completely present to her surroundings. Instead of smiling at the public like the other dancers, she is thinking about her sick child, left behind while she works, and whom a brief insert shows us lying in bed. Hence blurredness, in this case, is not used in its habitual fashion, simply to mark the passage from a scene taking place in a conscious situation to a scene describing a dream and vice versa, but, rather, to manifest a character's state of 'absorption', where the character is so preoccupied that she appears – literally and metaphorically – partly absent from the image. The use of a partial filter creates an exogenous zone at the centre of the image, the undefined appearance of the figure implying its dual spatio-temporal belonging: it is as if Sibilla's slightly hazy form were wavering between two places, here at the cabaret and, at the same time, there, with her child. In this case, therefore, blur is not the sign of a faulty vision, nor is it the expression of a lack or deficiency on the part of the character, but, rather, the manifestation of an exacerbated sensitivity, which the softening of contours and details expresses, yet also envelops in a protective veil. But the show is about to begin, and as the other performers call Sibilla to attention, the whole image becomes sharp.

Commenting on the strangeness of this composition (which L'Herbier repeats later, when Sibilla starts dancing), Gilles Deleuze described it as the confusion of the 'regardant-regardé': a confusion of the 'seer' with the 'seen'.[11] The eye of the camera does not align itself with that of the observers – the cabaret audience that could serve, as in Laura Mulvey's classic description of the construction of the male gaze, as a relay for the spectator's own gaze. Nor is it shadowing that of the character in a subjective point of view – showing what she is distractedly looking at. It is an objective, distant shot; yet by allowing the partial 'withdrawal' of the character's form from the image, it expresses an empathy with her state of mind. Hence the blurring effectively evokes Sibilla's detachment from her surroundings, her tormented self-absorption, in a manner more evocative of the eighteenth-century painterly techniques described in Michael Fried's classic study than of the theatricality of cinema's early melodramas.

In his writings on Diderot and painting, Michael Fried draws on the philosopher turned art-critic's accounts of the *salons* to describe a trend that flourished in the second part of the eighteenth century.[12] Reacting against the theatricality and spectacular, ornamental quality of Rococo art, a number of artists (the painter Greuze is Diderot and Fried's most recurrent case in point) turned to depicting intimate scenes or moments, focusing on characters who are sleeping or day-dreaming, or who appear wholly absorbed in their thoughts, sometimes in their reading or playing. Such a choice of subject matter has deep implications in terms of the viewer's place and engagement with the work. Theatrical compositions overtly display themselves for someone's gaze, the *mise en scène* implicitly or explicitly acknowledging the viewer's presence, including him or her as extensions of an in-frame audience, or offering the best possible point of view on the scene. The absorbed characters of the non-theatrical painting, on the other hand, appear to shut off any other reality than the one they inhabit, and in doing so, throw the spectator back on to her or his own absence from the represented scene.

If Fried developed his theories principally in relation to painting and contemporary art, he did acknowledge the closeness of some of his conclusions with Stanley Cavell's writing on film.[13] For Cavell, cinema, more than any other medium, has the capacity to grant its audience its 'wish for invisibility'.[14] A film presents us with an autarkic universe; a result of cinema's dual 'automatism' (as photographically recorded and projected moving image), the denial of co-presence with the audience is part and parcel of the experience of the screened image and of the magic of the cinema; in turn, however, this condition of invisibility imbues that experience with an inbuilt sense of voyeurism or displacement.[15]

Hence, whereas Cavell and Fried initially concur, they differ on the spectator's response: for Fried, absorption in painting need not be equated with voyeurism. Taking his cue from Diderot's careful descriptions, Fried observes that if scenes of 'absorption' appear to exclude the spectator, they do, in turn, encourage a different kind of spectatorial involvement: one that is attentive, empathetic and non-voyeuristic at the same time.[16] In her classic study of cinema and haptic visuality, Laura U. Marks described the experience of haptic film in closely related terms, insisting on the viewer's willingness to 'give herself up' to the image rather than to attempt merely to master it by deciphering its content.[17] At the same time, to behold Marks's critique of art historians' recurrent blindness to those material qualities of painting, such as the visible brushstrokes, that enhance the tactile dimension of the work, is to point to a dimension largely missing in both Fried and Cavell's accounts.[18] Consideration of the material qualities of the image, and, in particular, of the kind of haptic vision that low definition or blur can elicit in the spectator, complements Fried's observations and complicates Cavell's arguments.

In *Absorption and Theatricality*, Fried repeatedly refers to the similarity between the type of works favoured by Diderot, and that of earlier schools of paintings, most particularly the major figures of seventeenth-century art, including Caravaggio, Rembrandt and Vermeer. Artists discussed by Fried as part of his theory of absorption demonstrate a preference for the kind of soft touch that recalls earlier techniques developed by the masters of the Dutch school in particular: a favouring of subdued, filtered light and loose brush strokes, resulting in a slightly hazy rendition of the figures. In turn, the attenuated or even unfinished rendering is part of the qualities for which Diderot occasionally shows appreciation in the work of artists like Greuze and Chardin.[19] Though Fried hardly engages with these specific questions of form, they suggest that the effect of 'absorption' also grows out of a painting style that encourages engagement with atmosphere and mood rather than with narrative content.

If these observations resonate with the visual treatment of the feminine figure in early melodramas, it is not merely because the conventions of the genre encourage filmmakers to take absorption as a motif, but also because, as intuited by L'Herbier, the genre, in its depiction of inner states, opened itself to visual experimentation outside the needs of representational clarity. Though, as a theorist and essayist, Epstein was at pains to differentiate cinema from other art forms, his own cinematography, engaging with techniques that push the image beyond the requirement of readability, often evokes painterly effects, not only in his depiction of landscapes, but also in the creation of scenes of absorption. Like L'Herbier, Epstein had the ability to experiment even within the conventional confines of the melodrama, and as L'Herbier did in *El Dorado*, in *Cœur fidèle* (1932) Epstein uses defocus to evoke the despairing mood of his heroine.

The film's central protagonist, Marie, is being exploited by her foster parents, who also forbid her to see the man with whom she has fallen in love. In one early scene, as her lover has just been thrown out of the café where she works, she seeks refuge close to the door, where she falls into melancholy day-dreaming. Epstein captures the young woman in medium shot, framed by a window, and inverts the familiar sharp foreground/out-of-focus backdrop ratio. The camera focuses not on her face, in the foreground, but on the space behind. In the far background, the hazy silhouette of a boat passes by, and it is the stone wall, blocking the middle ground, that appears sharp in the image. From its blurred contours, to the frothy mass of her hair and the pools of darkness that hide her eyes, the young woman's outline is all softness, but it is also opaque: it is as if the image were infused with the confused and remote murmur of her thoughts.

The shot is brief, hardly a few seconds. Yet it remained in my memory long after I had first seen the film. What is it that *touches* me in such images, even when I am aware that the frontier between expression and mere sentimentality might be wearing thin? Possibly, it is the way that the images, with their indefinite, painterly quality, shift perception from the purely visual to the

Figure 4.1 *Cœur fidèle* (Jean Epstein, 1932).

tactile. For it may be through their affinity with the most deeply buried part of our sensory memory, the memory that precedes speech, that blurred images draw their affective power.[20] Or, possibly, the way that they mirror human vision when it is disrupted by tears.

Here, as in Fried's discussion of the evolution of painterly styles, there is a sense of silent cinema's moving away from theatrical acting (even if in both films one still finds examples of it). In Epstein, as in L'Herbier, the topic and situation are part of the genre's familiar tropes (a woman and her sick child, a woman separated from her lover, a woman at her window). Yet here both filmmakers rely on the expressive power of the image itself, rather than on dramatic gesturing, to express the pain felt by the character. No twisting of one's arms or pulling of one's hair: in both instances the – to our contemporary eyes – theatrical externalisation of emotions typical of early melodramas is replaced by a subdued mood.

It seems natural that absorption, as a subject matter and as a style of filmmaking, finds its place in melodrama: if the softening of the image definition evokes a contemplative sadness and arguably encourages us to empathise, it also protects the figure of the pained character from our preying gazes. In the so-called soft-style cinema, however, the use of filters and oblique light to obtain the classic, idealising close-up on the face had a different aim: absorption became, first and foremost, a mark of the star's inaccessibility. Self-absorbed even when looking at the camera, these portraits exemplify

Cavell's concept of the cinema as a training ground for the learning of human subjectivity as a form of distance, the self as dissociated from the world. As such, and although the soft-style close-up of the face remains a cinematic figure characteristic of classic silent film, it anticipates certain tropes of modernist cinema where the expression of human emotions, or of their absence, comes to mirror existential uncertainty.

In *Absorption and Theatricality*, Fried posits the trend for 'absorption' in painting as a reaction against the theatricality of Rococo art in particular. In turn, he outlines the contrast between eighteenth-century art and modern painting, as epitomised by Manet, whose figures boldly gaze out towards the viewer as if to confront him or her. Whilst Fried's account of the shift to modernism resonates with Cavell's reflection on modern art cinema's attempt at breaking the illusion of film as self-contained and objective, here, again, the question of the material quality of the image, in particular where it explores the formal possibilities and painterly effects of low definition, complicates matters.

The classic opening credit sequence of Ingmar Bergman's *Persona* (1966) systematically undermines the affinity between touch and empathy, the sense of affective reversibility entailed by touch and translated visually by the blurred image. In the shots that depict the confrontation of the young boy with the enlarged, entwined image of the mother and the nurse, the feminine figure's absorption is cruelly equated with aloofness and indifference. The physical and emotional proximity that characterises the mother–child relationship in our contemporary Western culture is here implied, yet at the same time denied, and, by the same token, the relation of identification of the spectator with the character is unsettled. The maternal figure is inaccessible: sublimated by the soft focus and light, the face appears absorbed and remote: it is, in the end, but a cold and flat surface on which the child's hand glides. Absorption thus spells distantness: the boy, like the film spectator, is effectively shut off, and in the end, it is with a sense of absence that, following Cavell, the viewer possibly identifies.[21]

Contemporary with *Persona*, Andy Warhol's *Poor Little Rich Girl* (1965) explores similar tropes, focusing on a figure that features recurrently in the paintings examined by Fried: the sleeping subject.[22] The first few images of the film are almost abstract: white, curvaceous forms that we identify retrospectively as a young, reclining woman's arm. The camera remains defocused and slowly pans until it frames her face. This blurred sequence is the result of a mistake: a wrong choice of aperture, which Warhol corrects in the course of the shooting. Yet he did not reject these opening images, instead adopting their woolly, druggy quality, the manifestation of a form of absorption more toxic than sleep.

The model is one of Warhol's muses, Edie Sedgwick. For more than 3 minutes, the camera gazes at her almost immobile face, a milky surface where features are mere outlines. The image as a whole is blurred: hence the double sense of absorption that it creates. Absorbed by sleep, the figure is also absorbed in the grainy matter of the image. It is thus pulled beyond figuration, towards the formless.

In the introductory sequence of *Poor Little Rich Girl*, as in the shots from the films of L'Herbier, Epstein and Bergman previously discussed, stillness, combined with defocus, reinforces the painterly effect while also pulling the film image towards still photography. Yet blur born out of movement (that of the camera or of the filmed body) can also draw together cinema and painting, eliciting a different kind of absorption to that described by Fried.

Jean-Luc Godard's *Sauve qui peut (la vie)* (1980), the film that marked his return from television to film, remains exemplary in its sweeping synthesis of movement and stillness that explores the endless plasticity of cinematic blur. By the same token, in an era where the medium was arguably emulated by television, Godard's film stood as a reaffirmation of cinema's status as an art in dialogue with photography and painting.

Caught in slow motion, and rendered in the halting rhythm characteristic of step-printing, the bodies in *Sauve qui peut (la vie)* evolve according to their own, secret schema and the contours of their figures eschew sharpness – just as, as subjects, the characters appear to escape fixed identities. Whether cycling, working or playing, the characters in Godard's film are not only absorbed in their activity, but protected by the image's visual resistance to definition – a resistance that marks a fragile opening of potentiality or freedom,[23] and a space where the plasticity of the film image is put to the test. With its blurred slow-motion sequences and its Richterian style of shots, evocative of the smeared photo-painting technique, *Sauve qui peut (la vie)* thus prefigures Godard's recent experimentation with digital film and 3D. His feature *Adieu au langage* (2014) extends cinema's encounter with painting not only in its foregrounding of the plastic versatility of the digital and 3D image – a fusion of impressionism, pointillism and tachism with the flux of the moving image – but also as a celebration of blurred images' denial of the exercise of the possessive, all-consuming gaze.

In the time period between the releases of these two films by Godard, a number of filmmakers pushed the cinematic treatment of the human form towards the limits of figuration, deploying low-definition techniques that radically undermine the integrity of the figure. David Lynch, Philippe Grandrieux, Leighton Pierce, Lucien Castaing-Taylor and Véréna Paravel, to name but a few, are amongst the filmmakers whose cinematography makes extensive use of blurred effects, often bringing the figure close to dissolution.

Figure 4.2 *Sauve qui peut (la vie)* (Jean-Luc Godard, 1980).

From 16 mm and classic 35 mm film to digital video, including Go-pro cameras, the choice of medium, techniques, genre and subject matter varies greatly, but the filmmakers share a willingness to experiment with the kind of distortions produced not only by defocus and low light, but also by camera movement (most typically, the shaky image characteristic of the handheld camera) and motion blur created by the movement of bodies caught in long exposure.[24] Such techniques produce a markedly different set of painterly references from those so far evoked. In effect, if the kind of cinematography that emerged in the 1990s has been described as characteristic of a cinema of sensation, it is partly in relation to the paintings of Francis Bacon, as well as Gilles Deleuze's classic study of the artist's work, *The Logic of Sensation*.[25] In this case, the process of exchange between cinema and painting is thus circular: it is common knowledge that Bacon was inspired by Jules-Étienne Marey's chronophotography, including, no doubt, the ghostly shadows that shrouded the blurred silhouettes of some of Marey's series of moving (and fighting) bodies, later emulated in futurist photography.

In Deleuze's words, in Bacon, we 'see everywhere the reign of the blurry [*flou*] and the indeterminate, the action of a depth that pulls at the form'.[26] The warped, blurred figures are not likenesses of bodies but visual renderings of an experience of corporeality, of the body traversed by sensation: 'What is painted on the canvas is the body, not insofar as it is represented as an object, but insofar as it is experienced as sustaining *this* sensation.'[27] The foundation of this process, the input of the painter's hand, is not hidden; on the contrary, the visible marks, the brushing, the fading, serve to 'break up the sovereign optical organization: one can no longer see anything, as if in a catastrophe, a chaos'.[28] As a time-based medium of flux, cinema is arguably a perfect vessel for the manifestation of the chaotic and formless (which, as Deleuze is at pains to point out in Bacon's case, never transforms into pure abstraction).[29] In the hybrid zone where art and experimental cinema meet, filmmakers frequently elect to foreground the process of filming over the legibility of the figurative content, and to treat the human form as the manifestation of an intensity or sensation – in this cinema, the human figure often seems on the brink of fusing with its surrounds. The end sequence of Lynch's *Lost Highway* (1997), with its striking motion blur defiguration, remains one of the most direct cinematic citations of Bacon, and Nicole Brenez's account of Lynch's cinematography for this film points to obvious similarities: 'David Lynch produces a form that fuses the optical and the tactile, the abstract and the figurative, the blurredness of the shot and the clarity of the concept, and pushes the image to the limits of figurativity.'[30]

Absorption, in this context, loses its connection with the representational content and takes on different meanings from those derived from Fried's study. As well as the immersive mode of filmmaking, the term evokes the 'depth that pulls at the form': the literal, material absorption of the figure by the rest of the image. But just as it was for Deleuze experiencing Bacon's painting, absorption may also aptly describe the experience of the spectator herself, as she yields into a world imbued with a logic of visual uncertainty bordering on confusion: 'As a spectator, I experience the sensation only by entering the work, by reaching the unity of the sensing and the sensed.'[31]

Whether shot on analogue film or digitally, a cinema of sensation exploits those qualities of film that tend to be played down in mainstream filmmaking: the capacity to create visual confusion, to elicit a sense of uncertainty or wonder that encourages the spectator to engage with the image's material appearance. But as the twenty-first century dawned, filmmakers also paid increased attention to the variations in image quality in relation to the expressive potential afforded by the cohabitation of digital and analogue film. At stake was the resistance to high-definition imaging's increasingly normative representations of the human figure, as well as the manifestation of visuality as a historical phenomenon: just as variations in artistic techniques and media stand for different periods of our pre-industrial history, so have variations in the quality of the film stock, including its definition and resolution, come to encapsulate the changing times of the industrial and post-industrial era.

The opening sequence of Chantal Akerman's *La Captive* (2000) offers a striking reflection on such issues via its initial *mise en abyme* of cinema. On the one hand, the film looks back towards its own beginnings as a medium, to the opposing pull – between art and science, mystery and disclosure – that presided over its early years, and later, over the emergence of a diversity of film formats. On the other hand, the film's introductory sequence self-reflexively captures the complexities of a modern cinema (and of modern subjectivities) caught between the logic of the spectacle and the resistance to the kind of hyper-visibility that heightened definition and new modes of interactive viewing appear to foster.

Akerman's film is a loose adaptation of Marcel Proust. It focuses on the fifth volume of *Remembrance of Things Past*, *La Prisonnière* (*The Captive*), a study of obsessive love. It starts with the recollection of a scene at the beach, an evocation of Proust's description of Balbec, where the hero discovers the object of his future attachment.

The opening credit sequence unfolds to the sound of waves and against the backdrop of images of the sea that are initially shot out of focus: confusion in nature is here magnified by blur as technical choice, the effacement of detail attuning the eye to the spectacle of the *clear and confused*, the visualisation of obscure knowledge.[32] This original shot vanishes with the credits, to be replaced by images recorded on 8 mm film. At the same time, the sound of a projector replaces the sound of the sea, thus aligning, *in fine*, the sound and the vision of the film with the ceaseless movement and sound of the waves.

The images show a group of young women at the beach, going for a swim or absorbed in a game of ball, their brightly coloured swimming costumes contrasting with the more muted palette of the sand, water and cloudy sky. The slightly unstable gaze of the camera, as it attempts to catch up with the group, captures a sense of collective absorption and shared, carefree vitality. Ostensibly at the request of the operator, the young women eventually assemble in front of the camera, first for a group portrait, then for individual portrait shots.

It seems like an obvious choice for a filmmaker seeking to adapt Proust to opt for 8 mm film: in projection, it has the trembling, breathing quality of the films of the silent era; the softness of its finish, as well as its association with amateur practice makes it a perfect format for the evocation of memory, both intimate and incomplete. When used to shoot seascapes, 8 mm also has a particular painterly quality that Akerman fully exploits here: it is reminiscent, in texture, light and hues, of watercolour (the association with analogue film extends to the physical qualities of the medium: one watercolour technique consists in scattering sea salt on a wet surface before painting).

The effect of the grain of 8 mm film, which comes out so strikingly in the close-ups where skin and film seem to blend, is also reminiscent of the *pointillés* or circles of confusion often associated with Vermeer's painting (possibly a reminder of Marcel Proust's own fascination with Vermeer's style). The confusion or exuberance of the real so readily manifested in the spectacle of the sea is enhanced by the painterly treatment: the erasure of the superfluous, the softening of contours, encouraging a shift from the *reading* of the image to a less precise, more synaesthetic perception.

The sequence soon shifts to 35 mm, however, revealing the lone spectator who also operates the 8 mm projector. The incarnation of the possessive Proustian lover, driven by the need to know, the projectionist seems oblivious to the quality of elusiveness from which the film draws its charm. We watch him stop, rewind and project the same few frames. He is trying to read the lips of two closely shot young women whom he suspects to be lovers. As in dubbing, he puts words in their mouths. Is it 'I love you' or is it 'I like you'? The process brings to mind one of Georges Demenÿ's experiments in chronophotography. In 1891, the engineer famously photographed himself saying 'I love you' as an exercise in the decomposing of speech for the purposes of lip reading. Demenÿ's series of chronophotographs manifests a tongue-in-cheek interest in the scientific, practical applications of the animated image, while also foreshadowing the advent of sound cinema and, with it, the need for images sufficiently defined and stable to communicate a spoken message clearly.

In Akerman's silent, 8 mm version, however, the image resists the possessive viewer's drive to uncover its secret. The faces are alternately obscured and imprecisely delineated, and the projectionist, acting like a jealous spectator and casting his shadow over the projected images, is left to speculate. Even as the young women face the camera and look directly into its lens, the soft, shivering quality of the 8 mm image creates a distance, shrouding the figures in a protective veil of pastness, their gaze not a sign of presentness, but a form of haunting. There are striking echoes between Daniel Arasse's writing about Vermeer's portraits and Akerman's use of 8 mm film. Arasse talks about the relationship between an image's quality of indefiniteness and its capacity to elicit, in spite of the temporal divide, a sense of presence. 'Such an image', he says, 'is not destined to make its object known, but to turn the viewer into the witness of presence.' For, he adds, what is being showed is not 'the secret of the object that is being observed, but a mystery, internal to the image itself, and to the visibility of its figures'.[33]

In the end, the projectionist lets the film run its course and the young woman who had been singled out in close-up escapes back to the sea, like the mermaid of the fairy tale, who was separated from her sisters but rejoins them in the end. In contrast with the hazy quality of the 8 mm sequence, the precise visual and sound treatment of the following shot, filmed on 35 mm with pristine definition, heralds the young woman's new status as her lover's 'captive'.

Figure 4.3 La Captive (Chantal Akerman, 2000).

From Proust to popular entertainment, there may seem to be little in common between Akerman's film and Douglas Gordon and Philippe Parreno's *Zidane, a Portrait of the 21st Century* (2006); yet with this foray into the world of international football, the two artists offer their own, complex study of absorption and memory. As in the introduction to Akerman's film, the diverse range of image quality and definition deployed in *Zidane* undermines the theatricality that always threatens to rule over the recording and viewing of moving images today.

Gordon and Parreno's deployment of a maverick filming apparatus for their project is well known, as is their insistence on taking their seventeen cameramen to the Prado to look at the work of Goya and Velázquez. Shot in the course of a 90-minute match, the film forms a dazzling montage of shots, selected from the footage filmed by seventeen cameras set around the football pitch, but also from satellite images, as well as the refilming of the TV screens from which live footage of the event is chosen for broadcast. The richness of the film's audio and visual construct thus stems not only from the cubistic assemblage of a multiplicity of perspectives, but also from the continuous shift in image quality, from high-definition footage to heavily pixelated images.

In *La Captive*, the projectionist, who is alone, and able to pause the film, revert and start again, stands in for the contemporary spectator armed with a remote control: a possessive, rather than contemplative spectator,[34] bent on investigating that part of the film image that resists exposure. In Gordon and Parreno's film[35] the spectator finds herself mirrored and infinitely multiplied in the image of the match's live audience, which is included in the spectacle and subjected to the same variations of low definition and defocus as the star player who is the overt subject of the film.

Entirely absorbed by the game, the football player appears oblivious to the many cameras, as well as the gazes of the 80,000 fans that follow him. The shifts between focused and blurred shots reflect the tension that builds in the course of the film, between the sense of intimacy that the recurrent close-ups and the constancy of the camera gaze establish, and the extreme exposure that the match and the filming imply. Yet as the player falls in and out of focus, and occasionally fades out of sight, becoming but a mere blot in the field of vision, so does the audience, enfolded in the collective absorption that the match elicits, come in and out of sight. The sound, likewise, alternates between the wavering rumour of the crowd as a whole and the sudden, ephemeral insert of a precise, isolated sound – Zidane's breathing, the noise of his shoe scraping the pitch, a member of the audience shouting or coughing. The overall effect is that of a shared absorption. By the same token, the film offers its subject matter an alternative outlet, away from television's heavily normative grammar and its increasingly narcissistic regime of spectatorial engagement.[36]

In its bold appropriation of a football match as experimental art object, Gordon and Parreno's film remind us of the long-lasting link between avant-gardist art and popular culture – an association where film features prominently, sometimes in relation to painting. As their content shifts from almost abstract blocks of colour to precisely delineated figures and then again to blurred silhouettes caught in the flux of the images, Gordon and Parreno's shots are fleetingly reminiscent of Nicolas de Staël's series of paintings *Les Grands Footballeurs* (1952).

Conclusion

To consider the cinematic image at its most elusive, where it leaves the realm of the immediately legible to enter that of the indeterminate and fluctuating, is to envisage it at a point where it opens itself most readily to a dialogue with other art forms. This chapter addresses only a few aspects of this interchange taking place between the painterly and the cinematic. In particular, it strives to show how the notion of absorption, though initially associated with the history of painting, may be productively deployed in the context of the moving image where it points to shifting regimes of representation and spectatorship. Most crucially, however, and even when restricted to the treatment of the human figure, the theoretical and formal resonances that surface in the encounter between film and painting point to the historically meaningful implications of the film image's versatility and plasticity. For, in cinema as in painting, the multiplicity of material qualities and the various degrees of image definition draw the eye away from the narrowly standardised image. Pulling the gaze towards uncharted, indefinite territories where it can wander, they are also intrinsic to the medium's historicity, its capacity not only to record the realities of its time, but to account for evolving perceptions, sensibilities and subjectivities.

Notes

1. This article is an extension of the book *L'Attrait du flou* (Crisnée: Yellow Now, 2017).
2. As Leonardo da Vinci famously proposed, a few stains on a decrepit wall might be the best stimulation for the imagination. Similarly, Ernst Gombrich argued that the extent of the spectator's 'share', of her active engagement in perceiving and interpreting the image, depends on its partial legibility or incompleteness. Léonard de Vinci, *Traité de la peinture* (Paris: Calmann-Lévy, 2003), p. 216. E. H. Gombrich, *Art and Illusion: A Study in the Psychology of Pictorial Representation* (Princeton, NJ: Princeton University Press, 1960). See also Georges Didi-Huberman on the spectator's productive 'épreuve du non-savoir' (the trial of not-knowing) in *Devant l'image* (Paris: Minuit, 1990), and Bernd Huppauf, 'Between imitation and simulation: Towards an aesthetics of fuzzy images', in B. Huppauf and C. Wulf (eds), *Dynamics and Performativity of Imagination: The Image between the Visible and the Invisible* (London: Routledge, 2009), p. 231.
3. Jean Epstein, *Écrits sur le cinéma*, vol. 2 (Paris: Cinéma Club/Seghers, 1975). On the difficulty of defining the concept itself, see Louise Merzeau, 'De la photogénie', *Les Cahiers de médiologie*, 15 (2003), pp. 199–206.
4. On Epstein's complex relationship with painting, as a critic and as a filmmaker, see Prosper Hillairet, *Cœur fidèle de Jean Epstein* (Crisnée: Yellow Now: 2008), pp. 68–9.
5. See Siegfried Kracauer's discussion of the Lumière brothers' films and his description of 'camera-life', the 'flow of Life' and the 'indeterminate' as intrinsic qualities of film in *Theory of Film: The Redemption of Physical Reality* (Oxford: Oxford University Press, 1960). See also Martine Beugnet, 'Introduction', and Erika Balsom's chapter, 'One hundred years of low definition', in Martine Beugnet, Allan Cameron and Arild Fetveit (eds), *Indefinite Visions: Cinema and the Attractions of Uncertainty* (Edinburgh: Edinburgh University Press, 2017).
6. On the soft-style see David Bordwell, Janet Staiger and Kristin Thomson, *The Classical Hollywood Cinema: Film Style and Mode of Production to 1960* (London: Routledge, 1988), pp. 288–92.
7. See Beugnet, *L'Attrait du flou*.
8. See Beugnet, *L'Attrait du flou*, and Dominique Païni, 'The silent ruins of films', in François Fontaine, *Silenzio!* (Paris: Les Éditions de l'Œil, 2012), pp. 36–7.
9. See Martine Beugnet and Richard Misek, 'In Praise of Blur', *[in]Transition* (July 2017). Available at <http://mediacommons.org/intransition/2017/07/11/praise-blur> (accessed 1 September 2017).

10. E. H. Gombrich, *Art and Illusion*.
11. Gilles Deleuze, *Cinéma 1: L'Image-mouvement* (Paris: Minuit, 1983), pp. 105–7.
12. Michael Fried, *Absorption and Theatricality: Painting and Beholder in the Age of Diderot* (Berkeley: University of California Press, 1980).
13. Fried, *Absorption and Theatricality*, p. 182, note 13. Fried further associates film and painting, suggesting that film provides 'an equivalent for the beholder's simultaneous exclusion from and presence within the scene of representation' (p. 235, note 81).
14. Stanley Cavell, *The World Viewed: Reflections on the Ontology of Film* (Cambridge, MA: Harvard University Press, 1979), pp. 41–5.
15. Though, as Philipp Schmerheim points out, the possibility of being discovered, which defines voyeurism, is lacking. *Skepticism Films: Knowing and Doubting the World in Contemporary Cinema* (London: Bloomsbury, 2015), p. 102.
16. Fried, *Absorption and Theatricality*, p. 31.
17. Laura U. Marks, *The Skin of the Film: Intercultural Cinema, Embodiment, and the Senses* (Durham, NC and London: Duke University Press, 2000), pp. 183–4.
18. Marks, *The Skin of the Film*, p. 167
19. Fried, *Absorption and Theatricality*, p. 43. See also his citation of Diderot, p. 118.
20. Interestingly, Fried evokes Diderot's account of dreaming as a heightened state of sensory perception 'that restores the conditions of a pre-theatricalized mode of perception', and goes on to suggest the closeness of such an experience with that of film viewing (*Absorption and Theatricality*, p. 235, note 81).
21. Cinema, Cavell argues, fosters a sense of presentness imbued with a form of absence, making 'displacement appear as our natural condition' (*The World Viewed*, p. 41).
22. Fried's concept of absorption has also been mentioned in connection with contemporary video works that address the issue of theatricality and absorption, as does, for instance, Sam Taylor-Wood's *Beckham Sleeping* (2004, 1 hour 7 minutes continuous loop on a 40-inch 4:3 plasma screen).
23. In 'On Potentiality', Giorgio Agamben takes to task the dualist conception according to which potential exists only as part of a process of actualisation. Where blurred images cease to be regarded merely as sharp images in the making, then potential rhymes with blur. Agamben's conclusion connects potentiality with freedom – a state of non-definition that aptly describes Godard's characters' eschewing of fixed identities. *Potentialities: Collected Essays in Philosophy* (Stanford: Stanford University Press, 1999), pp. 183–5.
24. For a study of body distortion in digital video art, see Allan Cameron's definitive chapter, 'Facing the glitch: Abstraction, abjection and the digital image', in Beugnet, Cameron and Fetveit (eds), *Indefinite Visions*, pp. 334–53.
25. Gilles Deleuze, *Francis Bacon: The Logic of Sensation* (1981) (London: Continuum, 2003).
26. Deleuze, *Francis Bacon*, p. 29 (French in original text).
27. Deleuze, *Francis Bacon*, p. 35.
28. Deleuze, *Francis Bacon*, p. 101.

29. Deleuze, *Francis Bacon*, p. 103 and ff.
30. Nicole Brenez, *De la figure en général et du corps en particulier: L'Invention figurative au cinéma* (Louvain-la-Neuve: De Boeck Supérieur, 1998), p. 424 (my translation).
31. Deleuze, *Francis Bacon*, p. 35.
32. G. W. Leibniz, *New Essays on Human Understanding* (Cambridge: Cambridge University Press, 1996). See Chapter xxix, 'Of clear and confused ideas', and p. lii for Leibniz's classic example of the perception of the sound of waves.
33. Daniel Arasse, *L'Ambition de Vermeer* (1992) (Paris: Adam Biro, 2001), p. 162.
34. The terms are coined by Laura Mulvey in *Death 24x a Second: Stillness and the Moving Image* (London: Reaktion Books, 2006).
35. *Zidane* is also presented in galleries as a multi-channel video installation.
36. More often than not, the image that the TV spectator watches is also on display on giant screens in the stadium – a broadcasting loop feeding on itself. As soon as a member of the live audience catches their own image live on the screens, they spring to attention and wave to the camera. Fusing surveillance with exhibition, new regimes of representation herald the return to a theatricality that also rests on a reinforced illusion of 'co-presence': the spectator who waves at the camera waves to me, ostensibly acknowledging my gaze with uncanny instantaneity.

Part 2

The Intermedial Avant-gardes

CHAPTER 5

From the Periphery to the Interstices: Avant-garde Film, Medium Specificity and Intermediality, 1970–2015
Christopher Townsend

The late 1960s and early 1970s witnessed an efflorescence of publishing on what can be loosely categorised as 'the avant-garde film', at the same time as those years witnessed a global surge in experimental filmmaking. The two phenomena were not unrelated. Titles ranged from the sensationalist, through the general trade, such as Sheldon Renan's *An Introduction to the American Underground Film*, to the specific and scholarly, with Peter Gidal's monographic study of Andy Warhol. Nor was this flowering limited to Anglophone scholarship: Birgit Hein would publish *Film im Underground* and contribute to Christian Michelis and Rolf Wiest's collection *XSCREEN*.[1]

I identify two particular tendencies within this period that established overarching concerns and conceptual frameworks which have influenced the subsequent study of modernist, experimental filmmaking, and trace their disciplinary effects over the last forty-five years. This outline is sketched through overviews of the histories and effects of particularly influential journals and monographs. If the study of avant-garde film early on was conducted at the margins of widely separated disciplines, notably Film Studies and Art History, I suggest that it has now moved to the spaces between increasingly interconnected disciplines, and become the object of literary scholarship in the scrutiny of intermedial relationships between films and texts. Both approaches, the one characterised by technical competence and an over-romanticised conception of modernist avant-gardism, the other by an inspiring breadth of scope but loss of historical and technical attentiveness, bring particular benefits and particular problems.

The 1970s saw publications by practising filmmakers such as Hein and Gidal, along with David Curtis and Malcolm Le Grice.[2] These writers attended to recent developments in their field and sought to establish a degree of historical continuity between what they conceived as their own late-modernist avant-garde and older practices. Secondly, there was the more closely focused historical investigation of experimental filmmaking in the early twentieth century. This was conducted variously through new research

– for example, in Standish Lawder's *The Cubist Cinema*, which developed from a Yale doctoral thesis; from the publication of memoirs by surviving participants, such as Hans Richter's *Dada: Art and Anti-Art*; and from the republication of key period texts, including László Moholy-Nagy's *Painting, Photography, Film* (1925), which appeared in English translation in 1969, Roger Manvell's *Experiment in the Film* (1949), republished in 1970, and Paul Rotha's *The Film Till Now* (1930), republished in 1967.[3] I want to make a generalising observation about the context for all of this activity, representing as it does the first extensive, scholarly scrutiny of the cinematic avant-garde: that it emerges from the framework of the visual arts, whether within the academy or where it touched on the public sphere. That is, scholarship comes either from the domain of Art History – the department in which Lawder took his PhD – or the only newly established, and still to a degree inchoate, register of Film Studies, where it was worked through in the nascent technical and theoretical rhetoric of the discipline. Whilst the introduction to *The Cubist Cinema* reflects that the study of film has emerged piecemeal from departments of English, Drama, History, Sociology or audio-visual studies, I would argue that the dominant concern is with modernism's reconfiguration of the visual field. Le Grice, for example, begins *Abstract Cinema* with a framing commentary on Cézanne.

The second observation I would make is that these writers, even when they were university scholars, were also filmmakers. Their attentiveness depended in part upon their technical competence. Lawder, for example, was seemingly appointed to his chair at Harvard because, having begun 'exclusively as a scholar, he had become so interested in film as an expressive medium that he was equally devoted to making his own movies'.[4] Those who regarded themselves principally as filmmakers were also teaching within creative schools or academic institutions: Le Grice at Central Saint Martins School of Art, Curtis in Birmingham, Croydon College of Art and the John Cass School. Publication of essays was often in the context of commercial, contemporary art magazines such as *Artforum* or *Studio International*, or small 'enthusiast' titles rather than in academic journals, even when the content was historically and theoretically rigorous and even when, as in the case of *Framework*, begun in 1974, such journals quickly acquired scholarly authority.

The lack of formal training in established disciplines, coupled with issues of linguistic competence and the aesthetic and ideological preferences of these artist–scholars, along with the scarcity of authorities who might rigorously peer-review publications, certainly led to lacunae, errors and biases that would be repeated in later studies. For example, Le Grice's still-vital book neglected the prewar influence of Oskar Fischinger in the USA on filmmakers such as Dwinell Grant, because he did not use, or perhaps even know of, the Hilla von Rebay archives – already in the Guggenheim museum at that point – with their extensive documentation of Solomon R. Guggenheim's patronage of American abstract film production; the battery of translators for *Framework* of Ricciotto Canudo's key essay (in which the modernist avant-garde embraces film as early as 1911) made some serious errors of translation that are now perpetuated in republication ('agriculture' for 'architecture' in the first paragraph, for starters) and they omitted an entire, crucial paragraph.[5] But equally, traditionally trained art historians such as Lawder would make erroneous statements that became unchallenged facts for the discipline in future. For example, Lawder claimed the influence of Keystone's *Heinze's Resurrection* (1913) – a lost film, which he could not have seen, but only known through studio records – on Picabia and Clair's *Entr'acte* (1924).[6] The speculative association of influence that ignores historical evidence is a persistent habit that has accompanied the shift of avant-garde film studies from the margins of art historical scholarship to the interstices between different schools of the humanities.

However, in general, their experience as filmmakers gave these commentators a command of the technical possibilities and limitations of their medium. As I show below, the loss of this competence – in part a consequence of a disciplinary schism between theory and practice – now bedevils contemporary intermedial and literary approaches to the study of the avant-garde film. An equally persistent problem that derives from this scholarship is the degree to which imagined continuities of practice and philosophy render a construction of the historical avant-garde in these artist–scholars' own image. The British avant-garde of the 1960s and 1970s, as it aggregated around the rubrics of Structural Film and Expanded Cinema, was antipathetic towards narrative, antipathetic towards mainstream industrial practices, antipathetic perhaps towards anyone except its own subscription and understood its project – at least within Structural Film – as a modernist endeavour fundamentally concerned with medium specificity and the meaning of form rather than content. Whilst not without larger theoretical paradigms for that antipathy to the mainstream (for example, Peter Bürger's *Theory of the Avant-Garde* – and here I am assuming a competence for readers in German before its English translation) and that concept of rhetorical purity as characteristically modernist (Clement Greenberg *passim*), this cenacle's conception of its own isolation and purity profoundly coloured its reconstruction of historical avant-gardism. A good example of this, and one with persistent effects, is Deke Dusinberre's seminal work on POOL Group and its publication *Close Up* (1927–33). Dusinberre's research rested on original investigation – including interviewing Oswell Blakeston, a key POOL affiliate, when no one else had the slightest interest. In a republication of his essay in the 1990s, Dusinberre acknowledged the limitations of his research, describing its observations and conclusions as 'intellectually obstetric'.[7] However, he clearly understood the POOL project within the intellectual framework lately outlined by Douglas Mao and Rebecca Walkowitz as characteristic of mid-twentieth-century modernist studies:

> for many years modernism was understood as, precisely, a movement by and for a certain kind of high (cultured mandarins) as against a certain kind of low (the masses, variously regarded as duped by the 'culture industry', admirably free of elitist self-absorption, or simply awaiting the education that would make the community of cognoscenti a universal one.[8]

Dusinberre saw *Close Up* as a representative of an alternative film culture that existed largely at the level of criticism rather than production as 'avant-garde' because of its opposition to mass culture.

> The term 'avant-garde' is intended towards those films (and that film criticism) which seek an alliance with modernism in the other arts, which demand a consistent interrogation of the medium; they challenge the industry not only on the levels of content and of production/distribution/exhibition, but also on the level of the aesthetic/representational postulates on which the industry's commerce is based.[9]

Dusinberre clearly understood that formation of the 'avant-garde' as originally a critical project of literature, noting that *Close Up*'s 'cultural sympathies [. . .] are suggested by its publication of contributions from people such as the imagist poet H.D. (who often wrote reviews and criticism and occasional poems), Gertrude Stein [. . .] and Man Ray'.[10] This operating principle would subsequently determine James Donald, Anne Friedberg and Laura Marcus's approach in their celebrated selection of essays from *Close Up*, published in 1998. The cultural allegiance of 'avant-garde' film was understood to adhere to an existing body of work that was, first of all, literary; secondly whose aesthetics were incompatible with the rhetorical forms of mass culture (Stein being a particularly good exemplar); and thirdly, which sat outside and above that culture. Yet to achieve this conclusion Dusinberre had to make an oddly focused analysis of *Close Up*'s contributors that presaged the editorial bias of Donald, Friedberg and Marcus: Stein published just two pieces across three early issues, whilst Man Ray published only once, in the second issue. The most frequent contributors to *Close Up* were not literary modernists: they were practising filmmakers, screenwriters, technicians and professional film critics, and most of them (including Blakeston) were not completely antipathetic towards the industry where they earned their living. Rather, they and the magazine existed in a dialogic relationship with the cinematic mainstream.[11]

By the mid-1970s, Film Studies was more fully established as a discipline. It was evolving what was understood as a rhetorically specific mode of critique – with that specificity in part a legacy of the late modernism of pathfinders such as Peter Wollen – whilst engaging wholeheartedly with structuralist and post-structuralist theory and identity politics. Where this discourse touches upon avant-garde film it is often associated with the decade's fashionable modes of experiment, and where it undertakes historical reclamation reflects the prejudices and knowledge of those scholars and practitioners associated with particular journals. A good example of this is *October*, founded in 1976 after a cataclysmic rift between junior staff at *Artforum* and their editor, John Coplans. Whilst *Artforum* had carried a number of significant contributions about modernist film – for example, Barbara Rose's early appreciation of Man Ray and Moholy-Nagy – those essays never approached either the scrupulous level of attention or the rhetorical density manifest in *October* from its first issue.[12] Firstly, the journal embedded late-modernist experiments within a loosely post-structuralist critical matrix, as both the films emerged and the theoretical discourse evolved. *October* immediately recognised the significance of the contrasting, contemporary projects of Michael Snow, Hollis Frampton and Richard Serra, and provided paradigms for the reception of their work.[13] Secondly, living up to its title, the journal promptly undertook a theoretical and historical reappraisal of Soviet cinema, and of the montage technique in particular.[14] Whilst it was not alone in this enterprise – the 1970s and 1980s witnessed a renaissance of studies in the field – *October*'s commitment to a radical stance led it to privilege those modes, tropes and techniques that endowed its currency with a historical legitimacy. The rediscovery of Vertov, therefore, appeared initially not in historical or aesthetic terms so much as in those suited to the uses to which he was put in political filmmaking elsewhere in the 1960s and 1970s, for example by Godard and Gorin's 'Groupe Dziga Vertov'. This position was, perhaps, best summed up in an aside in a later essay by Annette Michelson, one of *October*'s founding editors, that the underpinning hypothesis for the cinematic avant-garde in the 1920s was that it 'now disposed of a new and powerful cognitive instrument which gave him (*western man*) access to a clearer and fuller understanding of existence in the world'.[15] This was an epistemological adequacy that modernism, with its problematising of language, would surely never have acknowledged, beyond the purlieus of the Soviet avant-garde and its affiliates – and, to be fair, Michelson's remark comes from an essay where she distinguishes the artist–filmmaker Francis Picabia from this stance. But any attentive study of those avant-garde projects which apparently espoused such ends – for example, Walter Ruttmann's *Berlin, Symphony of a Great City* (1927) – would have quickly exposed the deeper flaws in Michelson's claim. *October*'s insistence on the primacy of Soviet montage and its makers also exposed its blind spot, one where critical theory and contemporary politics overrode attentiveness to historical detail.

There was a significantly different approach to Soviet film elsewhere in the 1970s and into the 1980s. In 1979, Richard Taylor would publish *The Politics of the Soviet Cinema*. Taylor possessed a linguistic competence only rarely matched by later Anglophone scholars of Soviet film and undertook a detailed analysis of the archives rather than using a theoretical model. Taylor's historical attention and linguistic rigour are sustained by contemporary scholars such as Philip Cavendish, who grounds the aesthetic innovations of Soviet film in a meticulous analysis of its technical practices, and John MacKay, with his attention to the politics of form and medium, especially in the work of Dziga Vertov.[16] Indeed, *October*'s 'New Vertov Studies' issue of 2007 might be seen as an example of the journal's recent revisionism, with its inclusion of essays by MacKay, Oksana Sarkisova and Yuri Tsivian. Tsivian complicates and corrects the facile associations and assumptions about Vertov and Constructivist art that had been made by early proponents of intermediality.[17] One of the key indicators of this revisionist turn has been *October*'s regular publication since 1999 of profoundly important essays by Malcolm Turvey: these have sought to establish the historical contexts of avant-garde practice, framed by an appreciation of intermedial relations, and undertaking an archaeology of theory – notably in his monographic study of Epstein, Vertov, Balázs and Kracauer.[18]

However, for a journal premised on the elision of boundaries in art practice in the 1970s, in its treatment of avant-garde film *October* at times resembles a bastion of Film Studies – even if the revetment's architecture is not exactly traditional. That is to say, it often resists the allure of establishing hybridised relations between moving image media and the other arts to insist on medium specificity. For example, in spring 2008, *October* published an issue, edited by the Arte Povera specialist Claire Gilman, dedicated to 'Postwar Italian Art'. Exactly a year later, it published 'Postwar Italian Cinema: New Studies', framed with an introduction from Michelson. With the exception of an essay by Jaleh Mansoor that dealt with Lucio Fontana's problematising of painting in the age of television, there was absolutely no correspondence between the two fields. Strangely, given the journal's early attention to sophisticated concepts of an expanded cinema, its scholarship concerned with the filmic avant-garde's scrutiny of the conceptual and material limits of cinema has been restrained, though what it has deigned to publish has been profoundly influential.[19] As we shall see, such caution may be well warranted.

A history of the scrutiny of the intermedial relations between experimental film and other art forms might, oddly enough, go back to Lawder, for the thesis in *The Cubist Cinema* is very much that 'Modern Painters Discover the

Cinema' (as its first chapter is indeed titled) and then to test it through the relationship of Léger's œuvre to *Ballet mécanique*. As Malcolm Turvey has shown, in one of the exemplary essays of *October*'s revisionist moment, that thesis does not really work out, since by the time he makes *Ballet mécanique*, Léger has moved on from the fragmented picture planes of the works that Lawder cites, such as *La Ville* (1919), into a wholly Purist phase. Indeed, one of the problems in facile appraisals of *Ballet mécanique* is that it does not really look like anything Léger might have painted in 1923–4 – even if there are works that clearly derive from it, including a number of paintings, and text and image works such as the 'scenario' *La Joconde amoureuse de Charlot* (1924–33) that are clearly corresponding with it. It is through this void of non-relation that recent promotion of alternative authorships has entered the field, notably by James Donald and Susan Delson.[20] I would suggest that if we are to use intermediality as a framing concept by which to understand the relationship of different media within an œuvre, or indeed as one that frames exchanges *between* œuvres, we need to forget resemblance. After all, the first theorisations and paradigms of intermediality, as they emerged primarily in German scholarship in the 1980s, were concerned with relations between the ineffable – music – and the material, painting or the textual, and then between the textual and the painterly. No one thought much about cinematic exchanges with other media, and how complex those exchanges might actually be. Certainly, they were not considering a direct visual correspondence between symbols.

Where film, text and art were seriously attended to as sites of exchange within modernism was, first of all, within the study of Dada and Surrealism that emerged around the University of Iowa under the influence of Stephen Foster and Rudolf Kuenzli in the 1970s and 1980s, and especially in the journal *Dada/Surrealism*. As early as issue 3 (1973), this explored the interaction of film and theatre in these modernist movements, returned to the topic with an overarching psychoanalytic, theoretical approach in issue 6 (1976), attended to visual poetics in issue 12 (1983) and culminated in a special film issue (volume 15) in 1986 that would, eventually, be republished as a book that – in academic terms – would be wildly popular. All of these volumes are notable for the attention that they pay to the relation between film and the poetic text in Surrealism: this occurs most notably in Inez Hedges's revelation of the extensive collaboration between Man Ray and Robert Desnos on *L'Étoile de mer* (1929), one that the filmmaker largely erased in his memoirs. What Hedges discovered, through forensic attention to a document 'known' since 1972, was the profound interaction of poetic text and film in a process that was something more than adaptation.[21] That special issue of 1986 also, with Peter Christensen's ground-breaking essay on

Benjamin Fondane, led scholars towards concepts of the paracinematic text and intermediality.[22]

In appraising intermediality as a currently fashionable scholarly concept for understanding avant-garde activity I want to stress both its utility and its significant flaws. The transformational exchange of tropes and motifs across media is valuable because it moves us beyond the critical myth of modernism's medium specificity, with its privileging of non-representational painting.[23] Most modernist movements, from Symbolism through Futurism to Dada, to Fluxus, were not medium-specific. Artists within those movements experimented in a wide variety of media and did not define motifs according to the medium in which they were deployed. So, intermediality allows us to look at migrations both within œuvres and, indeed, across them, from one artist to another. However, intermediality becomes a problem in two ways – at least – and these might encourage us to use the concept with greater sophistication and to deploy it with a certain degree of caution. Firstly, if 'intermediality' becomes a catchphrase to nominate the blindingly obvious, the first reaction is that this is just jargon – much like 'deconstruction' when used as a substitute for 'critical analysis'. If *Ballet mécanique* did actually look like Léger's paintings of 1924, then we would not need intermediality to explain it. That is to say, figural migration involves, in the border crossing, a certain translation or even outright shape-shifting that may also necessitate the reconceptualisation of the figure by the artist concerned. Intermedial analysis can be very useful in working through that process, but it may then be work that demands total familiarity with all aspects of an œuvre, along with the historical and technical conditions of that œuvre's production. Such analysis would include its subject's relation to the works of others. This would mean, therefore, reading *Ballet mécanique* not only through Léger's painting and writing, but through his important paracinematic text and image collaborations with Blaise Cendrars (*La Fin du monde* (1919)) and Yvan Goll (*Die Chapliniade* (1920)), his performative collaborations, especially with Canudo, for the Ballets Suédois, and peripheral works in the Léger œuvre such as *La Joconde amoureuse de Charlot* (1921–33). We might also attend to the writings of influential members of Léger's circle such as the art historian Jacques-Élie Faure. Once we do that, a far more nuanced conception of the authorship, style and philosophy of *Ballet mécanique* emerges.

More worryingly, intermediality may become a tool of academic recuperation and reification. This is particularly the case with the alleged cinematicity of non-filmmakers who are canonical figures in other media. Research on the marginal aspects of established œuvres becomes a means of attending to the canonical artist whilst mapping out what looks like an original field for research. Given the amount of recent scholarly literature devoted to the cinematicity of Virginia Woolf as a writer, say, or Pablo Picasso as a painter, one hardly dares imagine what would have happened if either had, actually, made a film.[24] An example of how this process works is the treatment of POOL Group, within English Literature scholarship. As a collective, POOL's activities embraced filmmaking, journal publication and book publication, with those books – both fiction and non-fiction – not being limited to core members of the group but extending to affiliates, notably Robert Herring and Oswell Blakeston, who were also crucial to its journal production. If we were to appraise the extended group in terms of its importance in filmmaking and the sheer volume of critical commentary, we might rank its members in this order: Kenneth Macpherson, who made four films, of which only *Borderline* survives in substance, and was the most prolific contributor to *Close Up*; Blakeston, who worked in the film industry as a camera assistant in the late 1920s and made at least three films, of which only the collaborative *Light Rhythms* survives; and Herring together with Ernest Betts, both professional film critics for national British newspapers and regular broadcasters on the BBC from the late 1920s. (A note in Blakeston's archive suggests that Herring also made, or wrote the scenario for, a lost film, *Between the Lines* (1928).) Yet, if we approach the group from another angle, that of significance in the literary canon, we emerge with a wholly different order, and it is this order that is indeed reflected in the intermedial scholarship on POOL Group. That order is, of course, H.D., followed at a distance by Dorothy Richardson, and then Bryher. H.D., because of her canonical standing as a poet, is the subject of numerous analyses of the relationship between her writing and theories of film, whereas Bryher – so far regarded as important to modernism principally for her financial support of others – receives little attention, and Macpherson, incidentally the author of two ciné-novels that attempt to transfer the techniques of modernist film to literature (*Poolreflection* and *Gaunt Island*), before he has made a film, is given none at all. Furthermore, commentators from within the literary humanities, lacking both the technical knowledge that characterised early scholars of the avant-garde film and a broad research framework, sometimes in consequence commit solecisms that go unchecked. For example, Rachel Connor ascribes Eisenstein as an influence on Blakeston; yet one of the films Connor cites is wholly abstract and the other she cannot have seen, since it was destroyed in World War II.[25] The editing style of the abstract *Light Rhythms* is not influenced by Soviet montage, but by Len Lye's technique of developing patterns of movement within the shot rather than through edited juxtaposition, seen as early as the animation *Tusalava* (1929) and praised accordingly by Blakeston in *Close Up*.[26] This is an influence that Blakeston acknowledged in the 1930s in his writing for various film journals.

This critical bias towards the literary canon also excludes POOL affiliates like Herring (poet and novelist, including the Bryher-subsidised *Cactus Coast*) and Blakeston (also a novelist and poet, with a POOL-published ciné-novel, *Extra Passenger* (1929), to his name). And what of another POOL affiliate, Dorothy Richardson? There is more literature on Richardson in the context of POOL Group than on founder members Macpherson and Bryher. A significant part of Donald, Friedberg and Marcus's selection from *Close Up* is devoted to Richardson. Certainly, she was an important contributor to the journal, though not as frequent a writer as Blakeston or Herring, or even Ralph Bond or Andor Kraszna-Krausz. But Richardson is an important English novelist of the modernist era – the writing in the novels can be extended to include the film writing and both deemed cinematic. Indeed, Jane Garrity sees a 'narrative montage' unfolding in sections of Richardson's *Pilgrimage* that were written long before she ever wrote for *Close Up* and, in fact, before any Soviet montage films had been seen in the West, or even made.[27] Intermediality here, the imagined influence of experimental film form on literary form, works as a tool of disciplinary recuperation and expansion when it might, more properly, be used to examine the relation between still image, moving image and text in Macpherson's œuvre, say, or Blakeston's.

The shift from a primarily pictorial to a primarily textual framework for analysis through intermediality may thus be less about finding new paradigms through which to address subaltern modes of filmmaking and more about exploiting under-researched and under-theorised niches in the œuvres of hegemonic figures within literary studies. Such approaches can get into deep trouble, technically, when they touch on film – and here I want to return to my early comments on the technical aptitude of the early scholar–practitioners of avant-garde film. Susan McCabe brilliantly charts an imaginative relationship between modernist poetry and film: however, here also is an example of a literary scholar being carried away by theoretical speculation, and without the necessary technical knowledge of the realities of 1920s filmmaking to maintain a balance.

> The hysteric body in this period functioned not only as a reminder of corporeal fragmentation but of sexual fluidity. Spliced bodies of modernity, like the surrealist game of 'exquisite corpse,' or the body in René Clair's experimental film *Entr'acte* (1924) with its male head sutured on to a female ballerina's torso, exposed the way in which the body might be cut into and refashioned.[28]

If you wanted an example of that sort of cutting and mounting, you might indeed look to Dada collage: on paper. Hannah Höch would be the obvious starting point. However, a Film Studies scholar – or a filmmaker – would know that, with the splicing and printing techniques of the 1920s, it would look a bit obvious if, a frame at a time, you *sutured* a male head – one bit of film – within another bit of film that showed a female dancer's body from which the head had been excised. Practically, it could not be done. It is difficult enough today to make such a combination look convincing in Photoshop or Blender! One cannot imagine Le Grice or Lawder committing such a solecism. What we have in *Entr'acte* is not *suturing* in either the material sense of collage or the cinematic, theoretical sense of spectatorial identification: it is the substitution of bodies between shots; the cutting is not enacted *on* the body, as it is in 'exquisite corpse', but *between* bodies. Close examination of the sequence that includes the bearded ballerina shows that first we see a female dancer shot from below, through a glass floor: we do not see the male head and the movements are those of a trained ballerina *en pointe* – movements that are physically impossible for a male dancer. There is a cut. When the camera slowly tilts up the body to reveal the head, we see not photographic suture, but an organically whole male body and head, that of the conductor of the orchestra in the Théâtre des Champs-Élysées, Roger Desormière, who, at that moment in the performance, would have been conducting Erik Satie's music for the film. There is another cut. The sequence ends with another shot that, in its final frames, fades, but none the less shows the female dancer in her entirety. Picabia and Clair's sequence is thus more complex than McCabe realises, since rather than simply being about sexual mobility, it is, first of all, self-referential – as so much of the film is – addressing both the performance and the expectations of the audience of what a ballet should be; given this, we might even speculate that Desormière's conducting gestures in the film accord with those he might have made in the pit for that particular section of Satie's score. Secondly, the sequence shares wider themes of gender substitution and displaced perspective within Picabia's œuvre that would become apparent on an intermedial reading that McCabe elides. In Picabia's *Cinésketch* (1924) for example, Jean Börlin, the lead dancer and choreographer of the Ballets Suédois, appeared dressed as a ballerina; in 'Un Effet facile' (1922) Picabia remarks, 'We should look at men and women from below.'[29]

In part, this particular use of intermediality has been encouraged by disciplinary tendencies: as Film Studies departments are increasingly orientated around industrial practices and histories, and encouraged to move towards the domain of the digital, so study of the historical activity of the avant-garde has devolved upon English and Modern Language departments. The migration of this scholarship from the margins of Film Studies to the interstices of textual studies and Art History has brought with it substantial benefits. If we have, regrettably, lost technical competencies along with medium specificity, the literary disciplines mean we have acquired a new and welcome capacity of close reading between media. If McCabe and Connor typify an approach in which close reading is deployed within one medium – text – whilst the others are there as subaltern support, there remain numerous models of detailed, careful analysis that eschew the obvious and look for the deeper structural relationship and the processes involved in translation between media. Perhaps the next step is to cultivate a generation of young scholars indifferent to boundaries, whether of discipline or medium; equally at home with a Standard 8 camera and film stock and contemporary technologies; equally comfortable within modernist literature, painting and film, and mindful of Frederic Jameson's dictum that, even as we theorise, we must always historicise.

Notes

1. Sheldon Renan, *An Introduction to the American Underground Film* (New York: Dutton, 1967); Peter Gidal, *Andy Warhol: Films and Paintings* (New York: Da Capo Press, 1971); Birgit Hein, *Film im Underground* (Frankfurt: Ullstein, 1971); B. and W. Hein, Christian Michelis, Rolf Wiest (eds), *XSCREEN: Materialen über den Underground Film* (Cologne: Phaidon, 1971).
2. David Curtis, *Experimental Cinema* (London: Dell, 1971); Malcolm Le Grice, *Abstract Film and Beyond* (Cambridge, MA: MIT Press, 1977).
3. Standish Lawder, *The Cubist Cinema* (New York: New York University Press, 1975); Hans Richter, *Dada: Art and Anti-Art* (London: Thames & Hudson, 1965); László Moholy-Nagy, *Painting, Photography, Film* (Cambridge, MA: MIT Press, 1969); Roger Manvell, *Experiment in the Film* (New York: Arno Press, 1970); Paul Rotha, *The Film Till Now: A Survey of the World Cinema* (London: Spring Books, 1967).
4. Daniel Robbins, 'Introduction', in Lawder, *The Cubist Cinema*, pp. xiii–xiv.
5. Ricciotto Canudo 'The birth of a sixth art', trans. by Ben Gibson, Don Ranvaud, Sergio Sokota and Deborah Young, *Framework*, 13 (1980), pp. 3–7, reprinted in Richard Abel (ed.), *French Film Theory and Criticism: A History/Anthology. Volume I: 1907–1929* (Princeton: Princeton University Press, 1988), pp. 58–66.
6. Sennett's film is the most frequently cited reference point for the funeral chase sequence and eventual resurrection in *Entr'acte*. See William Camfield, *Francis Picabia: His Art, Life and Times* (Princeton: Princeton University Press, 1972), p. 213, note 59 ('Professor Stan Lawder has also brought to the attention of this author the similarity between *Entr'acte* and Mack Sennett's comedy, *Heinze's Resurrection* (1913), particularly in the funeral, grand chase and final scene'). This influences Paul Sandro, 'Parodic narration in *Entr'acte*', *Film Criticism*, 4 (1979), p. 53. *Heinze's Resurrection* is known only from production records and stills in the Sennett archive. The film may not have contained such a funeral sequence: we do not know. The surviving *He Wouldn't Stay Down* (1915), which Sennett scholars suggest draws on *Heinze's Resurrection*, does not include a funeral sequence. See Douglas Blair Riblet, *The Keystone Film Company, 1912 to 1915*, PhD thesis,

University of Wisconsin-Madison (1998), p. 272; Brent E. Walker, *Mack Sennett's Fun Factory* (New York: McFarland, 2013); and Rob King, *The Fun Factory: The Keystone Film Company and the Emergence of Mass Culture* (Berkeley: University of California Press, 2008). I am indebted to Prof. Rob King for his advice here.

7. Deke Dusinberre, 'The avant-garde attitude in the thirties', reprinted in Michael O'Pray (ed.), *The British Avant-Garde Film, 1926 to 1995: An Anthology of Writings* (Luton: University of Luton Press, 1996), p. 67. When Dusinberre began his research, few of the films made under POOL's aegis were identified, or thought extant; nor could he use the Bryher/H.D. papers.
8. Douglas Mao and Rebecca Walkowitz, 'The new modernist studies', *PMLA*, 123–3 (2008), p. 738.
9. Deke Dusinberre, 'The avant-garde attitude in the thirties', in Don MacPherson (ed.), *Traditions of Independence: British Cinema in the Thirties* (London: BFI, 1980).
10. Dusinberre, 'The avant-garde attitude in the thirties', in MacPherson.
11. For a reappraisal of the contributors to *Close Up*, see Chris Townsend, 'Close Up, after *Close Up: Life and Letters To-Day* as a Modernist Film Journal', *Journal of Modern Periodical Studies*, 9–2 (2019), pp. 245–64, and Chris Townsend, 'A Deeper, Wider POOL: Reading *Close Up* Through the Archives of its Contributors', *Papers on Language and Literature*, 55–1 (2019).
12. Barbara Rose, 'Kinetic solutions to pictorial problems: The films of Man Ray and Moholy Nagy', *Artforum*, 10–1 (1971).
13. Hollis Frampton, 'Notes on composing in film', *October*, 1 (Spring 1976), pp. 104–10; Annette Michelson, 'About Snow', *October*, 8 (Spring 1979), pp. 111–25; Annette Michelson, Richard Serra and Claudia Weyergraf, 'Richard Serra's films: An interview', *October*, 10 (Fall 1979), pp. 69–104; Scott MacDonald, 'Interview with Hollis Frampton: The early years', *October*, 12 (Spring 1980), pp. 103–26.
14. Sergei Eisenstein, 'Notes for a film of *Capital*' (1927), trans. by Maciej Sliwowski, Jay Leyda and Annette Michelson, and Annette Michelson, 'Reading Eisenstein reading *Capital*', *October*, 2 (Summer 1976), pp. 3–26 and 27–38.
15. Annette Michelson, 'Painting. Instantaneism. Cinema. America. Ballet. Illumination. Apollinaire', in *Francis Picabia: Máquinas y Españolas* (Seville: IVAM Centre Julio Gonzalez, 1995), p. 193. Exhibition catalogue.
16. John Mackay, 'Film energy: Process and metanarrative in Dziga Vertov's *The Eleventh Year* (1928)', *October*, 121 (Summer 2007), pp. 41–78; the all-encompassing survey *Dziga Vertov: Life and Work*, beginning with Vol. 1, 1896–1921 (Brookline: Academic Studies Press, 2018); and Philip Cavendish, *The Men with the Movie Camera: The Poetics of Visual Style in Soviet Avant-garde Cinema of the 1920s* (London: Berghahn, 2013).
17. Yuri Tsivian, 'Turning objects, toppled pictures: Give and take between Vertov's films and constructivist art', *October*, 121 (Summer 2007), pp. 92–110.
18. Malcolm Turvey, *Doubting Vision: Film and the Revelationist Tradition* (Oxford: Oxford University Press, 2008).

19. See, for example, Pavle Levi, 'Cinema by other means', *October*, 131 (Winter 2010), pp. 51–68; Jonathan Walley, 'The material of film and the idea of cinema: Contrasting practices in sixties and seventies avant-garde film', *October*, 103 (Winter 2003), pp. 15–30.
20. James Donald, 'Jazz modernism and film art: Dudley Murphy and *Ballet mécanique*', *Modernism/modernity*, 16–1 (2009), pp. 25–49; Susan Delson, *Dudley Murphy: Hollywood Wild Card* (Minneapolis: Minnesota University Press, 2006).
21. Inez Hedges, 'Robert Desnos's and Man Ray's manuscript scenario for *L'Étoile de mer*', *Dada/Surrealism*, 15 (1986), pp. 207–19. It became clear to Hedges – familiar with both artists' archives – that a scenario for the film in the MoMA New York archives, thought to originate with Man Ray, was in fact wholly authored by, and in the handwriting of, Desnos. The dates for that scenario problematised all accounts of the film's authorship and production process. Oddly, though she cites Hedges in her bibliography, even a recent work such as Katherine Conley's biography of Desnos treats the film as a work by Man Ray 'inspired' by Desnos – that is, in the terms that Man Ray describes its production in his autobiography. Katherine Conley, *Robert Desnos, Surrealism, and the Marvelous in Everyday Life* (Lincoln: University of Nebraska Press, 2003), p. 71.
22. Peter Christensen, 'Benjamin Fondane's "Scenarii intournables"', *Dada/Surrealism*, 15 (1986), pp. 72–85.
23. Clement Greenberg, 'Modernist painting' (1960), in John O'Brian (ed.), *Clement Greenberg, the Collected Essays and Criticism: Modernism with a Vengeance, 1957–1969* (Chicago: University of Chicago Press, 1995), pp. 85–93.
24. For Woolf see, inter alia, Winifred Holtby, *Virginia Woolf: A Critical Memoir* (1932) (London: Continuum, 2007), p. 117; Leslie Hankins, 'Virginia Woolf and film', in Maggie Humm (ed.), *The Edinburgh Companion to Virginia Woolf and the Arts* (Edinburgh: Edinburgh University Press, 2010); Maggie Humm, 'Virginia Woolf and visual culture', in Susan Sellers (ed.), *The Cambridge Companion to Virginia Woolf*, 2nd edn (Cambridge: Cambridge University Press, 2010), pp. 214–30; Maggie Humm, 'Cinema and photography', in Bryony Randall and Jane Goldman (eds), *Virginia Woolf in Context* (Cambridge: Cambridge University Press, 2012), pp. 291–301. Selected solecisms include Woolf's essay 'The cinema' (1926) presaging Eisenstein's theory of montage (published in Russian in 1923). For a useful critique of Holtby see David Trotter, *Cinema and Modernism* (Oxford: Blackwell, 2007), pp. 160–9. For Picasso see, inter alia, Natasha Staller, 'Méliès's fantastic cinema and the origins of cubism', *Art History*, 12–2 (June 1989); Bernice Rose, 'Picasso, Braque and early film in cubism', in *Picasso, Braque and Early Film in Cubism* (New York: Pace Wildenstein, 2007), pp. 35–147. Exhibition catalogue.
25. Rachel Connor, *H.D. and the Image* (Manchester University Press, 2004), p. 22.
26. Oswell Blakeston, 'Sketches by Len Lye', *Close Up*, VI-2 (February 1930), pp. 155–6.
27. Jane Garrity, *Step-Daughters of England: British Women Modernists and the National Imaginary* (Manchester: Manchester University Press, 2003), pp. 85–6. For a different approach to Richardson, see Zlatina Nikolova and Christopher Townsend,

'Dorothy Richardson's writing for *Close-Up* and *Life and Letters To-Day*', in Aarthi Vadde and Saikat Majumdar (eds), *The Critic as Amateur* (London: Bloomsbury Academic, 2019).
28. Susan McCabe, *Cinematic Modernism: Modernist Poetry and Film* (Cambridge: Cambridge University Press, 2005), p. 30.
29. Francis Picabia, 'Un effet facile', *Littérature*, 2nd edn, 5 (1 October 1922), p. 2.

CHAPTER 6

The 'Artist as Filmmaker': Modernisms, Schisms, Misunderstandings
Lucy Reynolds

In 1972, Annabel Nicolson wrote a provocative article for a special issue of the art magazine *Art and Artist*, devoted to artist filmmaking. Entitled 'Artist as Filmmaker', Nicolson addresses the potential role of the film medium (referencing predominantly the 8 mm and 16 mm gauges) in the art practices of herself and her contemporaries. As her article makes clear, through an argument at times passionate and polemic, artists were using the medium in two distinctive ways. Whilst some found it a useful means of documentation 'to deal with concerns arising out of other works',[1] others focused on its medium-specific qualities as a means of creative expression, which Nicolson describes as 'a fluent, organic approach to their material and an awareness of its structural implications'.[2] Nicolson builds her argument on close analysis of key works from artists associated with these stated tendencies, comparing the contrasting ways in which they were approaching the possibilities of the medium in their art practices. Despite recognising that both approaches came from the same fine art roots, Nicolson is, however, categorical about the divergent paths their use of film follows:

> It may seem tenuous to distinguish between artists and film makers, many of whom come from a background in painting i.e. Legrice [sic], Drummond, Gidal etc., but the use of film as an expedient for demonstrating concepts is diametrically opposite from structural use of film and still more so from the perceptual and psychological exploration identified with personal film makers.[3]

To make her case, Nicolson refers in particular detail to the conceptual use of the camera by Dan Graham, John Hilliard, the Canadian artist David Askevold and Jan Dibbets in Holland, whose work she was encountering as installations in the spaces of London galleries supporting less traditional art practices, such as the Lisson Gallery and Nigel Greenwood, the Institute of Contemporary Arts (ICA) and the Camden Arts Centre. In her analysis, she argues that film functioned for them as a documentation device for actions and ideas with a time-based dynamic, whether performative or photographic. In contrast, Nicolson argues for film to be considered as a creative medium in itself, where it might be assigned the same value as other forms of art media such as paint or plaster. She expresses frustration at how the 'plastic possibilities of film',[4] as she puts it, were not being realised by many of the artists from the conceptual field then beginning to pick up a camera. She contrasts Graham and Hilliard's conceptually driven use of the film camera as an instrument of documentation with that of artists such as William Raban and Chris Welsby, for whom the mechanics of filmmaking, such as camera speeds and exposures, become a visible and integral element of the image, rather than the means through which documentation might be produced. Writing of Raban's double-screen time-lapse film with Welsby, *River Yar* (1971), for example, she applauds how the 'different time analogues [. . .] are the most interesting in the use of film as film by providing scales to register different perceptions of time'.[5]

Nicolson clearly identifies herself in this latter camp. A painter who had recently finished a postgraduate course at Saint Martins School of Art, she had gravitated to the newly developed space for film, which Malcolm Le Grice had initiated within the sculpture department there. Her own films and film performances of this period also clearly show how a fascination with film's materiality is at the fore of her practice. As she stresses: 'What might appear didactic concern with the chemistry of the medium is an essential landmark in an overdue, radical re-examination of the nature of film.'[6] Her short film *Slides* (1971), for example, turns the 16 mm contact printer into an agent of magnification, arguing for the minutiae of her film's celluloid surfaces as a representational force more fundamental than cinematic fiction. In this regard, 'Artist as Filmmaker' might be read as a means of working through her own allegiances in the competing practices around film as a viable artistic medium. It is significant that her article is placed in *Art and Artists* alongside those of Peter Gidal and Malcolm Le Grice, two prominent fellow members and friends from the London Film-makers' Co-operative. Their contributions, 'Film as Film' and 'Real Time/Space', as the titles suggest, underline the common goal she also argues for in her article: both to define and to defend the medium-specific potential of film, which was central to the London Film-makers' Co-operative during this period.

Nicolson's close and often eloquent readings of the works themselves, rather than the theories or context around them, reveal what was at stake for her in terms of her own creative identification and questioning around the medium. In retrospect, she recalls the writing of her article as 'a way of working out what I thought about what was going on around me'.[7] But her article is also revealing in a number of unexpected ways for the retrospective reader. It offers a fascinating snapshot of how artists on the cusp of the 1970s were exploring the potential of the film medium within their artistic practices, at a point when video as an art form was still in its infancy, and not yet widely available for artistic experiment. In her discussion of these divergent experiments with the film medium, a record of the wider cultural networks, allegiances and art communities circulating in London and internationally during the early 1970s can be traced. Recognition of conceptual art practices came late to Britain, but it was already a well-established movement internationally, in which the films, photographs and performances of the artists whom Nicolson refers to, such as Graham or Dibbets, were well known. The year 1972 was a significant one for the emergence of conceptual art in London, where it was beginning to be taken seriously, in terms of both a number of exhibitions and writing around the phenomenon, particularly through the advocacy of Charles Harrison and Richard Cork, editors of the art magazine *Studio International*. Harrison was responsible for bringing the influential 1969 exhibition *When Attitudes Become Form* from the Kunsthalle Bern to the ICA, which introduced key practices and figures to a wider art audience in London. Nicolson's 1972 article reflects this flurry of activity, when Graham showed at the Lisson Gallery, and *The New Art* exhibition at the Hayward Gallery (17 August to 24 September 1972) provided one of the first British surveys of the movement,[8] whose key exponents were delineated by its curator Anne Seymour in the exhibition catalogue's foreword:

> The systems into which materials are fitted are arbitrary, quasi mathematical, always self-contained, often constructed directly out of the materials themselves. Among other things John Hilliard uses photography to discuss photography, David Dye film to discuss film, Art-Language philosophy to discuss philosophy, Long to discuss landscape.[9]

Experimental film was also in the ascendant, having now established a stable infrastructure of exhibition and production through the London Film-makers' Co-operative, in association with a wider Film Co-operative movement which spanned Europe to the US and Japan. The special artists' film issue of *Art and Artists* reflects a greater understanding from more traditional art quarters of the importance of film as an art medium, and acknowledges its widespread practice. As Cork remembers, this was a time 'when the centuries-old dominance of painting and sculpture gave way at last to a general acknowledgement that "art" could assume a far greater range of material identities'.[10] However, film was not yet to be found in the galleries of the Lisson, the ICA or the Hayward, unless it was connected to a conceptual practitioner such as Graham. Screenings of the single-screen and multi-disciplinary 'film actions' of Nicolson and other Co-op filmmakers

– however experimental in form – were limited to cinematic contexts, even those as informal as the Co-op cinema. Thus, for all the appreciation of film experimentation, which Nicolson and the Co-op were leading, their work was held separate from their conceptual art counterparts. Nicolson's argument for a greater appreciation of film's materiality could be seen as a response to this implicit division, and the lack of dialogue between two areas of practice that might have much to share. In the title of her article is imbricated the question of an identification in conflict between the contrasting modes of reception and endorsement associated with the gallery or the cinema. Where might the 'artist filmmakers' locate themselves in order to realise the potential of their work fully?

And were these two conflicting understandings of the film medium really as 'diametrically opposed' as Nicolson argues? As she insightfully observes: 'The lack of cross reference between artists' and film makers' films is disheartening since these polarities of conceptual and perceptual emphasis could throw illuminating perspectives on each other.'[11]

As I write from a time when the term 'artist filmmaker' is common parlance, Nicolson's prescient comparison of how film was used and understood within these two distinct fields of art practice may yet throw light on the elisions still occurring around the term, in both current curatorial practices and historical understandings of them. And by examining the slippages and distinctions, the similarities and the divergences raised in Nicolson's text, a picture emerges of how group identifications and institutional interests within the art community have come to obscure approaches to the medium's potential, which were not really so different after all. For, as this chapter argues, the questions which the camera brought to art practice, concerning time, process and technological mediation between artist, space and audience, were common to both artist filmmaker and filmmaker alike. To draw out these institutional determinants and shared concerns, my chapter begins with an examination of the contradictions inherent in Nicolson's foundational text, before turning briefly to a rare congruence between the 'conceptual and perceptual' in the film installations of the artist David Dye. My conclusion addresses the question which implicitly frames Nicolson's article: if much common ground can be found in the approaches that conceptual artist and structural filmmaker brought to film, why was there so little crossover between them?

RECIPROCITIES

To begin with Nicolson's critical analysis of the work itself: one of the key contentions that she levels at her conceptual art counterparts concerns their lack of engagement with the inherent properties of the film medium and its apparatus as a space of experimentation. Dan Graham's two-screen film work *Two Correlated Rotations* is held up as exemplary of this tendency. Seen by Nicolson at the Lisson Warehouse space in 1972, it demonstrates a reflexive use of the camera, which expressed for Nicolson 'reciprocity of process and content'.[12] Shot on Super 8 and projected on 16 mm on two walls adjacent and at right angles to each other, Graham's film documents two cameramen under instruction to keep each other in their cameras' sights whilst they spiral away from each other in different directions – turning inwards and outwards of a circle previously delineated by Graham on the floor.

But Graham's systematic brief yields no straightforward document of a performance to a set of instructions. The films do not only record the difficulty of the cameramen keeping each other in view, but the technological limits of the camera as a recording device, manifested as a series of disorientating rotational pans, blurred shifts and loss of focus. The incoherence of the images that register from this camera dance may certainly be seen as a record of the performance, which Graham has put in motion through the imposition of a given set of concepts. But instead of neutral recording devices, the cameras function like perceptual prosthetics, held close up against the eye and body of the performer. The shifts of focus and blurred images might thus be read as an assertion of the camera's own mechanical agency, which asserts its awkward and weighty presence in a reciprocal exchange of image creation with the camera holder.

Graham's notes on his intention for the work also suggest that he was as much interested in the nature of the documentation as in the ability of his performers to fulfil his instructions. He describes how, inspired by the Gestalt psychology of James Gibson in his book *The Perception of the Visual World*, the work intended to 'relate perception to perceived motion to the perception of depth/time'.[13] The work was also intended to act as an improvisatory dance, where its success depends on what Graham termed a 'learning process'[14] between the two participants as they circle with each other in their sights. *Two Correlated Rotations* might be seen to collapse the boundaries between form and content, where Graham's performative experiment actively foregrounds the technologies of film's apparatus in a way that would be familiar to Nicolson and other Co-operative filmmakers.

Turning to Nicolson's work, this dialogic interplay between performers and the film apparatus recalls her participatory film performance of the following year, *Precarious Vision* (1973), in which the artist involved performers (often volunteers from the audience) in a game of interruptions and instructions between screen, viewer and projectionist. She invites a volunteer to read aloud a short poetic text with their back to the screen, on which the same words – typed and filmed by Nicolson – are projected. Nicolson/the projectionist uses some playful cues to help the reader to keep pace with the writing on screen which they are unable to see. If they read too fast, Nicolson holds her hand over the projector lens, so the participant has no light to read and must stop until the words projected in the film have reached the same point in the text, when Nicolson lifts her hand and light is restored. If the reader is too slow, Nicolson uses the projector's freeze-frame mechanism to still the onscreen text until they have caught up with it. Like *Two Correlated Rotations*, *Precarious Vision*'s dialogic game of reading and speaking was also marked by fallibility and contingency as human comprehension is tested against the mechanistic pace of the projector, in a work that explores not only the keeping of time, but also the power dynamics of trust, instruction and control. These were elements also at play in a further performative piece, Graham's *2 Consciousness Projections*, which he tried out whilst in London, using televisual apparatus to mediate expressions of consciousness between two people.[15] Nicolson was already engaged in a fascination with 'the invisible space between projector and screen', suspending a series of small paper screens in her studio to explore the density of light at different distances.[16] Like these earlier works, *Precarious Vision* develops an idea of cinema as a form of 'light reading', in recognition of the light beam's role as a luminous transference of information from projector to projection surface in a game of reading and language. Common to conceptual artist and structural filmmaker alike, Nicolson and Graham use instructions or tasks to activate a performance in dialogue with the film or video apparatus, which will test the technology's limits as a transmitter of information and precipitate a complex reciprocity that is both human and mechanical.

In this regard, both artists could be understood as heirs to the discourses around cybernetics then circulating in exhibition and educational contexts, as Norbert Wiener's influential theories of 'information–communication' found their way into artistic practice, not only through early explorations of computational systems, but also through the use of feedback loops, dialogues between different people and groups, often with a social contextualisation. In Britain, I argue, art school pedagogy, particularly through Roy Ascott's influential 'groundcourse' programme at Newcastle School of Art, with its emphasis on the implementation of 'behavioural' exercises, and the teachings of Le Grice's colleague Peter Kardia at Saint Martins School of Art, encouraged students to explore the notions of reciprocal processes, and information systems, as potentially more relevant to their practices than traditional media.[17]

However, it is important to stress the different discursive emphases from which the work of Graham and Nicolson emerged. An image of *Two Correlated*

Rotations, for example, can be found in Lucy Lippard's 1972 book *Six Years: The Dematerialization of the Art Object from 1966 to 1972*. The inclusion of Graham's work in Lippard's paradigmatic index of conceptual art – devoted to works where 'the idea is paramount and the material form is secondary'[18] – exemplifies film as an instrument of dematerialisation rather than a focus in itself. Or, as Harrison put it in 'Against Precedents', his defining essay in the catalogue for *When Attitudes Become Form*:

> [i]t is no longer necessary for the artist to make his work finite in terms of area or form: it need be neither tangible nor visible so long as his particular intention will carry into 'mental space' without an object to remember it by.[19]

Harrison's assertion of the intangible as art addresses the spectre of its modernist forebears and the medium-specific creed of Clement Greenberg, whose influential 1961 book *Art and Culture* advocated art's material autonomy. Notably masticated and spat out by the artist John Latham in his piece *Still and Chew: Art and Culture 1966–1967* (1966), the perceived orthodoxies of *Art and Culture*, as Andrew Wilson argues, were consequential in the emergence of conceptual art, which he argues are a response to 'a crisis of modernism, driven by a reaction to the established edifice of Greenbergian modernism'.[20] Nicolson, on the other hand, tellingly commends the relation between the 'tactile potential of film' and the 'post-war unshackling of painting by the Abstract Expressionists',[21] and we see this attention to materiality in films such as *Slides*. Like many of her fellow Co-op filmmakers, she had come to film through a visual arts practice, but it could be argued that her touchstones – and those of her contemporaries – were not the burgeoning practices of art as idea but the earlier modernisms of process and medium that Graham and Lippard wished to leave behind. That she and her fellow Co-op filmmakers should still find potential in medium specificity returns us, I would argue, to Nicolson's point about the 'overdue, radical re-examination of the nature of film', which sought not only to challenge perceptions of the medium in the visual arts, but to use film's ontological specificity to argue for a different model of cinema from its commercial counterpart.

However, the dividing line that Nicolson draws between conceptual practice and materialist filmmaking is troubled by film's relationship to contexts outside art. To be self-referential with paint, as Greenberg argues in *Art and Culture*, requires an attention to its systems of support such as stretcher, canvas, or the reference to authorial performance found in the brush stroke. Yet film technology implies contexts that lie outside the studio and in the commercial arena of cinema production, distribution and exhibition. This was the argument later followed through by Peter Wollen in his polemic 1975 article 'The Two Avant-gardes', where structural filmmakers are cast as caught in a formalist endgame when a cinema of radical representation is sought. However, it could be argued that it is in structural film's attempt to purge film of cinema's indelible associations that its most interesting experiments are forged. For even the tropes of modernism cannot erase the intrinsic technological presence of the camera. Despite the artisanal settings created at the London Film-makers' Co-operative for singular control of its processes, film refers back irrevocably not only to its celluloid materiality, but also to its industrial contexts and origins. Whilst the films of Le Grice and his American counterpart, Ken Jacobs, both used found footage to explore cinematic beginnings, most famously in Le Grice's *Berlin Horse* (1971), it is the experimental attempts – and failures – to challenge this crucial element of film's identity as a technology harnessed to representational form that are often most compelling, as *Precarious Vision* or *Slides* shows. And whilst Nicolson or Le Grice might have seen art as an alternative model for filmmaking, less tainted by the commercial imperatives of cinema, so for the same reason their conceptual art counterparts were drawn to the camera for its quotidian associations with popular culture. Even if their positions might appear diametrically opposed with regard to how they identified themselves with modernism, both conceptual artist and structural filmmaker alike are exercised by the conundrum of how to assimilate film – and later video – technology into their practices and the wider cultural communities, and popular cultures, of which they were a part.

At stake for both is the question of representation and the film image. The concern for Nicolson stems primarily from a critique of mainstream cinema and its industrial contexts, manifesting through film's employment in the service of fiction film 'as a vehicle for literal and dramatic content',[22] a view shared by other Co-op filmmakers such as Le Grice, who, in the same issue of *Art and Artists*, refers to the 'prestructured substitute and illusory reality'[23] of conventional cinema representation. The root of this critique of cinema is indebted less to film theoretical sources than to the diverse, politically infused currents of counter-cultural ideas then circulating in London at hubs such as the Arts Lab,[24] from experimental music, cybernetics and the anti-psychiatry of R. D. Laing, to modernist literature and radical theatre. In retrospect, Le Grice relates their approach to a 'radical aspiration'[25] where 'we discussed philosophical questions and related them to the practice'.[26]

For conceptual artists such as Graham, representation in its widest definition was under scrutiny, rather than the representation associated with cinema in particular. Returning to Harrison's edict that art should occupy 'mental space', their interest was not in the optical certainties of film as a representational medium, but in the question of how the film or photographic document might function as a referent for actions and events, ephemeral in both form and idea. Andrea Tarsia has argued (with reference to the photographs of one of Graham's contemporaries, Richard Long) that artists of the period were concerned with the denotation of 'a field of representation, the allusion to something or some place other than the image or object before us'.[27] Tarsia suggests that representation becomes palpable only as a point upon which to reflect: 'our attention is drawn to the artist (conspicuously absent), his gesture, its mediation and our reception, holding us in the gap between artistic intervention and our own reception of that intervention'.[28] Following Tarsia's argument, the conceptual artist asserts the temporal and spatial remove at which representation has placed us from the scene of creative activity, whether it is two cameramen spiralling away from each other or a photographic record of a walk across a field. In this sense, Nicolson is indeed right that conceptual artists regarded 'film as an expedient for demonstrating concepts'. However, it could also be argued that the unique temporal and spatial capture of film technology was as integral to their creative enquiries as to her own. As Graham's work shows, the film projections for *Two Correlated Rotations*, projected on adjacent walls at the Lisson, assert the marks of the camera's technological presence, at the same time as they register the performers' attempts to stay in frame. In the films' inability to capture fully the movement of the turning performers is contained not only a record of a past performance, but a material assertion of the camera's technological struggle to represent the contingencies of another space and time. Nicolson herself describes this sensation in the work of David Askevold, writing that 'Askevold's films have a sense of somewhere just out of reach, they build their own space.'[29]

Confine

Graham's choreographic test of the limits of both human and technological movement could be said to find parallels in the time-lapse records of landscape produced by Raban and Welsby, which register not only temporal changes in the landscape, manifesting in weather and light, but the elusive presence of the film camera, and the artist, in the landscape. As Nicolson writes with regard to *River Yar*: '[T]he reflection of the camera in the window (closed because of heavy rain at night) provides a self-referential context at intervals.'[30] She also recognises 'parallels with the concerns of structural cinema'[31] in John Hilliard's serial photographic works and double-screen films, such as *Ten Runs Past a Fixed Point* (1971), and his twin-screen projection *From and Two* (1971),[32] for their use of 'camera variables, developing and printing factors determining and becoming the subject of photographs'.[33] But whilst Nicolson recognises the 'self-referential aspect' of his work, she implies that his 'controlled experiments' limit the richness of experience available to the viewer of structural film, which are, she explains, 'inevitably more subjective in that perceptual time plays havoc with one's responses'.[34] Her remark briefly crystallises an unspoken suggestion that threads through her article: about the more engaged relationship to film which she and her fellow filmmakers shared. As David Curtis has since observed: 'Both forms tend to reflect upon the nature of their medium and the process of their making, though *enjoyment* of the medium is supposedly unique to the structuralists.'[35]

One artist in Nicolson's article who appears to have straddled both conceptual and structural concerns was David Dye, a friend and fellow student at Saint Martins. Nicolson commends his work for its sensitivity to medium and critique of representation, acclaiming him as 'probably the only artist who consistently rejects the use of film as a retrospective reality referring to another time/space by initiating specific projection situations for each film for dialectic between image, process and content'.[36] Rather than rejecting representation, it could be argued that Dye practised a more nuanced dismantling of it through his playful exploration of scale and time frame. In his film performance *Confine* – presented during a one-week exhibition of his work at the ICA in 1972 – the artist holds an 8 mm projector which projects a film of a still photograph of himself on to the same photographic image of himself pinned to a wall. However, Dye has utilised a zoom lens on his camera so that the film image slowly zooms in to enlarge his picture, meaning that he must keep moving towards the photograph that has become the screen in order for his film image to match his unmoving still image on the wall correctly. *Confine* draws the mechanical time of the camera and the projector into a reciprocal equivalence, in which the performing artist becomes the intermediary, demonstrating the difficulty of a neat alignment. Nicolson praises the film as a 'radical divergence from conventional acceptance of projection as the relaying of an earlier completed activity'.[37] Here she reflects the enduring exploration in her own practice about how light relays information through 'the giving or withholding of information through light'[38] which is seen in *Precarious Vision*, when the projection beam is intercepted by the projectionist to reveal or withhold the words before they reach the screen.

However, Dye's performative interventions return us to Tarsia's point about how the gesture of the artist is instrumental in pointing us towards an undoing of the illusion which the technology of the photograph or film upholds – often through the artist's failure in relation to contingent factors such as environment and the inability to follow instructions correctly. Dye takes this notion of a destabilised authorship further in his installation *Unsigning for Eight Projectors*, presented in 1972 in the Hayward Gallery's *New Art* exhibition. A ring of eight 8 mm projectors each projects an image of Dye writing a letter of his name, but as the dangling screen in the middle twists and moves in accordance with movement in the gallery space, the letters jumble and superimpose, and those beams not caught by the expanse of the screen are cast unfocused and out of scale on the gallery walls around the circle of projectors. As Dye said: 'I wanted to do a work that was the opposite of the meaning behind the signature, identity fixture and projection and turn it inside out.'[39] But whilst this is a conceptual play on the artist's gesture of identity, and its negation, it also asserts the intrinsic properties of film projection – using the unpredictable turns of the suspended screen to draw attention to its beam of light as the conveyer of information that so interested Nicolson.

Nicolson was not alone in appreciating Dye's work. The young critic Richard Cork, a key advocate for conceptual art practices in Britain, also visited the show and writes enthusiastically in the *Evening Standard* of the potential of Dye's work to speak across fields of practice which had held themselves distinct. He praised:

> This was the excitement of Dye's exhibition: the realization it offered that the boundaries between two media of expression need not be tightly sealed off, that both sides can converge and yet succeed in defining their different priorities with exactitude.[40]

Yet it could be argued that what sealed off conceptual art from experimental filmmaking was the exhibiting context and its attendant endorsements, rather than the practices themselves. A further part of Dye's appeal to both conceptualist artist and structuralist filmmaker was his work's ability to cross the continued disconnect between the temporal and spatial conventions of galleries, designed to illuminate painting and sculpture, and the cinema's immersive auditoria. He was the only artist using film to be included in surveys of conceptual practices in Britain, such as 'The New Art' at the Hayward. Even though the relevance of film to dematerialised conceptual practices was acknowledged, it was not part of the major conceptual shows circulating in Britain and Europe at that time. One rare occasion to counter this cautious approach can be found in the third part of the ambitious *Survey of the Avant-garde in Britain* at Gallery House in 1972, based at the Goethe Institut's South Kensington address, where conceptual artists working with film were placed alongside their structuralist peers, thanks to the adventurous approach of the curators Rosetta Brooks and Sigi Krauss, whose intergenerational exhibition programme embraced radical art practices, from David Medalla and Gustav Metzger to younger conceptualists such as Hilliard. In their survey, John Latham's *Erth* might therefore screen before Peter Gidal's *Movie* or Anthony McCall's *Landscape for Fire Film*, adjusting to the durational conditions of the gallery through a number of repeating film programmes, situated in rooms adjacent to early video installations, such as David Hall and Tony Sinden's *60 TV Sets*.

However, with this notable exception, it was when film approximated sculpture – as was the case with Dye – that curators could more readily understand its relevance in the gallery. As Dye reflected in a 1972 interview with Simon Field, comparing his experience of showing at the Hayward and the ICA:

> The Hayward was a straight gallery situation in which it's not normal to see film. Although it is much more now. And so there are other kinds of problems involved about showing things, there are problems of presentation involved to begin with. Whereas with the ICA show, because I was there, projecting . . . it was strange because it related to a normal cinema situation, in a way, and yet it wasn't. It's very difficult to work out . . . they are very different situations. In a sense I learned as much from both of them because, in a sense, more than most, my work doesn't exist until it is being shown . . . it's hardly there.[41]

As his reflections suggest, it was through his performative interactions with visitors that Dye was able to resolve his initial ambivalence about the presentation of his films within the gallery, and it could be argued that it was his ephemeral and contingent presence that came to determine the experience of the work, not simply the film projections on display, nor their sculptural connotations. Dye's tentative comments also reflect the awkward place the film medium still occupied between two distinct cultural contexts, replete with established and very separate models of reception, exhibition and validation. Indeed, a case could be made that differences were less in the work itself – as Nicolson's close readings of Graham and Dye show – than in the contexts around them.

In his insightful dissection of the disconnect between conceptual artist and structural filmmaker, David Curtis argues that the Filmmakers' Co-op was both geographically and theoretically distant from its conceptual counterparts, making the Co-op cinema 'a place of film pilgrimage, attracting devotees only, offering little cross-over potential'.[42] As Dye's remarks already suggest, the tight-knit circles of the Co-op, with their distinctive approach to film, could also be seen as limiting to some in terms of exhibiting opportunities, as well as contexts for making work. By not aligning himself fully with the Co-op's structural film culture, Dye ensured he was not defined wholly with its associations, leaving him open to other exhibiting opportunities such as the Lisson Gallery or the attentions of Richard Cork or Charles Harrison. However, the institutional acceptance enjoyed by conceptual practitioners reflected for Nicolson an uneasy relationship to the supposed critiques made in their work. As she observes: 'I felt very uncomfortable with the values of the gallery system and how some artists whose work may have been considered radical at the time were co-opted into it.'[43] It could be argued that the facilities at the Co-op, low-cost and collective, enabled artist filmmakers such as herself to create an alternative system through which to find validation and afford to continue their work.

Furthermore, practical issues of display could be seen to determine the interest of galleries and exhibition curators, who were more comfortable with two-dimensional works and sculpture. Whilst Dye's ring of projectors could be supported in a gallery group show, what of an exhibition where time-based film performances and film installations were predominant, requiring the more immersive conditions of darkened spaces and regular maintenance? The opportunities that Dye received to present his film installations during 1972 and 1973 affirm how curators and critics at the time limited their dissemination and validation to artists who not only were able to position themselves within familiar conceptual art circuits of known galleries such as the Lisson or the ICA, but whose work was conducive to established models of reception: whether the gallery or the cinema. With this in mind, it is instructive that it was in the ad hoc and more indeterminate conditions of Gallery House that artists' experimental film was to find one of its first homes outside the Co-op and the cinema auditorium. The success of the *Filmaktion* exhibition at the Walker Art Gallery, Liverpool, in June 1973, with its ambitious programme of screenings, film actions and installations,[44] could also be attributed to the on-site expertise and maintenance provided by Co-op filmmakers such as Nicolson and Raban, which was not standard in art spaces more generally. Nicolson indeed observes that 'the alienation of distribution and unsuitable projection conditions are as unattractive to artists as to any discerning independent film maker'.[45]

At issue was how artist filmmakers located themselves within this divided cultural landscape. For Dye, like more conceptually aligned artists, film was one medium amongst others through which they addressed the question of representation: from their own bodies to still photography and diagrams. For artists working at the Co-op, on the other hand, representation was challenged through a thorough engagement – not disengagement – with film's materiality. However, as Nicolson's reading of Graham suggests, whether conceptual or structural, artist filmmakers were examining the temporal spatial implications of film and its ability to mediate representation and instrumentalise perception. Through their profound and singular probing of film's properties, Nicolson or Le Grice hoped to expose the fallacies of narrative cinema and unlock film's unrealised potential, whereas their conceptual contemporaries saw in the medium another means of undermining the orthodoxies of art practices still bound to the conventions of traditional art media.

'Artist as Filmmaker' is insightful on the commonalities that remain unacknowledged in accounts of conceptual art in Britain, both historical and contemporary. Nicolson recalls how she was 'interested in what those artists did, but did not feel close to it',[46] and in her close analysis of film's role in the art practices of her 1970s contemporaries, the reader can trace her curiosity about how other artists outside her immediate circle were exploring film. Yet, for all the profound differences of approach that she identifies between them, it is possible in retrospect to trace shared fascinations with how film and its technical apparatus had the ability to mediate representations of time, space and the artist themself. 'Artist as Filmmaker' suggests that the differences between conceptual artist and structural filmmaker are less about their interests in film's intrinsic qualities than in their level of engagement with the discourses and contexts of reception and exhibition surrounding the film medium. Conceptual artists still sought validation and visibility from Britain's established systems of publicly funded and commercial gallery spaces, whilst Nicolson and her peers found support and opportunity at the London Film-makers' Co-operative, and the circuits of co-operative film culture within which it operated. Returning to her point about the 'disheartening' lack of 'cross-reference' between 'polarities of conceptual and perceptual emphasis', Nicolson's article suggests that film might have been a possible bridge of common purpose, which – as history shows us – was not to be crossed.

Notes

1. Annabel Nicolson, 'Artist as Filmmaker', *Art and Artists* (December 1972), p. 20.
2. Nicolson, 'Artist as Filmmaker', p. 20.
3. Nicolson, 'Artist as Filmmaker', p. 20.
4. Nicolson, 'Artist as Filmmaker', p. 20.
5. Nicolson, 'Artist as Filmmaker', p. 26.
6. Nicolson, 'Artist as Filmmaker', p. 26.
7. Annabel Nicolson, in a letter to Lucy Reynolds, 2 February 2020.
8. A good example of Graham's positioning within the movement is provided by Richard Cork's review of his solo exhibition at the Lisson Gallery in March 1972. See Richard Cork, *Everything Seemed Possible: Art in the 1970s* (New Haven, CT, and London: Yale University Press, 2003), pp. 50–3.
9. Anne Seymour, 'Introduction', in *The New Art* (London: Arts Council 1972), p. 6.
10. Cork, *Everything Seemed Possible*, p. 10.
11. Nicolson, 'Artist as Filmmaker', p. 20
12. Nicolson, 'Artist as Filmmaker', p. 20.
13. Ronald Alley, *Catalogue of the Tate Gallery's Collection of Modern Art other than Works by British Artists* (London: Tate Gallery and Sotheby Parke-Bernet, 1981)

pp. 330–2. Available at <https://www.tate.org.uk/art/artworks/graham-two-correlated-rotations-t01737> (last accessed 10 November 2019).
14. Alley, *Catalogue of the Tate Gallery's Collection of Modern Art*.
15. In his contemporaneous review of Graham's 1972 exhibition, Richard Cork describes the work thus: 'A woman focusing attention only on a television image of herself has to verbalise her consciousness, while a man observing her through the camera connected to the monitor screen focuses only outside himself and verbalises his perceptions as well' (Cork, *Everything Seemed Possible*, p. 53). It should be noted that this is based on a preview of the piece, not his experience of it. For further discussion of Graham's interest in reciprocity through performance and film, see Birgit Pelzer, 'Double Intersections: The Optics of Dan Graham', in Birgit Pelzer, Mark Francis and Beatriz Colomina (eds), *Dan Graham* (London and New York: Phaidon, 2001) pp. 45–9.
16. As Nicolson explains in more detail, 'I was already working with projected light in my studio at the Dairy (1971–1975) where I had a series of small paper screens suspended at different distances from a 16mm projector. The beam of light became larger, but also dimmer, the further it was from the projector. It was this invisible space between projector and screen which continued to fascinate me.' Letter to Lucy Reynolds, 2 February 2020.
17. For a more detailed explanation of Wiener and his influence on art culture see Kristine Stiles, 'Art and Technology', in Kristine Stiles and Peter Seltz (eds), *Theories and Documents of Contemporary Art* (Berkeley: University of California Press, 1996), pp. 384–96.
18. Lucy Lippard, *Six Years: The Dematerialisation of the Art Object from 1966 to 1972* (Berkeley and Los Angeles: University of California Press, 1997), p. 2.
19. Christian Rattemeyer, *Exhibiting the New Art 'Op Losse Schroeven' and 'When Attitudes Become Form' 1969* (Vienna, London and Eindhoven: Afterall Books in association with the Academy of Fine Arts Vienna and Van Abbemuseum, 2010), p. 195.
20. Andrew Wilson, *Conceptual Art in Britain, 1964–1979* (London: Tate, 2016), p. 9.
21. Nicolson, 'Artist as Filmmaker', p. 20.
22. Nicolson, 'Artist as Filmmaker', p. 20.
23. Malcolm Le Grice, 'Real SPACE/TIME', *Art and Artists* (December 1972). Nicolson, 'Artist as Filmmaker', p. 20.
24. For a more detailed exploration of the relationship between the Arts Lab and structural film practices see Lucy Reynolds, '"Non-institution": Finding expanded cinema in the *terrains vagues* of 1960s London', in François Bovier and Adeena Mey (eds), *Cinema in the Expanded Field* (Zurich: JRP-Ringier, 2015).
25. Maxa Zoller, Interview with Malcolm Le Grice, *X Screen: Film Installations and Actions in the 1960s and 1970s* (Vienna: MUMOK, 2000), p. 143.
26. Zoller, Interview with Malcolm Le Grice, p. 143.
27. Andrea Tarsia, 'Introduction', in Clive Philpot and Andrea Tarsia (eds), *Live in Your Head: Concept and Experiment in Britain 1965–1975* (London: Whitechapel Gallery, 2000), p. 18.

28. Tarsia, 'Introduction', p. 18.
29. Nicolson, 'Artist as Filmmaker', p. 23.
30. Nicolson, 'Artist as Filmmaker', p. 26.
31. Nicolson, 'Artist as Filmmaker', p. 23.
32. With parallels to Graham's *Two Correlated Relations*, Nicolson quotes Hilliard's description of his installation: 'Cameraman A revolves filming cameraman B who is walking in a circle around him filming cameraman A. When the films are projected synchronously side by side, cameraman A is seen on one screen as what he is observing is simultaneously visible on the other screen. The only exception to these shooting rules is a short sequence where two cameramen film through a complete revolution of 360 back to back. Annabel Nicolson, 'Artist as Filmmaker', p. 23.
33. Nicolson, 'Artist as Filmmaker', p. 23.
34. Nicolson, 'Artist as Filmmaker', p. 23.
35. David Curtis, '"In the bloody basement again": Three observations about British conceptual and structural film', *Moving Image Review and Art Journal*, 6–1–2 (December 2017), p. 261 (author's emphasis).
36. Nicolson, 'Artist as Filmmaker', p. 22.
37. Nicolson, 'Artist as Filmmaker', p. 22.
38. Correspondence between Nicolson and Reynolds, 2004.
39. David Dye quoted in Alan Sheridan, 'David Dye Artist Filmmaker', in Avant-Garde Film in England and Europe issue, *Studio International*, 190–978 (November/December 1975), p. 207.
40. Richard Cork, *Evening Standard*, 1972.
41. Simon Field, 'David Dye: An interview with Simon Field', *Art and Artists* (December 1972), p. 16.
42. Curtis, '"In the bloody basement again"', p. 262.
43. Nicolson, letter to Reynolds.
44. For further details see Lucy Reynolds, 'Filmaktion: New directions in Film-Art', *Centre of the Creative Universe*, Tate Liverpool exhibition catalogue (Liverpool: Liverpool University Press, 2007).
45. Nicolson, 'Artist as Filmmaker', p. 20.
46. Nicolson, letter to Reynolds.

Figure 7.1 Johannes Vermeer (1632–75), *A Young Woman Standing at a Virginal*, reproduced with permission of National Gallery Picture Library.

CHAPTER 7

The Artwork/Statement as Intermedial Nexus: Paul Sharits's N:O:T:H:I:N:G
Barnaby Dicker

In 1969, Paul Sharits published a curated set of 'Notes on Films' in the influential American journal *Film Culture*. One set of notes is dedicated to his experimental film, *N:O:T:H:I:N:G*, completed the previous year, and contains a long passage from a letter to his renowned and widely revered peer, Stan Brakhage, also dated 1968. Here, Sharits states:

> During the final shooting sessions these past few months I've had Vermeer's 'Lady Standing at the Virginals'[1] hanging above my animation stand and have had the most peculiar experience with that work in relation to N:O:T:H:I:N:G. [. . .] As I began to recognize in the Vermeer the complex interweaving of all levels of 'gradation' (conceptually, sensually, rhythmically, proportionately . . . even the metaphoric level of subject making music, etc.) I began to see what I was doing in the film in a more conscious way. I allowed the feelings I was getting from this silent dialogue between process of seeing and process of structuring to further clarify the footage I was shooting. I can't get over the intense mental–emotional journeys I got into with this work and hope that the film is powerful enough to allow others to travel along those networks.[2]

N:O:T:H:I:N:G, like Sharits's other films of the period, is a minimalistic, heavily chromatic flicker film generated through stop-frame cinematography. As such, it conspicuously exploits cinematography's stroboscopic mechanisms – both technological and perceptual. The onscreen result is demanding and austere. Figurative images are minimal and fleeting, as is any semblance of movement. In stark contrast to the preceding statement, the film contains no obvious cues as to the significance of Johannes Vermeer, one of the most prominent masters of seventeenth-century Northern European Baroque painting. For over a decade, the relationship between Sharits's verbal confession and his film has fascinated me. In my view, once we acknowledge Sharits's account of the role of Vermeer's painting in the process of shooting *N:O:T:H:I:N:G*, it becomes an indelible part of the work, woven deep into the fabric of the film. And yet, Sharits's statement remains the irreducible carrier of this information: it cannot be directly recouped from the cinematographic statement of the film itself. I am continually left wondering how accessing the networks Sharits mentions takes place.

This case throws a number of contested relationships into productive relief: those between word and image, film and painting, abstraction and realism, and avant-garde and Baroque practice, embodied by Sharits and Vermeer. It is also particularly valuable in widening out our understanding of flicker films and experimental stop-frame cinematography, helping to lift these practices out of a self-enclosed, purely cinema- and screen-based debate to reveal their wider conceptual density and reach.

The artwork/statement relationship is central here. My starting point and fundamental premise is that, in some cases, an artwork and an accompanying statement form an intermedial nexus that problematises any simple distinction between artwork and statement, throws into question the location of the work under consideration and asks us to rethink its object: that is, what both artwork and statement are *about*. Readers must entertain the intermedial principle that such artworks and statements are not inherently inferior or superior but sit equal to one another. The statement cannot be regarded as a paratext or metatext that can be collapsed into the main, primary, text of the artwork. Rather, the scope or anatomy of the artwork must be expanded to include both the artwork, in its reduced sense, and the accompanying statement(s). In other words, the artwork spills out beyond the confines of some simple object; as Sharits puts it, 'A good deal of my art does not, in fact, "contain itself".'[3] Natalie Adamson and Linda Goddard have found a prevailing consensus between artists, critics and historians that there exists an 'uneasy, "non-isomorphic" rapport between statement and object'.[4] Moreover, they assert that 'as a declarative, "signed" source of artistic intentions, the artist's statement is the most essential, if problematic, irreplaceable companion to the artwork, but in many cases it becomes a proxy for, or even generative of, the artwork's very substance'.[5] This chapter contributes to attempts to clarify the artwork/statement relationship by seeking an alternative to the statement's dual companion/proxy status indicated by Adamson and Goddard. I take it as symptomatic of the problem in hand that it is hard to describe the artwork/statement nexus accurately. While artwork and statement certainly reflect and often support distinctions between practice and theory, the boundaries between these terms can, of course, be fluid, as we shall see. I also make no claim that *all* statements form an intermedial nexus with the artworks to which they relate. My concern is with one special case that, in my view, insists on such a relation. That said, a view is emerging that the significance of the statement to the development and, indeed, mechanics of avant-garde art has been somewhat under-estimated.[6] This prospect certainly helps us to understand how and why an intervention such as Sharits's arises in the form that it does.

The purpose of this chapter is not to 'solve' the *N:O:T:H:I:N:G* artwork/statement conundrum, but rather to celebrate it by picking at the warp and weft of their intermedial relation. The critical theory I have drawn on to guide the discussion is that of differential specificity: a notion found as far back as Aristotle[7] and as recently as Rosalind Krauss.[8] I primarily apply the term as set out by Louis Althusser in the 1960s and promptly applied to film and the fine arts by Marcelin Pleynet.[9]

Recent characterisations of intermediality find it occupying 'liminal',[10] 'in-between'[11] zones. In complementary contrast to such views, founding advocate of twentieth-century intermedia Dick Higgins offers an *expansive* conception of how such practices and artworks incorporate different media.[12] For Higgins, intermedia pave the way for the holistic reception of *all* artworks:

> To proceed further in the understanding of any given work, one must look elsewhere – to all the aspects of a work and not just to its formal origins, and at the horizons which the work implies, to find an appropriate hermeneutic process for seeing the whole of the work in [one's] own relation to it.[13]

Higgins articulates well the interminable, unstable and overdetermined prospect of intermedia. Studying the artwork/statement nexus provides one way to begin pursuing Higgins's proposition, with the statement operating as an 'elsewhere' to the artwork, in the reduced sense, but integral in its expansive sense. The artwork/statement nexus opens up a dynamic intermedial field where attendant discourses can be scrutinised through the themes, ideas, questions and philosophical, physiological and material problems found in an artwork. As Higgins makes clear, at stake here is something much larger than annotated lists of the material attributes of artworks comprised of more than one discipline, medium or object.

Differential specificity offers valuable tools for navigating the intermedial artwork/statement nexus, in particular in the case of Sharits. In 1969, the same year that Sharits's 'Notes on Films' appeared, Pleynet considered a most pressing question to be: 'Which films appear [. . .] determined by theoretical work – work, that is, which endeavours to consider the cinema in the manner of what Althusser calls "differential specificity"?'[14] Although Pleynet dismissed avant-garde and experimental filmmaking as a flawed bourgeois project,[15] he nevertheless acknowledged that 'there is more than one cinematic practice which could be inscribed within a theoretical perspective'.[16] Contra Pleynet, I see Sharits's avowedly avant-garde interventions clearly constituting a manifestation of such a practice. That Sharits published as much theoretical writing brimming with diverse references as he exhibited conceptually driven artworks is indicative of the deep inscription of a creative practice within a theoretical perspective to which Pleynet refers.[17]

Before turning to Althusser, it is important to clarify how Pleynet sees the theory/practice relationship in terms of differential specificity. In an essay on the Bauhaus, he ventures,

> It has always been the case that the painter, 'the artist,' considers the specificity of painting (if he considers it at all) as autonomous. [...] In order to outline a theory he must engage in a relation with literary language. He thus has to take into consideration the autonomy of the language he uses, the history of that language, and more precisely still the historical itinerary of the concepts (philosophical, for instance) that he is led to use. That is to say, he must contemplate his own discipline, painting, no longer in its specific autonomy but rather in its differential specificity (a specificity whose reality is equally constituted by what differentiates it from other disciplines and by the relation that it maintains with these differences).[18]

For our purposes, Pleynet is making the case for the intermedial operations of the artwork/statement nexus. While some artists might appear to abstain from theorising, Pleynet's insidious suggestion is that the formulation of any conception, principle or approach to making art – however private or threadbare – utilises theory and consequently generates or germinates some manifestation(s) of differential specificity, which, I would add, constitutes an intermedial fabric. Accepting Pleynet's rationale, artists who embrace the necessity of theory to practice occupy an advantageous, yet troubled, position where writing has quietly *also* become the artist's discipline, in addition to their 'own' named discipline. If not initiated by avant-garde artists in the late nineteenth century, the recognition of the power of theory to practice was certainly taken up by them vociferously, and the affiliation of theory with subsequent avant-garde practices has not diminished. Pleynet's formulation also suggests that any given iteration of differential specificity will be different to all others in specific ways. Thus, the aspects of *N:O:T:H:I:N:G* under consideration here are different from other aspects of the same project, to other works by Sharits and to other artists' works, be they by Vermeer or Brakhage – all the while potentially intersecting in specific ways with those very aspects of *N:O:T:H:I:N:G* being discussed.

This continual agitation, Pleynet makes clear, is a good thing: 'to insist upon theoretical activity in [...] painting implies [...] that the painter's work cannot turn back upon itself to form a closed oeuvre with no other consequence than its own closure'.[19] In other words, differential specificity acts as an instigator and guarantor of an artwork's intermedial mechanisms and its connections to debates that might otherwise appear to lie beyond it. While such considerations might feel more familiar if couched in terms of intertextuality, I believe that Pleynet is pointing to something else more aligned with brute form and operational structure than with semiotic reference. I take from Pleynet the insight that artwork and statement do not simply mirror each other at an intertextual level, but stand as divergent outcomes of a broader, all-encompassing, intermedial intent. This raises the question of the object of the theoretically rooted artwork/statement nexus. In this formulation, the statement is not simply *about* the artwork, and the artwork is not simply *about* a theory. Rather, both point towards some other object(s). That is not to say that statement and artwork cannot illuminate one another, but they do so to take us closer to those other objects.

This is where Althusser's conception of differential specificity asserts itself. Regarding Marx's *Capital* – a text about *something* – he states:

> we posed it the question of its *relation to its object*, hence both the question of the specificity of its *object*, and the question of the specificity of its *relation* to that object, that is, the question of the nature of the type of discourse set to work to handle this object.[20]

Clearly the basis for Pleynet's account of differential specificity in the arts, Althusser draws special attention to the *object* of any given study. But what kind of objects might we encounter when considering how certain forms of filmmaking might be 'inscribed within a theoretical perspective'?[21] Althusser states that 'the object of theoretical practice' is the 'peculiar raw material' underpinning knowledge,[22] which he understands as follows:

> The greater the progress of a branch of knowledge, the more elaborate [its] raw material becomes. [. . .] [And yet,] however far back we ascend into the past of a branch of knowledge, we are never dealing with a 'pure' sensuous intuition or representation, but with an *ever-already* complex raw material, a structure of 'intuition' or 'representation' which combines sensuous, technical and ideological elements in a peculiar '*Verbindung*' [combination].[23]

Subjecting Marx to his own critique of prior accounts of the distinction and relationship between epistemological objects and real objects, Althusser refutes the assumption that epistemological/theoretical work can ever access a real object and thus afford it some kind of primacy.[24] In addition, Althusser sees epistemological objects as being 'transformed'[25] by the production of knowledge, the outcome being any number of 'new differential sharpenings'.[26] This unending forward-/backward-looking process chimes with both Sharits's engagement with Vermeer and Higgins's expansive intermedial programme, as well as with a conception of the avant-garde being based on an evolving ecology of strategic interventions or 'moves' underpinned, to a greater or lesser degree, by theory. To be clear about the terms of differential specificity: we are dealing simultaneously with points of contact, parity, similarity *and* points of divergence, disassociation, alterity – all of which are often bound together.

There are no indications that Sharits was directly aware of the theory of differential specificity. However, aspects of his ways of working certainly chime with its principles, perhaps due in part to his interest in other contemporary structuralist and post-structuralist ideas. Sharits exploits the artwork/statement nexus as if precisely through a ludic exploration of the terms of differential specificity. He prefaces his 'Notes on Films' with an 'Overture': Antonin Artaud's declaration, 'All writing is pigshit. People who [. . .] try to define whatever it is that goes on in their heads are pigs'[27] – a cunning gesture that turns writing on itself and only superficially demotes the importance of writing in relation to the prospect that some other things might *not be* pigshit. Sharits follows this with his 'General Statement for 4th International Experimental Film Festival, Knokke Le Zoute', which opens,

> I am tempted to use this occasion to say nothing at all and simply let my films function as the carriers of themselves – except that this would be perhaps too arrogant and, more important, a good deal of my art does not, in fact, 'contain itself'.[28]

In one fell swoop, Sharits entertains two contrary positions by virtue of apparently opting for the latter. Thus, on Sharits's own terms, it is insufficient to approach a film such as *N:O:T:H:I:N:G* as a purely screen-based cinematographic work. Here, as elsewhere, Sharits leaves us with the feeling that his films may be seen as theoretical statements and his writings as literature animated by a well-crafted, almost performative polemical choreography.

Sharits's reference to Vermeer is not isolated. As mentioned, his writings as a whole consistently cite a diverse range of sources: philosophical, artistic and spiritual. In the entry on *N:O:T:H:I:N:G*, Sharits first discusses Buddhist and Hindu symbological theory, before moving on to Vermeer and ending with a postscript comprising a quotation on 'nothing' from René Descartes. Unfortunately, these other, equally important, references have had to be bracketed out of the present discussion due to space.

As the entry point to discussing Vermeer in his letter to Brakhage, Sharits defines his epistemological object(s) as follows: 'The film is "about" (it is) gradation-progression on many levels; [. . .] couldn't one construct inverse time patterns [. . .] [and] structure a felt awareness of really going thru negative time?'[29] How the film itself signposts its epistemological object(s) is far more difficult to divine. Is it light/colour? Stroboscopic perception? Audience engagement? Certainly, Sharits's description fits the film well enough, if only via the shifts in colour and the isotype-like lightbulb motif that acts as a marker of progression.

Echoing the contradictions of his Knokke Le Zoute statement, Sharits's public/private confession to Brakhage about the influence of Vermeer on

N:O:T:H:I:N:G shows the simultaneously centrifugal and centripetal forces that can connect an artwork and a statement. Despite addressing a well-informed, specialist audience – embodied by Brakhage – Sharits cannot help literally spelling out exactly what he hoped the film would convey on its own:

> Light comes thru the window on the left and not only illuminates the 'Lady at the Virginals' but illuminates the subjects in the two paintings hanging on the wall (which are staggered in a forward-reverse simultaneous progression creating a sense of forward and backward time) and the one painting on the inside lid of the virginal! The whole composition is circular, folds in on itself but implies that part of that circle exists out in front of the surface. What really moved me was the realization that the light falling across the woman's face compounded the light–gradation–time theme by forcing one back on the awareness of (the paradox of) awareness. I.e., one eye, itself dark, is half covered with light while the other eye is in shadow; both eyes are gazing directly at the viewer as if the woman is projecting music at the viewer thru her gaze (as if reversing the 'normal' role of 'perception') ... I mean, the whole point is that the instrument by which light-perception is made possible is itself in the dark).[30]

Sharits's thought-provoking analysis underscores the significance of the statement within the scope of the project, establishing a triadic rapport between Vermeer and Sharits's statement and film, the light/dark and circular themes echoing the film's stop-frame flicker forms and overall structure. The passage illustrates the depth of Sharits's inscription of his practice within a theoretical perspective – to paraphrase Pleynet. In other words, Sharits codifies Vermeer's painting in terms that are of use to his own artistic ideas and ambitions.

Sharits's singling out of Vermeer and *Lady Standing at the Virginals* is conspicuous in the 'Notes on Films' among the precise, but general, references to Buddhist and Hindu theory and the undeveloped closing Descartes quotation. Why Vermeer and not some other artist? Why not some other painting from his œuvre? What might have piqued Sharits's interest enough for him to 'hang' a copy of the picture above his animation stand?

Lawrence Gowing's seminal study of Vermeer, first published in 1952, offers much food for thought in terms of Sharits's interpretation of the painting and his own work, especially regarding ambiguities over the 'self-containedness' of artworks, the distinction between realism and abstraction, and, above all, the centrality of light and the question of the object of an artwork. While I have found no evidence of Sharits reading Gowing, I consider it a highly plausible source by which he could have informed himself about Vermeer; indeed, many similarities can be found.

Gowing asserts that '[Vermeer's] pictures contain themselves, utterly self-sufficient. In each of them the surface and design alike mark an act which is accomplished and complete. Its limits are unconcealed.'[31] Regarding the painting fixated on by Sharits, Gowing observes,

> The space around the *Lady Standing at the Virginals* is bound to her and to its frame [. . .] exactly [. . .]. We cannot think that this world extends behind the frame, it is complete and utterly enclosed. The space is revealed in its essence as a hollow cube.[32]

These claims chime with Sharits's aspirations for his films to 'function as carriers of themselves'.[33] And yet, signalling dimensions beyond any isolated artwork, Gowing also believes that 'pictures [. . .] communicate several kinds of information[:] [. . .] about visible things, about the painter's equipment to deal with them, and also, by inseparable implication, information about the nature of the artist himself'.[34] In terms of the latter, Vermeer is the apotheosis of enigma: 'However definite and recognizable the weave of paint in the style of Vermeer, inside it something is hidden and compressed.'[35] For Gowing, this raises significant ambiguity over the painter's identity.[36] Of course, this is all due to the relative absence of information — that is, primarily *verbal* information — about Vermeer's artistic intentions. We are left, essentially, with only the paintings and an invitation to engage in interpretive freefall, which Gowing and Sharits both accept — *through writing*. Gowing, in sum, takes Vermeer's work to be at once bound to the wider world, self-contained and impenetrable in the manner of a black box. The multi-valent appeal of Vermeer for Sharits, then, may well have been as something to unlock, a grand and mysterious role model to understand and an artistic precedent to be trumped via theory.

Gowing describes Vermeer's authorial comportment as 'detached', 'impersonal' and 'efficient':

> [his visual] description [. . .] always exactly adequate, always completely and effortlessly in terms of light. Vermeer seems almost not to care, or not even know, what it is he is painting. What do men call this wedge of light? A nose? A finger? What do we know of its shape? To Vermeer none of this matters, the conceptual world of names and knowledge is forgotten, nothing concerns him but what is visible, the tone, the wedge of light.[37]

Here, we are reminded of 'all writing is pigshit' as Gowing appears to place us at odds with theory and the peculiarities of Althusser's epistemological objects by casting Vermeer's concerns as being completely undefinable — with, significantly, the exception of light. Running against his own analysis, once more, Gowing speaks of Vermeer's 'vocabulary of formal representation',[38] 'his vocabulary of light' defined by 'his tonal method'.[39] We have, then, after all, *some kind* of syntax, system and codification, *some kind* of epistemological practice predicated on (the observation of) light.

But there is more. Gowing ventures: 'for [Vermeer] the play of light upon form not only conveys its substance but also subtly denies it. [. . .] Immediacy, touch, are excluded; his subject is the immutable barrier of space.'[40] The crucial proposition here is that Vermeer's paintings are not fundamentally *about* what can be recognised *in* them, but rather address 'the immutable barrier of space' *as articulated through light*. Light, too, is a central concern for Sharits. In his Knokke Le Zoute statement, he asserts his interest in 'light [as] energy rather than a tool for the representation of non-filmic objects; light, as energy, [. . .] released to *create* its own objects, shapes and textures'.[41] Much as both Sharits and Gowing seek to present light – and their own and Vermeer's perception and understanding of it – in some *pure* form, they cannot escape appealing to and utilising a codifying theoretical discourse. Sharits, for example, by referring to the painting's 'light–gradation–time theme',[42] binds himself and his own work to Vermeer and *Lady Standing at the Virginals*. Light thus exists, as Althusser would put it, as an epistemological object, both for Sharits and in Gowing's assessment of Vermeer.

Some other of Gowing's observations might also have endeared Sharits to *Lady Standing at the Virginals*. Gowing considers its motif to be original, in contrast to many of Vermeer's other music-themed paintings.[43] This 'originality' is likely to have attracted Sharits. 'There is hardly a detail [. . .] which does not contribute to [its] pervading emotional meaning,'[44] insists Gowing. This clearly aligns with Sharits's own emphasis of his powerful emotional response to the painting. However, notes Gowing, 'it is perhaps to the perceptible emotional tenor in its stylistic elaboration that [. . .] *Lady Standing at the Virginals* [. . .] owes its unpopularity with the painter's most devoted students'.[45] This outsider status, I think, would also have appealed to Sharits, not least because Gowing considers this to be a missed opportunity on the part of critics to 'come upon a deep pattern of Vermeer's thought':[46] namely, an interest in femininity that rivals the theme of light. For Gowing, the young woman, a human being, attended by 'erotic emblems' (the cupid and landscape paintings of the back wall), emerges as the subject of this late painting, 'her presence [carrying] the force of a challenge' that 'displaces the light' so coveted by the painter.[47] And yet, in closing the loop of a circular analysis, Gowing ultimately finds that the young woman disintegrates under scrutiny:

> we can almost gather the message of the picture from a single passage, the sleeves and shawl perhaps. [. . .] As the eye moves across the surface, from corner to corner along the rectangular avenues and returns, we are reminded again of the limit of its meaning, paradoxically both narrow and bottomless [. . .] [and its] claim [to] no greater depth than the play of light.[48]

Are these, perhaps, the same emotional networks of which Sharits speaks?

In terms of both interpretive insight and conceptual language, Sharits's analysis of Vermeer appears to echo Gowing. Sharits's advance is to integrate an analysis of Vermeer directly into his own work – during both the process of making and the formulation of a critical discourse (and, by extension, avant-garde film practice in general). When Gowing deduces that 'the critical point at which a change of tone becomes large enough to be worth recording appears to be decided by Vermeer optically, almost mechanically, rather than conceptually or in the interests of comprehensibility',[49] it is as if he gives Sharits the cue to hang up the picture and return to it between each exposure to consult it for an indication of what his next frame, his next cinematographic 'move', should be. Casting the shift from one tone to another as a question of emotion/perception and *not* of concept/legibility throws a veil of intuition over any amount of underlying theoretical activity. In relation to Sharits, this would serve to reassert the hermetic and independent identity of the artwork (in its reduced sense). If comparing Sharits's and Gowing's analyses of Vermeer confirms one thing, it is that, in terms of differential specificity, Sharits did not engage with *Lady Standing at the Virginals* purely as a painting – indeed, he may have never seen the original – but simultaneously took up the critical discourse around Vermeer, focused on light, colour and enigmatic meaning, in order to articulate his 'personal' response to it.

Let us take stock of the differential specificities attending the intermedial artwork/statement nexus unique to *N:O:T:H:I:N:G*. Beyond the basic, general distinction between cinematographic and written articulation, Sharits establishes specific differences between the film and the statement: that is, both convey information not replicated by the other, even while referring to each other – for example, the onscreen flicker effects and structures and the influence of a specific painting by Vermeer. Sharits distinguishes the shooting process of the film from its onscreen form, yet insists on their equivalence, envisaging that audiences can channel his own experiences in making the film under the influence of Vermeer. Colours are differentiated in specific ways; the frame-by-frame shifts are mapped on to Sharits's circular and repetitive interpretation of *Lady Standing at the Virginals*. In the 'Notes on Films', Sharits invokes different modalities of writing: catalogue entry, grant application, personal letter. He simultaneously links himself to and separates himself from Brakhage – *while Sharits speaks, Brakhage listens*. Somewhat boastfully, Sharits claims to have a special, deep connection with Vermeer; that he truly understands the painter and that his own work now speaks directly to that of his forebear. And yet, Sharits also distances himself from Vermeer by virtue of his theoretically driven writing and ideas. Again, *while Sharits speaks, Vermeer remains silent*. However, this time, Sharits dresses up Vermeer's silence as driving their 'exchange' with a power on which he can now draw. In sum, Sharits asserts that, for all the self-sufficiency of his film, it remains so advanced – even for specialist audiences such as Brakhage – that it requires further explication by its author. Naturally, this is a self-fulfilling prophecy, as Sharits's statement is the very thing that undermines the self-sufficiency of the film and announces the wider, intermedial status of the project.

The intermedial artwork/statement nexus under consideration here offers a glimpse of a radically alternative model of stop-frame cinematography in which Sharits's theoretically and emotionally driven meditation on Vermeer is recorded in *N:O:T:H:I:N:G*'s frame-by-frame structure, taking onscreen form in its fundamental cinematographic principle: its stroboscopic flicker effects. But Sharits's statement equally sets itself apart and draws attention away from – thereby undermining – the cinematographic specificity it apparently seeks to promote. This reflects the other, equally important, face of intermediality in which a dense, expansive fabric of connections and tensions – a work's differential specificities – contributes to shaping critical, legitimating discourses and practices. In this case study, we encounter a range of forces such as complementarity, contrast, difference, juxtaposition, contradiction, authorial assertion, spectatorial agency, overdetermined meaning, the disintegration of meaning, and the simultaneous primacy and disavowal of immediate perception and, analogously, writing/theory. This panoply of forces, I contend, should be apprehended positively.

Sharits was keen for his work to stand out. His orchestration of the intermedial artwork/statement nexus exemplifies what Griselda Pollock terms an 'avant-garde gambit', an idea that reveals the ecology of differential specificity in the arts. She writes:

> to make your mark in the avant-garde community, you [have] to relate your work to what [is] going on: *reference*. Then you [have] to defer to the existing leader, to the work or project which represent[s] the latest move, the last word, or what [is] considered the definitive statement of shared concerns: *deference*. Finally your own move involve[s] establishing a *difference* [. . .] both legible in terms of current aesthetics and criticism, and also a definitive advance on that current position.
>
> [. . .]
>
> To become cultural capital and cultural profit, the art work as product must be incorporated into a public discourse through recognition by a critical framework within which both the particular character of the product (the *difference* achieved by this gambit) can be named and its relation to an already valorized context of meanings can be identified (its *reference*).[50]

Much of Sharits's 'gambit' with *N:O:T:H:I:N:G* is performed via his statement, Brakhage and Vermeer standing, partially fused, as the notional cutting-edge with which he wishes to associate himself. Significantly, Sharits asserts that the difference between his and others' avant-garde work is not to be found solely in his film, but equally in his working methodology, articulated through writing. Such statements are clearly not unique. Sharits's claim to originality lies in the specific methodology he recounts: that is, his stop-frame meditation on Vermeer. The intermedial relay that Sharits sets up between artwork and statement generates innumerable 'networks'[51] that legitimate and insulate his intervention and promote his prowess on screen and in print.

Notes

1. The painting Sharits and Gowing refer to as *Lady Standing at the Virginals* is now known as *A Young Woman Standing at a Virginal*. It has been in the collection of the National Gallery, London since 1892. Signed but undated, it is believed to be one of Vermeer's last paintings. For the sake of clarity, I follow the title given by Sharits and Gowing.
2. Paul Sharits, 'Notes on Films/1966–1968', *Film Culture*, 47 (1969), p. 16.
3. Sharits, 'Notes on Films/1966–1968', p. 13.
4. Natalie Adamson and Linda Goddard, 'Introduction: Artists' statements: origins, intentions, exegesis', *Forum for Modern Language Studies*, 48–4 (2012), p. 364.
5. Adamson and Goddard, 'Introduction', p. 363.
6. See, for example: Griselda Pollock, *Avant-garde Gambits 1888–1893: Gender and the Colour of Art History* (n.p.: Thames & Hudson, 1992); Daniel Herwitz, *Making Theory/Constructing Art: On the Authority of the Avant-garde* (Chicago: University of Chicago Press, 1996); Linda Goddard, 'Artists' writings: word or image?', *Word & Image*, 28–4 (2012), pp. 409–18; Linda Goddard, '"Scattered notes": Authorship and originality in Paul Gauguin's *Diverses choses*', *Art History*, 34–2 (2011), pp. 353–69; Linda Goddard, '"The writings of a savage?": Literary strategies in Paul Gauguin's *Noa Noa*', *Journal of the Warburg and Courtauld Institutes*, 71 (2008), pp. 277–93; and Vladimir Feščenko, 'Dematerializing verbal and visual matter: Wassily Kandinsky's Bitextuality', in Sarah Posman, Anne Reverseau, David Ayers, Sascha Bru and Benedikt Hjartarson (eds), *Aesthetics of Matter* (Berlin and Boston: De Gruyter, 2013), pp. 94–103.
7. Aristotle, *Aristotle's Categories and De interpretatione* (Oxford: Clarendon Press, 2002), pp. 3–42.
8. Rosalind Krauss, *A Voyage on the North Sea: Art in the Age of the Post-medium Condition* (New York: Thames & Hudson, 2000), pp. 45, 53, 56.
9. Louis Althusser, 'From *Capital* to Marx's philosophy', in Louis Althusser and Étienne Balibar, *Reading Capital* (London and New York: Verso, 2009), pp. 11–75; Gérard Leblanc, Marcelin Pleynet and Jean Thibaudeau, 'Economic – Ideological – Formal', in Sylvia Harvey (ed.), *May '68 and Film Culture* (London: BFI, 1980), pp. 149–64; and Marcelin Pleynet, *Painting and System* (Chicago: University of Chicago Press, 1984).

10. Hans Breder and Klaus-Peter Busse (eds), *Intermedia: Enacting the Liminal* (Norderstedt: Books on Demand, 2005).
11. Ágnes Pethő, *Cinema and Intermediality: The Passion for the In-Between* (Newcastle: Cambridge Scholars, 2011).
12. See Higgins's 1995 *Intermedia Chart* reproduced in Dick Higgins, 'Intermedia', *Leonardo*, 34–1 (2001), p. 50.
13. Higgins, 'Intermedia', p. 53.
14. Leblanc, Pleynet and Thibaudeau, 'Economic – Ideological – Formal', p. 149.
15. Leblanc, Pleynet and Thibaudeau, 'Economic – Ideological – Formal', p. 163.
16. Leblanc, Pleynet and Thibaudeau, 'Economic – Ideological – Formal', p. 149.
17. For a recent survey of Sharits's career see Susanne Pfeffer (ed.), *Paul Sharits* (London: Koenig Books, 2015).
18. Pleynet, *Painting and System*, p. 122.
19. Pleynet, *Painting and System*, p. 100.
20. Althusser, 'From *Capital* to Marx's philosophy', p. 14.
21. Pleynet, *Painting and System*, p. 149.
22. Althusser, 'From *Capital* to Marx's philosophy', p. 45.
23. Althusser, 'From *Capital* to Marx's philosophy', pp. 45–6, translation modified.
24. Althusser, 'From *Capital* to Marx's philosophy', pp. 36–46.
25. Althusser, 'From *Capital* to Marx's philosophy', p. 46.
26. Althusser, 'From *Capital* to Marx's philosophy', p. 35.
27. Cited in Sharits, 'Notes on Films', p. 15.
28. Sharits, 'Notes on Films', p. 15.
29. Sharits, 'Notes on Films', pp. 15–16.
30. Sharits, 'Notes on Films', p. 15.
31. Lawrence Gowing, *Vermeer* (Berkeley: University of California Press, 1997), p. 17.
32. Gowing, *Vermeer*, p. 60.
33. Sharits, 'Notes on Films', p. 13.
34. Gowing, *Vermeer*, p. 18.
35. Gowing, *Vermeer*, pp. 18–19.
36. Gowing, *Vermeer*, p. 19.
37. Gowing, *Vermeer*, p. 19.
38. Gowing, *Vermeer*, p. 19.
39. Gowing, *Vermeer*, p. 26.
40. Gowing, *Vermeer*, p. 25.
41. Sharits, 'Notes on Films', p. 13.
42. Sharits, 'Notes on Films', p. 16.
43. Gowing, *Vermeer*, p. 156.
44. Gowing, *Vermeer*, p. 156.
45. Gowing, *Vermeer*, p. 28.
46. Gowing, *Vermeer*, p. 55.
47. Gowing, *Vermeer*, p. 61.

48. Gowing, *Vermeer*, p. 61.
49. Gowing, *Vermeer*, p. 21.
50. Pollock, *Avant-garde Gambits*, pp. 14 and 15.
51. Sharits, 'Notes on Films', p. 16.

Part 3

Technology, Apparatus, Affect

CHAPTER 8

Intermediality and the Origins of Cinema
Boris Wiseman

Until relatively recently, discussions of the origins of cinema have often focused on technological development.[1] They explained the advent of cinema as resulting from modifications made to technical objects. According to one such narrative, it was the development in 1888, by Étienne-Jules Marey (1830–1904), of a chronophotographic camera using mobile film that provided the technical basis for modern cinema.[2] Marey designed this camera to decompose movements, such as the opening and closing of a hand, that were too slow or insufficiently extended in space to be recorded sequentially on a fixed plate connected to a shuttering device. It was in creating a mechanism that stopped and started the movement of the sensitised paper (he used celluloid from 1890), which allowed the film to be exposed when the shutter was open and moved along when it was closed, that he is said to have laid the basis for cinematographic recording and projection such as it was later developed. The famous Lumière brothers' Cinematograph (patented on 13 February 1895) worked on the same intermittent basis. The film's moments of immobility were what allowed each still image to be seen before being carried off in the flow of other images, the brain taking charge of converting these stills into the illusion of continuous movement. A competing account of the origins of cinema that also focuses on technology traces the advent of the medium to early animations or 'graphic cinema', as it has been called.[3] These animations predate Marey's chronophotographic cameras. The stroboscopic discs created simultaneously by Joseph Plateau and Simon Stampfer in 1833 already deconstructed movement into its component parts and then reconstructed it for viewing. It was individual viewing, initially, but with later zoetrope drums the spectacle could be marvelled at by several viewers. These discs also showed images intermittently. They used shuttering mechanisms to convert a series of stills shown in quick succession into continuous motion. This is no less a form of cinema than that made possible by the invention of moving strips of film. What differentiates it from photography-based cinema is that its stills are hand drawn or painted. The key difference, at the time, didn't lie so much in the way in which the illusion of movement was created but in the means of its prior recording and analysis. Photography eventually became able to slow movement down and record phenomena that the eye couldn't see.

Both these accounts invoke technology as the basis for the invention of moving images. However, when we start to look more closely at the causalities at work in such accounts of the birth of cinema, they are less easy to discern. In a revealing aside, Laurent Mannoni suggests that the idea of the intermittent movement of film, so crucial to the successful exposure of Marey's sequential photographs, grew out of the physiologist's earlier, prephotographic experiments.[4] He traces the idea to the model of an artificial human heart that Marey created in 1857 while an intern at the Hôpital Cochin in Paris. It was designed to test the effects of the elasticity of arteries on blood circulation. Unlike prior models of the heart, it recreated, for the first time, the intermittent nature of the heart's pulses.[5] According to Mannoni, it was Marey's work on machines designed to record movement graphically that laid the basis for his later innovations in photography, said to be so important to cinema. In short, the movement of filmstrips is already contained in the movement of blood being carried away from the heart and back again. Mannoni goes on to identify yet earlier sources for mechanisms of cinematic projection. Louis-Léon Pajot's 1734 anemometer used spools to impart motion to a reel of paper on which a stylus traced the direction and force of the wind. It prefigures the way in which celluloid filmstrips are made to pass in front of the lens.[6] According to the Lumière brothers, their own device for moving film forward intermittently was inspired by observations of a sewing machine,[7] which similarly needs to stop the forward-moving fabric to allow the stitch to be made.

The further back in time we go, the further the point of origin recedes. The moment of cinematic rupture, of aesthetic innovation, is difficult to locate. It cannot be contained wholly and solely in changes made to technical objects. These changes are also conceptual, imaginative and hence dependent on a broader cultural context. In the above examples they are also dependent on a web of metaphorical free associations. Cinema cannot be traced to the innovations of single individuals. It is born from complex totalities, from culture itself, in the manner of the fairy tales and myths told by every known human society.

Viewing cinema as the result of technological innovations, such as the invention of the Lumière brothers' Cinematograph, obscures the many forms of the cinematic that preceded the moment of technological rupture. The Lumière brothers' famous 1895 projection, viewed retrospectively, seemed suddenly to give a definitive form to cinema. Philippe-Alain Michaud provides an alternative definition of film as 'a set of dissociated properties' that can be found across a broad spectrum of cultural products.[8] For example, for him, there is something essentially cinematic in Aby Warburg's *Mnemosyne Atlas*, that vast system made up of sequences of images assembled on panels and laid out so as to provide a visual comment on the afterlife of images borrowed from Antiquity.[9] Cinema as we know it – in its movie theatre incarnation – is only one of the possible forms of the cinematic, a culturally and historically determined way of configuring film. Michaud's notion of film fits what follows in this chapter, which explores moving images prior to what they became in the early twentieth century. My aim is to grasp cinema outside of itself and viewed in its inherent intermediality. These forms of moving images are not less perfect or less complete forms of the cinematic, preparing the advent of cinema proper. Cinema manifests itself whole and in its full complexity in each of its dissociated parts.

Moving images/cinema existed before it became possible to artificially create the illusion of moving of figures, before 'graphic syntheses' of movement.[10] The origin of moving images is undatable. Early camera obscuras, from Antiquity onwards, captured movement without recording it. It was a form of *cinema vivant*. We sometimes think of cinema as arising from the setting in motion of still photographs, as a result of the rapid successive presentation of a sequence of photographs. Before that, photography came about by freezing the moving images reflected in a camera obscura, by developing a process for extracting and copying a still from the continuous flow of images contained in a dark chamber. Arriving at this point took time. Until then, photographic images existed in an oddly in-between state – neither moving nor entirely still.[11] Nicéphore Niépce's trials with heliography, as he called it in his 1829 *Notice* (his manuscript presentation of his discovery), required such long exposures – at first an hour or more – that the resulting images blended together constantly shifting conditions of light, captured plural images, an expanse of time. A photograph, as we have come to know it, is a stoppage. Nothing remains of the trials that Niépce made before the shadowy *View from the Window at Le Gras* (1826–7), in part because the images he captured were so unstable. They darkened each time they were exposed to light, each time someone tried to look at one. They existed but could not be seen. Niépce later came to describe heliography as a method for using light to reproduce spontaneously the images received by a camera obscura, including their graded shadings. This was his success. But before the technology succeeded, it was something else, something I find more poignant in the stark choice it imposed between preserving the image and being able to view it, something laden with unrealised aesthetic/cinematic possibilities. Heliography, before it became photography, captured images of reality, only to plunge them into a process of chemical decay, a fade-to-black that engulfed, at each viewing, the very possibility of the medium. Nevertheless, these images articulate an idea of moving images, distinct from the representation of moving figures, rooted in the transformation of the properties of the image itself – not cinema as the illusion of movement, but cinema as the qualitative transformation of an image over time.

This form of the cinematic, different from the synthesis of movement, is integral to all forms of cinema, including narrative. It is also present in many kinds of optical device, popular from the eighteenth century onwards. These devices were a means of transforming images (initially, prints) by viewing them through various kinds of lens which framed the images, gave them depth, coloured them. Carlo Ponti's Megaletoscopio (1862), inspired by Daguerre's dioramas, was designed to view albumin photographs, mainly Ponti's own photographs of Venice (he was photographer and optician to King Victor Emanuel II of Italy). He photographed St Mark's square and the church of St Mark (repeatedly), the Grand Canal with the Palaces Cavalli and Barbaro, and the Basilica di Santa Maria della Salute, the Hall of the Grand Council, a gondolier in front of the Esclavons Quay and many other scenes. The images that the viewer placed in the Megaletoscopio were dual: black and white photographs on one side, a painted scene or highlights on the other. A system of shutters enabled the viewer to modify the strength and orientation of the light. When it was let in from above, the image refracted light and took the form of a photographic image. When the light was let in from the rear and the image viewed against the light, the painted scene on its reverse shone through. Day gave way to night, the realist black and white photograph to a coloured image. Garlands suddenly topped otherwise unremarkable lampposts. An empty town square filled with bustling revellers, yellow lanterns, visible through tiny pinholes, lit up the facades of palaces, enhancing the perspective and plunging the viewer deeper into the image. Photographic realism gave way to fantasy, static architectural motifs to atmospheric crowd scenes. Some of the lenses used by the device were stereoscopic (enhancing the illusion of depth) and also magnified the images, which were, in turn, surface, as photographs, and translucent medium, as paintings. In short, they were intermedial images and cinematic through their intermediality, in the sense that the light effects created a temporally unfolding narrative (the transition from day to night), and brought about a gradual qualitative transformation of the images over time. The lenses created an immersive experience whilst also operating shifts in scale. It is revealing, in the context of the argument that I am making here, that Ponti was concerned by the visual presence of the frame surrounding the scenes viewed in his Megaletoscopio. He wanted to avoid the eye being drawn towards the margins of the image at the expense of the 3D effect. He found ways of reducing the frame. In the process, the old painted image, the fabled window on to the world, was becoming something more cinematic whilst the viewer was invited to step into the frame.[12]

Cinema, in its graphically synthesised form, is often said to have been born from science. The narrative is that the first animations came about by 'applying' the experiments on vision of the great physicist Michael Faraday to the creation of a new kind of artefact: the Phenakistiscope. No doubt this narrative is in part true. But here too the causal connections are more ambiguous than first appears to be the case. Let us look more closely at Faraday's seminal work on vision, 'On a Peculiar Class of Optical Deceptions' (1831).[13]

Faraday was interested in 'the various modes in which [the eye] performs its office, the circumstances that modify its indications'.[14] His experiments set out to explain what happens to vision when it is interrupted at rapid intervals. It is a scientific exploration of retinal persistence, the '[eye's] power [to] retain visual impressions for a sensible period of time' (the eye's own cinematic projection).[15] Faraday created experimental devices of several types. One of them depended on viewing the radii placed on the periphery of a rotating disc reflected in a mirror. These images were viewed through the slits made in the disc itself, which formed a shuttering mechanism. The disc was placed between eye and mirror, its dark side facing the eye, its light side carrying the radii facing the mirror. Another device was set up to view a rotating picture disc through a second aperture disc, which could also be rotated. With this device, it was possible to vary the relative speed and direction of each rotating disc, thereby changing the visual effects: speeding up the cogs or radii, slowing them down, changing their direction of travel or stopping them altogether. Faraday devised another series of illusions by casting various shadows on a rotating wheel – shadows of other wheels or of parallel bars, for example.

A few years later, when Plateau took up Faraday's research, what he placed on the periphery of his disc were not cogs or radii but a human figure. At first, however, it was a figure made up of multiple versions of the same figure, a figure that therefore hovered immobile in the mirror.[16] This static figure is an important part of the history of cinema. The first disc made by Plateau did not recreate movement. It generated a static illusion, but one that could be maintained for a period of time – as long as the viewer continued to operate the disc's rotating mechanism. Later, he substituted, in place of the recurring image of the same figure, a figure that 'follow[s] some sort of series, passing by degrees from one form or position to another'.[17] The very first figure of this kind that Plateau hand painted in colour was a pirouetting dancer: 'the dancer turns further and further in one direction, eventually returning to the position from which he started while the ground beneath his feet remains identical in each of the sectors'.[18] Another disc showed a bee circling a flower. These discs usher cinema into existence as a graphic synthesis of the different phases of a movement. Before that, however, it already existed as a freeze frame.

Looking back at Faraday's wheels in the light of later stroboscopic discs, it becomes apparent that they do not just provide the technical principles for the subsequent discs. They already possess inherent cinematic qualities, to which Faraday himself was particularly sensitive. When making recommendations about how best to set up an experiment involving the observation of movement reflected in a mirror, he writes: 'The effect is very striking at night if a candle be placed just before the face, and near to it, but shaded by the wheel [. . .].' Much later, Edgar Degas tried something similar with a clay sculpture of a dancer, which he also illuminated with a candle and rotated so as to project 'a succession of shadows cast by [the sculpture's] silhouettes on a white sheet'.[19] Faraday's (and Degas's) dramatic division of light and dark, which places the viewer in darkness, splits vision so that the luminous spectacle of movement is offered from a place that is always other in relation to what is being seen, goes to the very core of the modern cinematic experience. It lays out, in a microcosm, the scenography of the movie theatre and sets the stage for modern cinematic viewing.

The results of Faraday's experiments are, as he puts it eloquently, 'curious spectra'[20] – cinema in an extended sense or perhaps abstract cinema. Later, Faraday devised an experiment in which these spectra were projected 'upon a screen', capturing, as it were, the illusion occurring naturally.[21] It used cast shadows. As he describes: 'The shadow is light where the wheels appear dark, for there the light has passed by the cogs; and dark where the wheels appear light, for there the cogs have intercepted most of the rays.'[22] He adds: 'the screen should be near to the wheels, that the shadow may be sharp'.[23] He then notes that if the wheels are placed obliquely in relation to the sun, this allows one 'to distinguish the shadow of each wheel' and observe 'how beautifully the spectrum breaks out where they superpose'.[24] This simple experimental set-up captures the transition, within the same space, from cast shadow to illusion and then back to shadow. The experiment foregrounds the area where the shadows superpose, which is where they transform into something else: a cinematic illusion.

Faraday's article on the deceptions of the eye does not just provide the scientific basis of cinema. It shows that science had already articulated an idea of the cinematic, that it was itself inseparable from cinema, in its very protocols and methods. Faraday's stroboscopic wheels make cinematic time perceptible in brute form, they manifest cinema as pure duration or, rather, as a series of artificially produced temporal intervals and rhythms, whose nature can be modified depending on the speed, direction and relative position of the rotating discs. They make manifest cinematic time as a product of mechanically produced, and hand-operated, projection.

Faraday's paper on optical deceptions is relevant to my exploration of the cinematic in another key sense. Faraday's first observations related to accidentally occurring illusions. Only later did he create devices for reproducing them experimentally. At the Maltby lead mills, he observed two cogwheels moving at such velocity that, at first, none of the cogs could be distinguished. Having moved to a vantage point from which one cog appeared behind the other, he is suddenly struck by the 'distinct though shadowy resemblance of cogs moving slowly in one direction'.[25] He then recalls an account of work carried out on the Thames Tunnel construction site that describes two wheels set in motion by an endless rope that, when seen from the right viewpoint, present 'the appearance of a wheel with immovable radii'.[26] Faraday finally relates these observations to various descriptions of the turning wheels of carriages as seen through the upright bars of a palisade or against their own dark shadow projected on to a brightly lit road. He remarks: 'the greater the velocity of the wheels the more perfect will be the appearance'.[27]

Faraday's first two examples of accidentally occurring optical deceptions (in the lead mill and Thames Tunnel) depended on wheels being propelled at speeds that could be sustained only by industrial processes. Seen as a product of industrial speed, cinema first existed in the form of a ready-made. Faraday built machines to experiment on stroboscopic illusions. Before that, these illusions were already being mechanically produced. The route that leads from the industrial machines to the cinematographic devices – the first set of machines belonging to the real world, the other cut off from it – is the route to modern cinema. Here, too, analogical thinking has a part to play. The function of the lead mill wheels was to generate force. These wheels were substitutes for large amounts of human labour. The process whereby they gradually gave rise to something else – an essentially unknowable creative process – was, in part at least, a neutralisation and repurposing of the industrial machine: not so much an evolution of technology as its deconstruction and reassignment. According to this viewpoint on to the origins of cinema, the machines themselves have agency in the process of invention. Or rather, agency is shared between the machines and those working on and with them. In the course of these transpositions, a form of proto-cinematic technology gradually migrated from the realm of industrial production to that of scientific and then aesthetic representation, a process that at some point also involved an epistemic cut, or several cuts, and a separation from earlier uses of the technology. Boundary crossing is an integral part of what generated cinematic technology.

Beyond their deterministic role in bringing about cinema, technical objects interest me here because they allow us to grasp better the different manifestations of moving images. Émile Reynaud's (1844–1918) *Pantomimes lumineuses* were probably the nineteenth-century form of entertainment closest to modern cinema, i.e., to moving images projected on to a screen in front of an audience made up of immobile spectators[28]. They were presented regularly from October 1892 at the Musée Grévin, three years before the Lumière brothers' famous Grand Café projection. *Autour d'une cabine*, one of the rare animations by Reynaud to have survived, is a comic sketch set at the beach involving bathers and a fancy Parisian woman who is spied upon whilst changing into her bathing costume.[29] The film is made up of more than 600 stills, hand-painted by Reynaud on to a supple strip whose length could be extended or shortened according to the needs of the story. *Autour d'une cabine* and other *Pantomimes lumineuses* were projected on to the rear of a translucent screen by means of Reynaud's *Théâtre optique*. The device grew out of his earlier *Praxinoscope de projection*, a single-person home-viewing device that used a stroboscopic disc made up of twelve views (a children's version was made with eight views). This earlier device gave the sequences a cyclical nature reminiscent of contemporary graphical exchange format (GIF) files. The extendible, unfurling painted strips that Reynaud used with his *Théâtre optique* allowed him to explore forms of temporality and visual narration that already belong to modern cinema. Here, we can see the importance of changing technologies. Animation had overtaken the photogram in the overdetermined story of the origins of modern cinema. From a technological point of view, what Reynaud developed with his *Théâtre optique* was a new way of setting images in motion, one that broke the physical boundaries of the earlier stroboscopic discs. The *Théâtre optique*, with its uncoiling strips of perforated film, resembles modern film. It also differs from it. It is both strange and familiar.

The *Pantomimes* required Reynaud to assemble two projected images using two magic lanterns, one for projecting the static décor, the other for the animated figures. These figures were mobile in two ways: the projection of moving stills allowed the appearance of the figures to change over time, but they could also be moved from one part of the screen or décor to another by modifying the angle of the mirror that projected the figures on to the rear of the screen. The projectionist ensured that the action always took place in the correct location (the screen was marked to this effect). He put the fancy Parisian woman in the water, submerged her and brought her out again so that she could enter a cabin and get changed.

Reynaud's *Théâtre optique* is unlike modern cinema, amongst other things, because the projectionist imparted movement to the filmstrip and because the filmstrip was designed to be manipulable, and minipulable by hand. The projectionist was free to modify the speed at which the action unfolded. He/she could slow his characters down or speed them up by altering the velocity at which the stills were being moved forward along the projection path. He/she could also stop the film, repeat a sequence and create loops similar to those associated with the older stroboscopic discs.[30] He/she introduced these effects (editing on the spot) in response to the reactions of the audience of the day, creating a slightly different performance each time. There must have been a shared sense that the projectionist, although hidden from view, was communicating with his audience through the characters he was known to be animating. And these characters, to some degree, must have seemed like extensions of the human being operating the device. The audience must have been aware of being part of a feedback look, of being involved, through response and counter-response, in the projection. The *Théâtre optique* gave rise to a form of cinematic projection that was close to the human body, that of the projectionist and the collective body of the audience. It placed the two in proximity to one another. Roger Leenhart's film, *Naissance du cinéma* (1946), provides rare glimpses of the *Théâtre optique* in operation. In it, Reynaud is played by his son, who had assisted his father in making his last animations and knew well how to operate the projection device. We see him standing behind the reel deck, bent forward, each hand on one of the spools which he is winding at slightly different speeds, adapting his gestures to the inertia of the uncoiling film reel and to what is happening on screen. What strikes me in this sequence is the eye of the projectionist constantly monitoring the little moving figures seen in reverse, on the back of the screen, an eye that is watching the outcome of what the hands are doing and adjusting their speed and direction accordingly. The relation between eye and hand, here, is not all that dissimilar to that of someone drawing from life. For the projectionist, the haptic and the visual are closely connected. Here, intermediality meets multi-modality, and connects the senses. The image of Leenhart that I retain from the film is not that of a projectionist but of a puppeteer, one who has substituted a system of mirrors and refracted light beams in place of the puppets' strings.

The different kinds of moving image considered so far, as well as being deeply intermedial (unlocatable in terms of the medium and the viewing spaces to which they belong), are also often self-referential. Frequently, it is the medium that is on display. Perhaps this was a natural consequence of the development of new technologies whose foreignness invited enquiry, called for a space for reflecting on the new forms of expression? This reflexivity is apparent, for example, in many of the subjects chosen by makers of stroboscopic discs. To an extent, it was inevitable. They invented circular movements for circular discs – a horse jumping through a hoop and a man somersaulting (same disc), a cyclist circling around a sphere. But the extent to which some of the early discs go to emphasise the medium suggests something deeper. Stampfer's *Toy Merry-Go-Round with Four Horsemen* is a coloured drawing that shows eight rotating merry-go-rounds, each supporting four horsemen.[31] The floor of each merry-go-round, shown in perspective, represents a stroboscopic disc (with green radii). It is attached by a vertical pole to the image of a complex mechanism made of cogs and wheels that mesh with a wheel depicted in 2D, itself superimposed on the centre of the stroboscope's actual axle, where real and represented movements mesh together. It is this borderline that seems to fascinate and that the device displays. Another Stampfer disc shows a hammer repeatedly striking an anvil.

Instead of being held by a human figure, it is machinery that is doing the pounding, in synchrony with the rhythm of the disc's rotations. Yet another disc shows a hand holding a quill. As the disc is rotated, the hand traces the letter 'a'. Reflexivity is present even in Faraday's wheels. I have suggested above that they are a form of abstract cinema. The cogs and radii that his

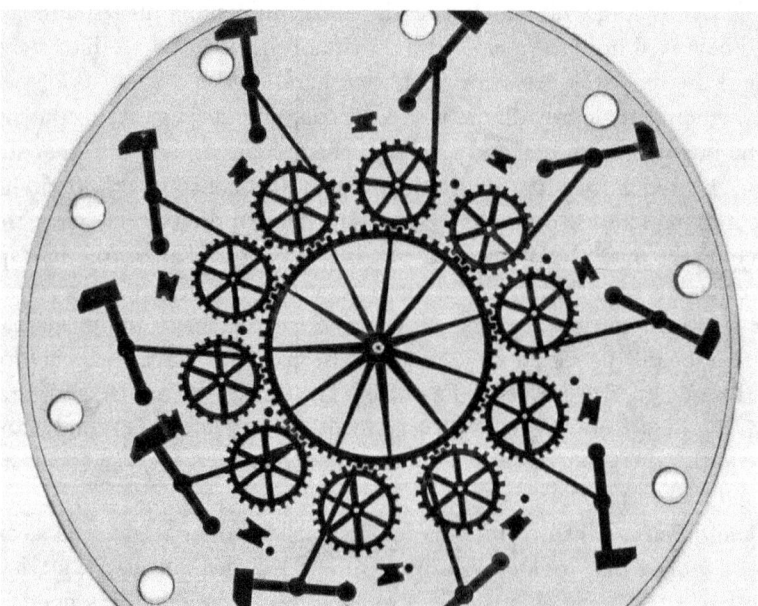

Figure 8.1 'Mechanical hammer set in motion by two wheels'. Patented 1833 (made in 1922). Cardboard with ten apertures and black and white ink drawing on one its sides. Collection of La Cinémathèque française. Photograph by Stéphane Dabrowski.

discs set in motion do represent something. They are cinema's first representations of itself as a medium, its first flickers.

The above are all technologies of enchantment, in the sense given to the phrase by anthropologist Alfred Gell: technologies that act upon us 'via the enchantment cast by [their] technical means, the manner of [their] coming into being, or, rather, the idea which one forms of [their] coming into being'.[32] Like the dazzling Trobriand canoe-board in Gell's essay, whose aesthetic qualities its viewers interpreted as being magical in origin, the optical discs described above also tell a story about their coming-into-being. Their subject is the origin of movement or rather of the illusion of movement. They signify the viewing technology on which they depend. Here, the agent designated as the source of the illusion/movement is not magic but a machine. The discs' motifs erase the human hand that is activating the mechanism. The magical source of movement is displaced on to a machine, whose fictionally created autonomy contributes to the enchantment. I am reminded of a magician showing his audience the inside of his empty hat.

The examples of moving images surveyed above show, time and time again, that cinema emerges, here and there, in different forms, including accidental, in between media, in between technologies, in between different kinds of viewing experiences and in between viewing spaces, as something at once tangible and imagined, in the world, in technology and in the mind's eye. It is not simply that these early forms of cinema incorporated or referenced other media. They show that cinema came into existence through intermedial displacements. This ambiguity of the medium is captured by the term later used by Baudelaire, among others, to designate optical discs: namely, scientific toys. The phrase points towards the unsettled status of these devices and to the historical process whereby technologies transited between one domain (science, research) and another (entertainment, aesthetics, storytelling), co-mingling in the process.

Reynaud's *Pantomimes lumineuses* are a case in point. They depended on the creation of a new kind of cinematic technology but also on a new genre and on a new space for cinematic projection. They drew on the popular nineteenth-century genre of the pantomime (itself a liminal art, bordering the spoken word), relocating it, in modified form, from the boulevards to the *cabinet fantastique* of the Musée Grévin.

The *Théâtre optique* was originally meant to be sold to fairground entertainers, but found no buyers because of its high cost and the difficulty in learning to use it. It was as a result of this commercial failure that Reynaud signed a contract with the Musée Grévin. Nevertheless, films such as *Autour d'une cabine* still bear the mark of the space for which they were first intended. It starts with a preliminary sequence unrelated to the comic sketch about a voyeur. Two characters in striped bathing costumes enter the frame along a diving board that projects frontally into the image. The first figure runs and jumps into the water, making a big splash. The second performs a front somersault and jumps in next. They both splash each other playfully before swimming out of the frame. A second pair enters the image the same way, via the diving board: a fat, bald man and another, slimmer, bather. The fat man looks down into the water. The slimmer bather jumps on to his back, making him fall in. He then jumps in himself. The rhythm is that of a clown act. The characters enter the stage, perform a slapstick gag and then exit. It is fairground entertainment – the circus ring – physically relocated to a space of cinematic viewing. When Reynaud's daily screenings were temporarily interrupted, they were replaced by a magician's act.[33]

The significance of the crossover between different viewing spaces in the creation of new forms of the cinematic is even more directly illustrated by the Phonoscope. It was created at the behest of Hector-Victor Marichelle (1862–1929), Director of the *Institut national des sourds-muets*, by Marey, who had already developed graphic systems for transcribing speech. It used no new technologies but combined existing ones (it is a zoetrope disc connected to a projection lantern) to show a series of striking photographic images – 'speaking photographs', as Demenÿ called them.[34] It was originally a pedagogical tool designed to help deaf–mute patients learn to lip-read by visually decomposing the positions of the mobile organs of the vocal tract during speech. Using chronophotography, short utterances were broken down into a series of frames – between eighteen and twenty for a sentence lasting about one second – and then projected. When the recorded images were shown to patients (without sound), they were able to decipher what had been said.[35]

What interests me about these 'animated portraits' (shown two years before the Lumière brothers' famous 1895 projection) is their presentation at the 1892 Exposition Internationale de Photographie by Marey's assistant, Georges Demenÿ. Strikingly, Demenÿ took himself as the subject of the sequence of photographs that he chose to project. And the sentence he decided to show himself uttering was far from anodyne: 'Je vous aime!' The event was an instantaneous success. It was reported on in many newspapers, earning Demenÿ world fame. Here is what one journalist wrote: 'The eagerness with which ladies queue up, sometimes several times, to look through the mysterious hole and behold the lips of a man articulating this phrase "I love you", is a sight to be seen.'[36]

Marey conceived and built the Phonoscope. But Demenÿ turned the Phonoscope into an extraordinary installation that he used to address his audience directly. His 'Je vous aime!' is wonderfully ambiguous. Was it Demenÿ's secret approach to someone close to his heart? Or was the declaration of love being sent to all viewers? Or, alternatively, is this the first love letter written to cinema itself? The answer does not matter as much as the fact that the installation put the viewer in the position of the addressee. It is in this respect, and not because of the technology it used, that Demenÿ's installation was profoundly cinematic. The Phonoscope created a psychological position for the viewer, inviting him/her to substitute himself/herself for the original deaf–mute viewers, in the process transforming the way in which the technology was being used and seen.

The nature of the medium changed as it migrated from a clinical setting to the floor of the Exposition Internationale. The act of display transformed the nature of the technology, turned it into a technology of enchantment. Looking through the peephole at Demenÿ's mouth forming the same sentence again and again demanded a different response to the images. The viewer was no longer in front of images whose meaning was contained entirely in what they showed: namely, the lip movements that needed to be deciphered. Instead, he/she became part of a circuit of communication, and was inserted in the chain of moving images. Images passed through him or her. The process underpinning enchantment here, the cinematic spell Demenÿ invented, was the becoming-machine (and image) of the viewer, the viewer's assimilation into the medium, which was the Phonoscope's own premonitory analysis of the future of cinema.

Notes

1. This model has been questioned for some time now. For an overview of current expanded and revised approaches to cinematic technology see the useful special issue of *1895*: 'Propositions pour une histoire des techniques en cinema', 82 (2017). This chapter explores the ways in which notions of the cinematic are reflected in so-called pre-cinematic technologies. It is concerned with the decentred view of cinema that these technologies provide. It questions the borderline between cinema and pre-cinema, as well as that between technical and aesthetic objects.
2. See Christian Salomon (ed.), *Marey, penser le movement* (Paris: L'Harmattan, 2008), p. 20; Caroline Chik, *L'Image paradoxale* (Villeneuve d'Ascq: Presses Universitaires du Septentrion, 2011), pp. 96–7.
3. Dominique Willoughby, *Le Cinéma graphique: Une histoire des dessins animés, des jouets d'optique au cinéma numérique* (Paris: Textuel, 2009).
4. 'Some of the devices [made by Marey] for graphically recording movement contain the seeds of future cinematographic systems.' Laurent Mannoni, 'L'Enregistrement du mouvement au XIXe siècle: Les méthodes graphique et chronophotographique', 4 vols, unpublished doctoral thesis, Université Sorbonne nouvelle-Paris 3 (2003), p. 306.

5. Étienne-Jules Marey, 'Recherches hydroliques sur la circulation du sang', *Annales des sciences naturelles, Zoologie*, 8 (1857), 329–64.
6. Marey, 'Recherches hydroliques sur la circulation du sang'.
7. Laurent Mannoni, 'Les appareils cinématographiques Lumière', *1895*, 82 (2017), pp. 52–85 (p. 61).
8. Philippe-Alain Michaud, *Sur le film* (Paris: Macula, 2016), p. 7; my translation.
9. Michaud, *Sur le film*, p. 7.
10. Willoughby, *Le Cinéma graphique*, p.102.
11. This paradoxical status of images, past and present, has been admirably analysed by Caroline Chik in *L'Image paradoxale*.
12. Based on the presentation of the device by the Cinémathèque. See <https://www.cinematheque.fr/fr/catalogues/appareils/collection/boite-doptiqueap-95-1613.html> (last accessed 5 August 2020).
13. Michael Faraday, 'On a peculiar class of optical deceptions' (1831), in *Experimental Researches in Chemistry and Physics* (London: Taylor and Francis, 1859), pp. 291–311.
14. Faraday, 'On a peculiar class of optical deceptions', p. 291.
15. Faraday, 'On a peculiar class of optical deceptions', p. 303.
16. The sequence in which this disc was developed is presented in Plateau's famous open letter to the scientific community. See Joseph Plateau, 'On a new type of optical illusion' (1833), trans. by Richard George Elliot, *Art in Translation*, 8 (2016), pp. 11–18 (Special Issue on *Cinematographic Art* edited by Barnaby Dicker).
17. Plateau, 'On a new type of optical illusion', p. 15.
18. Plateau, 'On a new type of optical illusion', p. 15.
19. Walter Sickert, *The Complete Writings on Art*, ed. by Anna Gruetzner Robins (Oxford: Oxford University Press, 2000), p. 416.
20. Faraday, 'On a peculiar class of optical deceptions', p. 303.
21. Faraday, 'On a peculiar class of optical deceptions', p. 302.
22. Faraday, 'On a peculiar class of optical deceptions', p. 303.
23. Faraday, 'On a peculiar class of optical deceptions', p. 303.
24. Faraday, 'On a peculiar class of optical deceptions', p. 303.
25. Faraday, 'On a peculiar class of optical deceptions', p. 291.
26. Faraday, 'On a peculiar class of optical deceptions', p. 292.
27. Faraday, 'On a peculiar class of optical deceptions', p. 292.
28. I take the description from Michaud's *Sur le film*, p. 8.
29. A version of it, restored by Julien Pappé in 1993 and transferred on to 35 mm film, can be viewed here: <https://vimeo.com/257109253> (last accessed 5 August 2020).
30. See Sylvie Saerens's lecture 'Les 10 ans du Conservatoire des techniques, trois anniversaires, hommage à deux pionniers : Émile Reynaud et Georges Demenÿ': <https://vimeo.com/257109253> (last accessed 5 August 2020).
31. Disc No. XVI in Simon Stampfer, 'Stroboscopic discs: An explanation', trans. by Jonathan Blower, *Art in Translation*, 8 (2016), pp. 22–33 (Special Issue on *Cinematographic Art* edited by Barnaby Dicker).

32. Alfred Gell, 'The technology of enchantment and the enchantment of technology', in Jeremy Coote and Anthony Shelton (eds), *Anthropology, Art and Aesthetics* (Oxford: Clarendon Press, 1992), pp. 41–63 (p. 47).
33. See video lecture by Sylvie Saerens.
34. Georges Demenÿ, *Les Origines du Cinématographe* (Paris: Henry Paulin, 1909), p. 18.
35. Demenÿ, *Les Origines du Cinématographe*, p. 18.
36. Gaston-Henri Niewenglowski and Albert Reyner, *La Photographie en 1892, première exposition internationale de photographie, progrès de la chromophotographie, union nationale des sociétés photographiques de France, enseignement de la photographie, etc.* (Paris: C. Mendel, 1893), p. 23; my translation.

CHAPTER 9

Cinematography's Blind Spots: Artistic Exploitations of the Film Frame

Gabriele Jutz

> I asked, 'Do you know how it is with the water and the moon? "The water flows on like this," but somehow it never flows away. The moon waxes and wanes, and yet in the end it's the same moon. If we look at things through the eyes of change, then there's not an instant of stillness in all creation. But if we observe the changelessness of things, then we and all beings alike have no end. What is there to be envious about?'[1]

Interrelationships between still and moving images take a variety of forms, involve diverse techniques, cut across different media and challenge the identity of both the medium and the apparatus or *dispositif*.[2] The richness and amplitude of the mutual relationships between instantaneous and time-based images have been the subject of numerous studies.[3] Cinematography is just one among many fields where this phenomenon can be observed. Broadly speaking, at one end of the spectrum, we find films that otherwise abound with movement, whose flow is blocked through the momentary intrusion of the 'freeze frame'[4] or a still photograph.[5] Such interruptions appear, for instance, in Dziga Vertov's *Man with a Movie Camera* (1929), François Truffaut's *Les Quatre Cents Coups* (The 400 Blows, 1959) and Wong Kar-Wai's *2046* (2004).[6] At the opposite end, there are entire films (and not just occasional shots) in which the impression of stillness is the default. This 'cinema of stasis'[7] is exemplified by Chris Marker's *La Jetée* (1962), composed almost entirely of stills; Andy Warhol's *Empire* (1964), a stationary eight-hour film of the Empire State Building; and Michael Snow's *Wavelength* (1967), consisting of a very slow zoom. In both cases – the sudden freeze frame and the quasi-static film – stillness is merely an illusion, considering that the filmstrip is always in movement once it has been placed in the projector and set into motion.

In contrast to these shot-based works, there are experimental films that call attention to cinematography's frame-based structure, usually occluded by the illusion of continuity. 'Flicker', the rapid alternation of light with dark frames and single-frame montage, for instance, creates a strong awareness of film's twenty-four-frames-per-second construction, as films by Tony Conrad, Peter Kubelka and Kurt Kren – among others – demonstrate. When we look back to the prehistory of cinema, it becomes evident that the interrelatedness of still and moving images started long before the advent of cinema. The endeavour to create movement by a quick succession of stills covers a broad spectrum of earlier visual practices, such as optical toys, dissolving slide shows or the serial motion studies of Eadweard Muybridge and Étienne-Jules Marey.

The objects of my own investigation here, however, do not fit into any of the categories just outlined. What I am interested in are artworks that focus on one (or more than one) isolated film frame, whether extracted from the strip of film, photographed from the viewing table, or, if the reel itself is not available, taking the form of a photographic frame reproduction taken from a book or a TV screen.[8] I have chosen the term 'film frame' (as opposed to 'film still' or 'photogram') because of its lack of ambiguity,[9] but also because it has the virtue of acknowledging the technical and material support of cinematography's smallest unit.

In theories of cinema the film frame has frequently been marginalised or even depreciated. Christian Metz is probably the best-known advocate of this tendency. Trying to identify a cinematic language and its grammar, he proposes the shot as the smallest unit of the filmic chain. According to Metz, the frame is only a distinctive unit lacking proper signification.[10] Roland Barthes's essay 'The Third Meaning',[11] in which the critic looks at frame enlargements from films by Eisenstein, appeared only a few years after Metz's *Film Language* (1971) and can be read as a defence of the filmic frame or the 'photogram', as the author terms it.[12] Barthes criticises the common opinion that regards the photogram 'as a remote sub-product of the film'.[13] Unlike Metz, Barthes grants the photogram an excess of meaning. Apart from their 'informational' and 'symbolic' meaning, photograms have a supplementary, 'third meaning', one that 'appears to extend outside culture, knowledge, information'.[14] Moreover, it is on the level of the individual photogram that Barthes locates the truly filmic, which 'cannot be grasped in the film "in situation", "in movement", "in its natural state", but only in that major artifact, the still'.[15] In accordance with Barthes, then, what is most filmic about a film reveals itself only when the projection comes to a standstill. Or, as Philippe Dubois puts it: 'Photograms are the only real images and the only invisible images in a film. This is the ontological paradox, which makes photograms into cinema's blind "spots".'[16]

The aim of this chapter is not only to discuss the aesthetic potential of the extracted and/or reproduced film frame, but also to grasp what is at stake when prominence is given to this invisible entity that is usually absorbed into the projection process. First of all, when a frame is torn away from the medium from which it comes, it risks losing its medial identity, as it no longer belongs to cinematography; nor does it fully conform with photography. But if intermediality challenges medium specificity, then it is equally important to map out how it alters core aspects of the *dispositif* – the medium in terms of its *use*. A related issue is the interrogation of the respective exhibition context, as the works to be discussed here tend to leave the movie theatre behind. Furthermore, a change of perspective from the diachrony of the sequence to the synchrony of the still (and vice versa) presumes a familiarity with working procedures, and the tools and materials used, and thus raises technical questions. Finally, but no less importantly, addressing the frame in its materiality reveals the ideological difference between a frame extracted from the continuum of the film strip on the one hand and the promotional production photograph made on the set on the other. The four works I intend to discuss are divided into two groups, each addressing the question of how these works deal with the frame: in the first, as a projection of serial images; in the second, as a static, image-object.

CREATING SERIALITY OUT OF STASIS

If one of cinematography's basic principles is to create 'something that is not present on its material base: animated pictures',[17] then Austrian artists Gebhard Sengmüller's *Slide Movie* (2007) and Peter Tscherkassky's *Motion Picture (La Sortie des ouvriers de l'usine Lumière à Lyon)* (1984/2008), the two projects under consideration here, are unambiguously cinematic. But things are more complicated than it seems, as these works' interest resides exactly in the gaps that separate them from cinematography.

Sengmüller's installation *Slide Movie* explores the slide show's cinematographic effect by turning a slide projector into a – not very efficient – movie projector. The artist first cut up a 35 mm filmstrip from a trailer of an action film into its single frames and fixed them into slide projector frames. Then he aligned twenty-four slide projectors, each of them capable of holding eighty slides, pointed them at the screen and ran them via electronic control at a rate of twenty-four frames per second. In doing so, the metronomical regularity of the images' apparition was enhanced by the mechanical clattering of the projector's changing slides. The 80–second film loop achieved by such an elaborate and time-consuming procedure is quite poor, as Sengmüller admits: 'The film is very bumpy, the brightness varies, and it takes some time for the eye to be able to recognize a moving image at all.'[18] From a utilitarian point of view, this hybrid machine is totally impractical. However, from a media-theoretical standpoint, Sengmüller's invention, which invests the slide projector with the power to project moving images, is far from being inopportune. It demonstrates – no more and no less – that medium specificity must be located elsewhere than in the technical support of the cinematic apparatus.

Tscherkassky's starting point for his 3–minute film *Motion Picture (La Sortie des ouvriers de l'usine Lumière à Lyon)* was not exactly a material frame extracted from the eponymous Lumière brothers' movie (1895), but a frame enlargement, found in a book and reproduced with a large-format camera. The resulting negative was then projected on to fifty strips of unexposed 16 mm film mounted on a wall and covering a rectangle of 50 by 80 cm. Next, Tscherkassky processed the exposed strips, arranged them on a light table to form a 50 by 80 cm duplicate of the original frame and edited the strips together, starting with the first strip on the left and proceeding to the right. The resulting single continuous film reel shows, when projected, completely abstract imagery: black and white blots, drained of all figurative content, as each frame of *Motion Picture* is just a very small section of the original Lumière movie.[19]

A description of these successive operations and working gestures reveals that the making of *Motion Picture* counteracts in several aspects standard cinematographic procedures, although it still results in a projected film. Firstly, Tscherkassky's piece is made without a camera. Its raw material does not consist of a temporal series of images (the discrete photographs on a strip captured by a movie camera) but of a single 'found' static image, which undergoes a process of spatialisation by being projected on to a rectangle of unexposed film strips. This enlargement causes the object, the men and women leaving the factory, to disappear and decomposes them into mere particles of light and darkness. As *Motion Picture*'s imagery stems from a projected image and not from the recording of a movie camera, the strip contains a single non-discrete image, and not a series of multiple contingent photograms. This initial lack of successive contiguous units is counterbalanced when the film is projected. Serialisation, the very condition of setting an image in motion, comes into play only through the intermittent mechanism of the projector, where the moving strip is stopped and briefly held still while the shutter opens and closes, and thus produces, despite its compound nature, the illusion of unbroken continuity.

Interestingly, the film's DVD version[20] hints at the making of *Motion Picture* by starting with a still image showing the arrangements of the film strips on the light table. This fixed image is not included in the cinematographic version of Tscherkassky's film, but – willingly or not – comes as a reminder of the Lumière brothers' earliest exhibitions, where the spectators were confronted with conflicting modes of appearing. As Gunning points out, 'the films were initially presented as frozen unmoving images, projections of still photographs. Then [...] the projector began cranking and the image moved.'[21]

Although very different in their technical operations and outcomes, both *Slide Movie* and *Motion Picture* each start from one (or more than one) single frame and end as projections of serial images. Although they create movement out of fixed images, as does the cinematograph, their respective proceedings vary widely from conventional cinematography. While *Motion Picture* demonstrates that there is more than one way to expose a filmstrip and that one frame can give birth to many by spatialisation, *Slide Movie*'s close mimicking of the mechanisms of a film projector fails to create a smooth flow and thus makes perceptible the material source of the impression of movement: the single image.

THE FRAME AS IMAGE-OBJECT

The frame transformed to a still image is given prominence in the photographic work of French artist Éric Rondepierre and in an installation by Austrian artist Susanne Miggitsch, entitled *Und ich blieb stehen. (Thames, London)* (2017). Rondepierre's method consists of selecting frames from films, capturing them with a simple 35 mm photo camera and enlarging them – usually without any modification – as photographic prints. For his earlier works, he viewed the movies very carefully and slowly on a video tape and 'froze' the selected image with the stop-motion of the video-player. Later, he explored film libraries and used a viewing table as his 'picking tool'. Rondepierre's photograms are particular, as they disclose 'moments of visual abnormality, moments of failure'[22] that are not supposed to appear clearly to the viewer when a film is projected at normal speed. These might be black frames that are present in some subtitled versions of films that are inserted so as to maintain the simultaneity between the image track and the sound track, as in his series *Excédents* (1989–97); or frames with superimposed written messages where the letters are formless, undecipherable spots that mask certain parts of the image, as in his series *Annonces* (1991–3). With his third series of photograms, *Précis de décomposition* (1993–9), a new element comes into play: Rondepierre's interest extended to materially deteriorated film stock, corroded by the passing of time and storage conditions. The photograms he selected feature spots, blisters, bubbles and blotches, and 'obey a very special representational principle', as Thierry Lenain indicates: 'What is at stake there is [...] a game of parallelisms between the iconic content of the image and the traces of deterioration which are equivalent to a catastrophic manifestation of its material medium'.[23] In *Confidence* (1996–8), for instance, one of the prints,

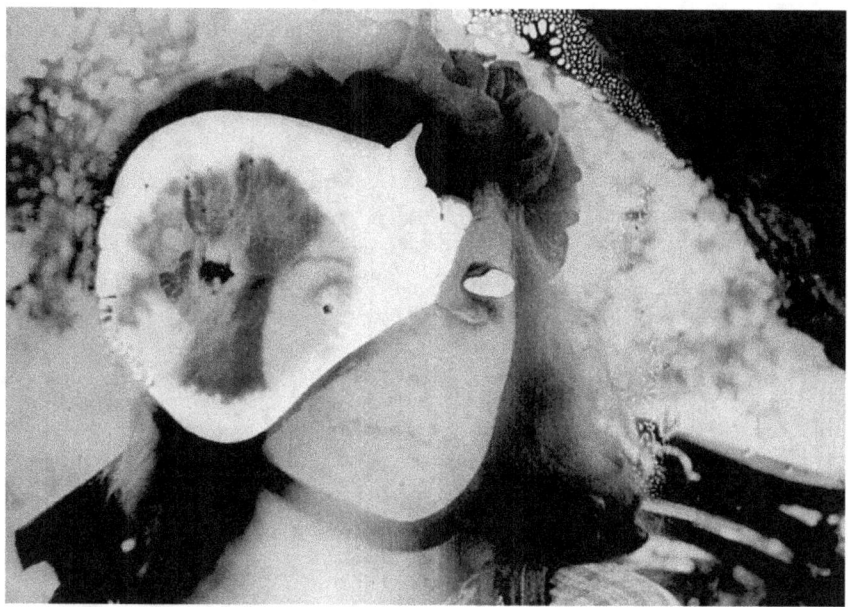

Figure 9.1 *R40* (Précis de décomposition – Masque) (Éric Rondepierre, 1993–5), silver print on aluminium, 47 by 70 cm. Copyright: Éric Rondepierre.

taken from a photogram and enlarged to 80 by 120 cm, features a kissing couple in a deep embrace; they seem to have grown wings due to the smudges of corrosion apparently protruding from their shoulders. Other prints from this series, such as *R40*, are less playful and express a more sinister tone, especially when marks of degeneration contribute to the deformation of spaces, bodies or faces. By making photograms in a state of partial decomposition the subject of his work, Rondepierre encourages close encounters with the underbelly of representation, one that is full of visual noise and disrupts an image's transparency.

While Rondepierre's frames are appropriated and derived from already existing films and thus lack personal expression, Susanne Miggitsch's approach involves subjective gestures. *Und ich blieb stehen. (Thames, London)*, a close-up of the gently rippling river Thames, is wholly dependent on the bodily presence of the artist and her camera at the river. Its mere 25–second length is determined by the Bolex camera being limited to this amount of time when manually wound. Pursuing her ongoing fascination with flowing water, Miggitsch watches and perceives, makes a decision to stop, and then chooses a place from which to shoot.[24] All of these elements point back to the subjectivity of the filmmaker and are expressed by the 'I' in the title ('And I stopped'). Nevertheless, this personal side does not prevent

Figure 9.2 *Und ich blieb stehen. (Thames, London)* (Susanne Miggitsch, 2017), 16 mm film installation, 25-second loop, with frame certificate. Installation view from the exhibition 'Slow Down! Cinematic Approaches on Reduction' at Kunsthalle Exnergasse, Vienna 2017. Copyright: Claudia Rohrauer.

Miggitsch from 'delegating' compositional decisions to the apparatus. The restriction to a single shot, without any editing, lasting as long as the camera runs, is based on impersonal and quasi-objective premises that obey the logic of the apparatus.

The film, presented as a 16 mm loop, is only one part of Miggitsch's installation. It comes with a 'film frame certificate', also exhibited, which consists of an isolated 16 mm frame extracted from *Und ich blieb stehen.*, fitted into a white A4–sized passe-partout. The minuscule photogram on white ground, displayed as an image-object, recalls a miniature etching in black and white. It is offered for sale and delivered to the buyer, including information regarding the exact position of the extracted frame (the frames are numbered consecutively), the number of prints and the artist's signature. (The certified frame is part of the installation; it is given to the buyer once the exhibition is finished.) Each frame that is sold is replaced by a black one in the original loop, so that, not unlike the portrayed river, Miggitsch's film remains in a constant state of flux, never fully formed. Moreover, *Und ich blieb stehen.* creates a series of echoes: the constantly changing film echoes the constantly changing body of water; the 25–second loop can be seen as a sample from a larger continuum, just as the frame offered for sale is extracted from something larger than itself. In addition, a formal element emerges, which picks up and doubles this coming to a halt inherent in the title: the full stop at the end of the sentence (*Und ich blieb stehen.*).

MODES OF DISPLAY

Each of the four works discussed here possesses a particular mode of presentation, mostly related to a move away from the theatre. The passage from the 'black box' – the film frame's ancestral home – to the 'white cube' of the gallery inevitably has an impact on the *dispositif*. As opposed to the term 'apparatus', the mechanical parts of the machine as well as its flexible constituents, the term *dispositif* is conceived as a relatively stable, fixed arrangement between heterogeneous elements; among them are the body of the machine (the apparatus, including its parts), as well as the body of that machine's user – be it artist/producer or viewer/receiver (including his/her eyes, hands and so on). The *dispositif* approach facilitates an investigation of media technologies in terms of their use, and it is only within a *dispositif* that a medium's identity fully realises itself. Nonetheless, as Raymond Bellour argues, the cinematic *dispositif* and the *dispositifs* offered by gallery-based environments have to be clearly distinguished. While the former is highly standardised, the other invents, in each of its manifestations, its own specific arrangement[25] – as the artworks under consideration demonstrate.

Tscherkassky's *Motion Picture* not only is available as film (and, as mentioned, on DVD), but also has been presented as a gallery installation on several occasions. So, for example, it was shown in Vienna at Galerie nächst St. Stephan in 2008. In this version, it consisted of the 16 mm film loop projected on to a wall, and a wooden box atop a low pedestal containing the original filmstrips arranged side by side in a rectangle. Exhibited in this way, visitors were given the opportunity to experience the visual *and* material quality of *Motion Picture* at the same time.

Sengmüller's *Slide Movie*, calling itself a 'black cube installation', is designed primarily for festival or gallery exhibition. As continuous operation of the slide projectors would impair the slides and the machines, visitors are invited to press the power switch, which starts the projection and stops after eighty seconds. The audience is mobile: visitors can walk around, watch from a distance or linger in the path of the projector's beams. As for the economic aspect, both Sengmüller's and Tscherkassky's installations can be purchased – in limited editions – by private or institutional collectors.

Rondepierre shows his works in the form of enlarged prints hung on the wall, either framed or adhering to an aluminium plate. Although he follows the conventional way of presenting two-dimensional pictures ordinarily in a

Figure 9.3 *Motion Picture (La Sortie des ouvriers de l'usine Lumière à Lyon)* (Peter Tscherkassky, 1984/2008). Installation: object (wood, glass, 16 mm filmstrips), 16 mm loop projection. Installation view Galerie nächst St. Stephan, Vienna, Austria, 2008. Copyright: Galerie nächst St. Stephan/Rosemarie Schwarzwälder.

gallery, it is in the difference from the cinematic *dispositif* – room plunged in darkness, seated bodies and so on – that his mode of display – single enlarged and printed frames displayed as photographs – should be situated.

Finally, Miggitsch's mode of exhibition can be understood as a satirical allusion to the art market's 'limited-edition model',[26] all the more so as a certificate of authenticity is an integral part of the installation. As Jonathan Walley expounds, the same medium – film – can undergo strikingly different economic models. While avant-garde film production is generally not financially profitable, the sale of limited-number prints of so-called 'artists' films',[27] made for gallery exhibition, is virtually the norm. These prints are 'purposefully scarce, as scarcity is what makes them valuable in the art market'.[28] The irony of Miggitsch's investment in forms of scarcity lies in the fact that her own 'selling model' rejects and embraces the art market's laws at the same time. On the one hand, she does not provide a complete print for sale, but only a tiny sample of it, a snippet of celluloid of very small size (and value). On the other, compared to the limited edition, where a restricted number of copies of the *same* artwork is offered, Miggitsch's isolated frame truly represents an 'original copy', a unique object of an edition of only one, as two consecutive frames on a film strip would already differ, however slightly. Moreover, the artist hands the destiny of her film over to potential buyers, as every purchased frame, when replaced by a black one, contributes to the film's 'dying' and eventually disappearing into total blackness.

IDEOLOGY OF THE FRAME

An explicitly ideological perspective on the frame was already offered in 1971 by French film critic Sylvie Pierre Ulmann in an article published in *Cahiers du cinéma*, recently made available in English by Barnaby Dicker.[29] According to Pierre Ulmann, early in the twentieth century the film industry realised that literal reproductions of photograms no longer suited its commercial purposes and thus began to assign still photographers to film productions. Compared with extracted photograms, the technical quality of these promotional photographs made on the set with a photo camera was impeccable, bearing no traces of the material state of the given copy, such as marks, scratches, blurs or distortions. This innovation had far-reaching consequences, as Pierre Ulmann explains:

> from this point forward the photographic language of film about film became a metalanguage of ideology. It conformed to the idea of film that *its producers wanted to send out* so that it would be consumed in a certain way in keeping with the dominant ideology [. . .][30]

These 'parasitic photographs', as Pierre Ulmann calls them, support an idealist reading and are 'nothing other than a manipulation that allows for the separation of the image of the film from itself, from its imperfect, perishable materiality'.[31] In contrast to production photographs, which meet ideological requirements of 'legibility' and 'beauty', the extracted photogram reveals what is repressed by these demands: namely, 'meaningfulness' on the one hand, and 'formlessness' on the other.[32] Pierre Ulmann's explicit reference to George Bataille's notion of the 'formless' is well worth pursuing, as it is also able to clarify the ideological implications of the artworks considered here.

The term 'formless' (*informe* in French) was coined by Bataille in a mock dictionary he edited for the journal *Documents* in 1929 and 1930. According to the French author, the imperative of form, so omnipresent in our lives, can be countered only by an uncompromisingly rigorous 'lowering', a destabilising act that serves to bring things down [*déclasser*] in the world.[33] The formless was explicitly linked to twentieth-century art practices in the 1996 exhibition *L'Informe: Mode d'emploi* at the Centre Pompidou in Paris, curated by Yve-Alain Bois and Rosalind Krauss. The curators insisted that Bataille's *informe* 'is not so much a stable motif to which we can refer, [. . .] as it is a term allowing one to operate a declassification'.[34] The formless must be considered as a never-ending performative process, a 'falling into the *informe*', which contributes to a corruption of form, reduces meaning and decreases value – in sum, the formless punctures ideologically connoted categories.

AFTER THE SPECTACLE HAS BEEN SILENCED

Whether actually picking up one (or more than one) frame from a continuum, as Miggitsch and Sengmüller do, or capturing an isolated frame photographically, as in the cases of Tscherkassky and Rondepierre, all of these practices conform to the 'photogrammatic letter of the film text',[35] as Pierre Ulmann would put it. The fact that the dissected frame belongs to the same order as the film is a decisive point in Pierre Ulmann's argument in favour of the (extracted) photogram, which, according to her, has the potential to bypass ideological claims. Pierre Ulmann's opposition between the 'imperfect' frame and the idealised promotional photograph, which has lost any material connection with the 'letter' of the film, can be productively extended to the above-mentioned 'freeze frame' and the quasi-static film, as their impression of stillness is illusionary – another ideologically loaded term. Unlike the promotional photograph, the projects under discussion here are exempt from the debris of illusionism, as the frames they cope with are actually (rendered) still, obdurate, before they are integrated into new contexts. Moreover, the gestures involved in the making of these works (extracting a photogram, reproducing it) are able to silence the cinematic spectacle from which these frames are disconnected, be it an early motion picture (Tscherkassky), an action trailer (Sengmüller), various fiction films (Rondepierre) or one's own footage (Miggitsch). As a matter of fact, seeing a frame necessarily means not seeing the film. At the same time, these works' withdrawal from the spectacle is a withdrawal from 'legibility' and 'beauty'.[36] Once the spectacle has been silenced, the scene is set for the *informe*.

Tscherkassky's *Motion Picture* is composed of abstract – some would say meaningless – black and white spots. Sengmüller's *Slide Movie* represents a kind of technically poor 'primitive' cinema. Rondepierre literally 'stalks' what one could call waste: marks of deterioration, image-less black frames and undecipherable writings. Though Miggitsch's extracted photograms look flawless, even precious, their extraction contributes to the continuous disappearance of the film from which they are taken. The particular *use* that all of these works make of the frame prevents them from being reinscribed into ideological categories. It is exactly their varying degrees of illegibility and their destabilisation of 'good form' that release the subversive power of the photogrammatic text and shed light on cinema's blind spots.

Notes

1. Su Tung-p'o, 'First prose poem', in *Selected poems of Su Tung-p'o*, trans. by Burton Watson (New York: Copper Canyon Press, 1994), p. 96.
2. The English term 'apparatus' covers two distinct French terms, *appareil* and *dispositif*. *Appareil* – the technical apparatus – denotes the mechanical parts of the machine, as well as its flexible and changeable constituents (such as camera roll and filmstrip, for instance); *dispositif*, however, adds to this the relation between the mechanical device and the user, and all that this implies.
3. See Noam M. Elcott, 'The cinematic imaginary and the photographic fact: Media as models for 20th century art', *PhotoResearcher*, 29 (2018), pp. 7–23; Sylvie Pierre Ulmann, 'Elements for a theory of the photogramme' (1971), in Barnaby Dicker (ed.), *Art in Translation*, 8–1 (2016), pp. 108–27; Justin Remes, *Motion[less] Pictures: The Cinema of Stasis* (New York: Columbia University Press, 2015); Steven Jacobs, *Framing Pictures: Film and the Visual Arts* (Edinburgh: Edinburgh University Press, 2011); Laurent Guido and Olivier Lugon (eds), *Between Still and Moving Image* (New Barnet: John Libbey, 2012); Karen Beckman and Jean Ma (eds), *Still Moving: Between Cinema and Photography* (Durham, NC and London: Duke University Press, 2008); David Campany, *Photography and Cinema* (London: Reaktion Books, 2008); David Green and Joanna Lowry (eds), *Stillness and Time: Photography and the Moving Image* (Brighton: Photoforum and Photoworks, 2006); Raymond Bellour, *L'Entre-images: Photo, cinéma, vidéo* (Paris: La Différence, 2002); Jan-Christopher Horak, *Making Images Move: Photographers and Avant-Garde Cinema* (Washington, DC and London: Smithsonian Institution Press, 1997).
4. As Laura Mulvey puts it, 'the freeze frame is a series of identical frames repeated in order to create an illusion of stillness to replace the illusion of movement'. See Laura Mulvey, *Death 24x a Second: Stillness and the Moving Image* (London: Reaktion Books, 2006), p. 81.
5. Bellour, *L'Entre-images*; Mulvey, *Death 24x a Second*.
6. Raymond Bellour, 'Concerning "the Photographic"', in Beckman and Ma (eds), *Still Moving*, pp. 253–76.
7. Remes, *Motion[less] Pictures*.
8. Though it is true that, in material terms, a photographic reproduction of a frame is not the same as a frame extracted from the continuum of a film reel, it can be regarded as its equivalent because photography in this case is just a simple means of capturing the image.
9. A film still is generally understood to be a section of the film, literally stilled for illustration purposes, whereas the term 'photogram' also includes a photographic

practice executed by the imprint of an object directly placed on to a light-sensitive surface, as Man Ray's *rayograms*, for instance, demonstrate.

10. Christian Metz, 'The cinema: Language or language system?', in Christian Metz and Michael Taylor (eds), *Film Language: A Semiotics of the Cinema* (Oxford: Oxford University Press, 1974), pp. 31–91.
11. Roland Barthes, 'The third meaning: Research notes on some Eisenstein stills', in Roland Barthes and Stephen Heath (eds), *Image Music Text* (New York: Hill and Wang, 1977), pp. 52–68.
12. Barthes called these frame enlargements 'photogrammes', translated into English as 'stills' ('The third meaning', pp. 52–68).
13. Barthes, 'The third meaning', p. 66.
14. Barthes, 'The third meaning', p. 55.
15. Barthes, 'The third meaning', p. 65.
16. Philippe Dubois, 'Éric Rondepierre or working with photograms (between spot and texture)', in *Éric Rondepierre* (Brétigny-sur-Orge: Espace Jules Verne/Galerie Michèle Chomette, 1993), p. 28.
17. André Gaudreault, 'One and many: Cinema as a series of series', *History of Photography: An International Quarterly*, 31–1 (2007), p. 34.
18. Dominik Landwehr, 'Fictive media archeology: Interview with Gebhard Sengmüller, 2007', in Dieter Daniels and Barbara U. Schmidt (eds), *Artists as Inventors – Inventors as Artists* (Ostfildern: Hatje Cantz, 2008), p. 137.
19. Peter Tscherkassky, 'How and why? A few comments concerning production techniques employed in the making of the CinemaScope trilogy', in Maximiliano Cruz and Sandra Gómez (eds), *Desde el cuarto oscuro: El cine manufracturado de Peter Tscherkassky/From a Dark Room: The Manufractured Cinema of Peter Tscherkassky* (Spanish/English) (Mexico City: Interior 13/UNAM International Film Festival – FICUNAM, 2012), p. 114.
20. Peter Tscherkassky, *Films from a Dark Room* (Index DVD 08) [no year].
21. Tom Gunning, 'An aesthetic of astonishment: Early film and the (in)credulous spectator' (1989), in Leo Braudy and Marshall Cohen (eds), *Film Theory and Criticism* (Oxford: Oxford University Press, 1999), p. 822.
22. Dubois, *Éric Rondepierre or Working with Photograms*, p. 30.
23. Thierry Lenain, 'An example of withstanding the mass media in the arena of contemporary art: Eric Rondepierre and his critique of cinematographic vision', in Candido Mendes and Enrique Rodriguez Larreta (eds), *Media and Social Perception* (Rio de Janeiro: Unesco/ISSC/Educam, 1998), p. 391.
24. Telephone interview with Susanne Miggitsch, 28 February 2019.
25. Raymond Bellour, 'Reprise', in *La Querelle des dispositifs: Cinéma – installations, expositions* (Paris: P.O.L., 2012), pp. 49–63.
26. Erika Balsom, *After Uniqueness: A History of Film and Video Art in Circulation* (New York: Columbia University Press, 2017).
27. Jonathan Walley distinguishes between 'filmmaker films' and 'artists' films': 'In avant-garde cinema, film is the artist's primary, often sole medium (sometimes excepting video). In artists' films, however, film is one medium among many,

and artists' films are often part of a body of related works in a variety of media.' See Jonathan Walley, 'Modes of film practice in the avant-garde', in Tanya Leighton (ed.), *Art and the Moving Image: A Critical Reader* (London: Tate, 2008), p. 189.
28. Walley, 'Modes of film practice in the avant-garde', p. 188.
29. Pierre Ulmann, *Art in Translation*, pp. 108–27.
30. Pierre Ulmann, *Art in Translation*, p. 112
31. Pierre Ulmann, *Art in Translation*, p. 113.
32. Pierre Ulmann, *Art in Translation*, p. 114.
33. Georges Bataille, 'Informe' (1929–1931), in Georges Batailles and Bernard Noël (eds), *Le Dictionnaire critique: Note de Bernard Noël* (Paris: L'Écarlate, 1993), p. 33.
34. Yve-Alain Bois and Rosalind E. Krauss, *Formless: A User's Guide* (New York: Zone Books, 1997), p.18.
35. As Barnaby Dicker, the editor of Pierre Ulmann's article, elucidates in a footnote, the 'photogrammatic letter' 'speaks to a sense of cinematographic specificity – in contrast, here, to that of (still) photography – while nevertheless inviting us to grasp this specificity in linguistic terms' (Pierre Ulmann, *Art in Translation*, p. 124).
36. Pierre Ulmann, *Art in Translation*, p. 114.

CHAPTER 10

Filming and Feeling between the Arts: Pascale Breton, Suite armoricaine *and Eugène Green,* Le Fils de Joseph

Marion Schmid

Ever since André Bazin's seminal 1952 article 'In Defense of Mixed Cinema', there can be no doubt about cinema's status as an 'impure' medium traversed and shaped by other art forms: its narrative and dramatic antecedents literature and the theatre (which are of particular concern to Bazin in this piece),[1] but also music, painting, sculpture, architecture and photography, not to forget dance. Referenced and remediated, incorporated and recontextualised, sources of emulation or objects of rivalry, the other arts have played a crucial role in the medium's self-definition and its struggle to be recognised as an art form in its own right. In our digital age, with its enhanced possibilities for the combination and merging of media, they continue to nourish the filmic medium, contributing towards an ever increasing hybridisation between the arts.[2] 'All the arts flow through cinema,' Alain Badiou – together with Jacques Rancière, one of the philosophers to have thought most extensively about cinema's interrelation to its sibling arts – states in an interview with Antoine de Baecque. 'It doesn't just use them or intermingle with them; it defies them and presents them with challenges hard to meet: to achieve by themselves, on their own what cinema is able to do with them.'[3] Cinema, according to Badiou, both draws on the other arts and 'magnifies' them, raising them to a 'simultaneously impure and heightened power that affords [them] a new timelessness'.[4]

If film critics have consistently drawn on the other arts for their theoretical formulations, over the last three decades Film Studies as a discipline has been greatly enriched by interdisciplinary works focused on cinema's interactions with its sister arts. Ground-breaking studies by Pascal Bonitzer, Jacques Aumont, Angela Dalle Vacche, Raymond Bellour, Giuliana Bruno, Jean Cléder and Steven Jacobs, to name only a few scholars, have opened up new paradigms for understanding film as a site of encounter and dialogue between different art forms.[5] Though, for practical and disciplinary reasons, the majority of work in this area isolates specific media interfaces – such as, for instance, cinema and literature, or cinema and painting – several recent studies take a broader, trans-disciplinary approach. Important forays towards a more comprehensive study of cinematic intermediality have been made by Ágnes Pethő in her excellent *Cinema and Intermediality: The Passion for the In-Between*, as well as in Lúcia Nagib and Anne Jerslev's edited collection, *Impure Cinema: Intermedial and Intercultural Approaches to Film*, and, most recently, in Jørgen Bruhn and Anne Gjelsvik's *Cinema between Media: An Intermedial Approach*.

What these recent works throw sharply into relief is that instances of cinematic intermediality cannot always be contained within one particular interface, even though studies of cinema's interactions with one particular art are extremely valuable as theoretical tools and heuristic templates. Looking beyond specific media constellations, we are able to grasp the wide array of artistic practices and traditions engaged by certain filmmakers, and we become attentive to the multi-faceted ways in which cinema 'insinuate[s] itself between the arts among which it has so swiftly carved out its valleys', to use Bazin's geological metaphor.[6] Just as important, an approach that is open to crossovers between different media helps us understand better how film harnesses the other arts in its signifying processes.

With these considerations in mind, the following chapter will explore the dialogue with other art forms in two recent French films, Pascale Breton's *Suite armoricaine* and Eugène Green's *Le Fils de Joseph* [The Son of Joseph]. Both released in 2016, the two works evince astonishing parallels in their use of intermediality as a vehicle to interrogate questions of belonging, personal growth and transmission. In the former, Proust's novel of remembrance and the art of landscape painting are enlisted in the story of an art lecturer's rediscovery of her cultural roots. In the latter, Caravaggio, Georges de La Tour, Baroque music and the Bible become the vectors of a humanist meditation on parenthood and filiation. In-between media, the two filmmakers carve out a space where literary and painterly motifs are reimagined in a contemporary reflection on the transformative, nourishing function of art. In my reading, I will argue for the significance of artworks in the two films as a way of giving expression to thoughts and affects that are not articulated directly, by making 'sensible' central human concerns without recourse to language. From an intermedial perspective, I will also examine the various 'migrations'[7] – on both a thematic and a formal level – effected between the artworks and the cinematic image in the two films.

SENSITIVE LANDSCAPES: *SUITE ARMORICAINE*

Released twelve years after her remarkable debut feature *Illumination* (2004), *Suite Armoricaine* confirms Pascale Breton as one of the most original voices of contemporary French cinema – a director who broaches profound human questions in a vibrant, poetic film style. Where *Illumination* had taken its inspiration from the landscapes and imaginary of the director's native Brittany, here she delves into academic life, in a campus-based work shot at the University Rennes 2 with the participation of local students. The film's multi-layered plot interweaves the lives of art historian Françoise (Valérie Dréville), who has left a prestigious post in Paris for a lectureship at Rennes, and geography student Ion (Kaou Langoët), a former foster child struggling with the reappearance of his alcoholic mother (Elina Löwensohn). Different in age, experience and itinerary, the middle-aged lecturer and the student suddenly find themselves confronted with a past they had evacuated from their lives, the former, according to Breton, having chosen landscape painting as a screen against memories of her native Finistère, the latter studying geography 'to ward off the menace of the no man's land'.[8] Linked through their mutual concern with landscape, history of art and geography become a means for the characters to understand their place in the world and to decipher the sensitive maps of their lives. The seventeenth-century *Carte du pays de Tendre* (Map of the Land of Tenderness) that Françoise evokes in a conference paper – a map which, in the words of Giuliana Bruno, 'visualises, in the form of a landscape, an itinerary of emotions'[9] – is emblematic of landscape as a form of affective geography in the film. As we will see in more detail, painted landscapes and landscapes of the soul become, to a certain extent, porous as the two characters embark on a journey of self-discovery.

In both its narrative construction and its visual aesthetics, *Suite armoricaine* sketches out an intermedial poetics, signalled from the outset in its paratext. If the title suggests a continuity with her first feature, equally set in Brittany, it above all alludes to the musical form of the 'suite', consisting of several movements that contrast in rhythm and mood (usually dance pieces), yet which are thematically linked. During the shooting, the director also likened her approach to fresco painting, with reference to the technique of mural painting executed on freshly laid plaster, particularly associated with Italian Renaissance and Baroque art. *Suite armoricaine*, comments Éric Thouvenel, 'is a film *a fresco*, because it was written and shot like one walks in fresh paint, producing traces that become a part of us'.[10] The film's division into chapters, on the other hand, alludes to literary forms of expression, the handwritten titles superimposed upon the image gesturing towards a 'written screen' in the tradition of Godard.[11] In treating the filmic image like a page of writing, the director visually crosses the boundaries that traditionally separate text-based from image-based media, positing her filmmaking as a form of authorial écriture.

The film's main subject, according to Breton herself, is the substance of time.[12] Following the unravelling of an academic year, punctuated by the cycle of the seasons, in its most literal form this is a work that seeks to capture time in its duration. Yet, cautious of any linear conceptions of temporality, on a more philosophical level *Suite armoricaine* interrogates the individual's permeable position with regard to time, notably in our capacity to relive moments of the past through processes of remembrance. In its preoccupation with time lost and regained, as well as its attentiveness to memory as a sensuous phenomenon residing in the body, the film exhibits a distinctly Proustian sensibility that has not been lost on its critics.[13] Referenced in one of the dialogues, as well as in the last chapter title, 'Le Printemps retrouvé' ['Spring Regained', a variation of Proust's 'Time Regained'], Proust's *In Search of Lost Time* provides a narrative foil for Françoise's retrieval of a past which she had expelled from her consciousness. While she reconnects with her roots, the filmic present becomes increasingly porous to the past through flashbacks to her student days in the 1980s. At first triggered by visual aids (notably a photograph of 1981, showing her among a group of friends) and through the familiar melody of the Breton language, Françoise's journey of remembrance culminates in a series of epiphanies at the end of the film, when, accompanied by Ion, she returns to the farm where she grew up. Amidst the Breton countryside in spring, teeming with colours and scents, she lives a Proustian 'fragment of time in the pure state',[14] as memories of her childhood are restored to her in their full affective and sensorial richness. As suggested by the figure of her grandfather – a traditional healer – the lecturer's reconnection with her roots marks a process of personal healing, but it also becomes a gift of transmission as she reaches out to the student, whose homeless mother – her former friend Moon – has tragically died from hypothermia.

If a modernist literary text provides the structure for the female protagonist's rediscovery of her past, Baroque painting underpins the two characters' emotional journey. At the heart of the filmic enquiry lies the trope of Arcadia, mediated by Nicolas Poussin's *Et in Arcadia ego* (1637–8), with which Françoise opens her lecture series on landscape. One of the masterpieces of Baroque allegory, the painting invites a meditation on time and mortality: grouped around a sepulchral monument, four Arcadian shepherds receive what Erwin Panofsky, in a famous reading, calls the 'silent message of a former fellow being: "I, too, lived in Arcady where you now live; I, too, enjoyed the pleasures which you now enjoy"'.[15] Arcadia as the metaphor of a lost paradise, often associated with the time of youth, becomes key to understanding the sentimental map of Françoise's life. Standing in front of the projector while offering a close reading of the painting, the lecturer's face and body are suffused by its translucent images. As painting, dissolved into the pixelated images of a photographic projection, takes on the immaterial qualities of the cinematic image, the human figure in turn becomes one with the picture, the exterior world of the painting hinting at the 'interior landscape' of the character.[16] Imprinted on Françoise, the painting makes palpable the abyss that separates the middle-aged woman not only from her student days, playfully evoked in the lecture, but from the child of the filmic prologue, who, mindful of the dangers of amnesia, reminded herself: 'I'll have to remember myself as I am now. Otherwise, were will I have gone?' On a more collective level, Arcadia as the locus of unspoilt wilderness, celebrated in Renaissance and Baroque painting, becomes an allegory for the Brittany of the protagonist's youth, sacrificed to the French State's infrastructure projects of the 1970s and devastated by the 1978 Amoco Cadiz oil spill, both evoked in the archival footage of the title credits. This was a destruction that not only led to local protest movements – equally referenced in the credits – but gave birth to the vibrant punk-rock scene of the 1980s that shaped the young woman's emotional journey: '[s]ince the damage was done, Eden lost, we needed this dark music and a new romanticism, built on the night, physical love and the criticism of collective utopias', comments the director in reference to her own youth.[17]

For Ion also, painting affords a deeper understanding of himself, triggering a process of personal growth. Adopting a technique of temporal 'rewind' (poetically called 'maritime drift' by the director), used for all of the encounters between lecturer and student,[18] the film offers two versions of a scene in Rennes' Museum of Fine Arts. At first shot from Françoise's point of view, we follow the art historian's gaze as it navigates a series of landscape paintings. Zooming in on details and scrolling over the canvas, the camera reveals the rich textures and colours of the paintings, while also animating the still images of landscapes populated by human figures. As in the lecture scenes, where paintings are navigated by means of a cursor, painting changes its ontological

Figure 10.1 Painting as sensitive landscape (Pascale Breton, *Suite armoricaine*, 2016).

nature, taking on the characteristics of the moving image. Fragmented into sections, as Bazin explains in an influential article on painting and cinema, 'the space of the painting loses its orientation and its limits and is presented to the imagination as without boundaries'.[19] In an adjacent room, Françoise catches sight of a young man sitting in contemplation before Georges de La Tour's *The Newborn Child* (c. 1648), who, aware of her presence, leaves hastily. In the reiteration of the scene from Ion's perspective some twenty minutes later, by contrast, the young man's gaze first wanders among female nudes, evincing his fascination with the female body. Scrutinising representations of infancy, his eyes come to rest on the newborn child in the La Tour painting and, finally, on the mother figure. Where, for the art lecturer, the pastoral landscapes of which she has made a research specialism resonate with her inner search for the Arcady of her youth, for the foster child La Tour's Nativity, which abstracts a religious motif into an intimate depiction of maternity, heralds a belated reconciliation with his mother, beyond death. 'Deeply rooted in the real world'[20] and without idealisation, the painting conveys the tender care of the mother for her newborn son, its profound emotion helping the young man make peace with a difficult childhood. Apprehended in its spiritual dimension by the Baroque painter, the mystery of birth marks a rebirth for the wounded adult.

At once mirrors and catalysers of the protagonists' inner journey, the paintings in *Suite armoricaine* engage a wider meditation about the finitude of our earthly existence, the role of art in our lives, and our capacity for empathy and compassion. It may be helpful to think about the role of painting in the film in terms of what Badiou calls the 'breached frontier' between cinema and its sibling arts. For the philosopher, cinema acts upon the other arts, subtracting them from themselves. He writes:

Figure 10.2   Rebirth through art: Georges de La Tour's *The Newborn Child* (Pascale Breton, *Suite armoricaine*, 2016).

> The allusive quotation of the other arts, which is constitutive of cinema, wrests these arts away from themselves. What remains is precisely the breached frontier where an idea will have passed, an idea whose visitation the cinema, and it alone, allows.[21]

Chiming also with Proust's anti-intellectual, sensorial stance, in *Suite armoricaine* painting serves as a conduit for ideas that cannot be grasped by the intellect alone, opening a breach through which essential human questions can be communicated in non-verbal form. Transmuted by the camera, the paintings make ideas sensible, without them needing to be articulated in words. Shifting cinematic expression towards what Pethő calls 'non-discursive domains and more sensual modes of perception', painting in the film opens up an alternative mode for apprehending thought and feeling.[22]

Where, on a structural level, the paintings serve as a vector for the non-verbal transmission of ideas, on a visual level, the film stages a series of what, borrowing a concept from another leading thinker of intermediality, Jacques Aumont, we may call 'migrations' of themes, techniques and *mise en scène*. For Aumont, it is not so much the practice of citation that defines the relationship between painting and film, but, rather, the more complex ways in which a film revisits an artwork, movement or aesthetic tradition by means of its own specific language and expression. In the wake of Aby Warburg, who uses the notion of migration to account for the subterranean passage of artistic figures and motifs across centuries, geographical space and even seemingly unconnected cultures, in *L'Œil interminable* Aumont asks: 'What migrates in the cinema? Ready-made images (citation), themes, forms, formulas, devices? What work must the film image do to welcome these "migrants"?'[23] The concept of migration is elucidated further in the later *Matière d'images*, where he explains: '[t]he artist is a critic to the extent that he practises an art that reproduces *in its own form* the work of the past, transformed, metamorphosed. Migration *is* this power of translation.'[24]

In *Suite armoricaine*, tropes, themes and settings from the paintings discussed in Françoise's lectures migrate into 'real' life, most prominently in the sequence where the students are having a party in the woods bordering campus, which immediately follows the lecture on Poussin's *Et in Arcadia ego*. Cutting from a detail of the painting straight to Ion and his friends drinking, making music and dancing, the editing posits student life – and, by extension, the university – as a possible modern-day Arcady. In her re-enactment of the trope, the director puts particular emphasis on the multi-cultural composition and diversity of the student body (the party consists of students from mixed ethnic backgrounds and includes an assertive blind student), making inclusiveness a defining criterion of any contemporary Arcady. More subtly, an insert shot of a rocky islet, ominously placed after Françoise's last encounter with Moon before the latter's death, evokes Arnold Böcklin's symbolist painting *The Isle of the Dead* (1880). Though this particular work is not shown in the film, a few minutes later Françoise's discussion of Böcklin's *Prometheus* (1883), in her closing lecture of the year, creates a visual bridge to the inserted landscape shot.

Just as important, though more diffuse, a painterly mode informs the overall aesthetic of the film in its predilection for long takes, soft lighting and tableau-like compositions. In their use of chiaroscuro and warm, reddish brown hues, the shots of the child in the prologue and of Françoise on her bed scrutinising the photograph are reminiscent of La Tour's famous 'night paintings'. What is more, in interview, Pascale Breton reveals that the lush greens in her images of nature were adjusted digitally in post-production according to late nineteenth-century treatises on colour mixing.[25] The final shot of a meander of the River Aulne, opening out into the surrounding countryside, is paradigmatic for the wider transmutation between the painterly and the cinematic that underpins *Suite armoricaine*. With its elevated point of view and depth of field, the shot composition recalls Joachim Patinir's *Landscape with Charon's Bark* (c. 1521), discussed in one of Françoise's lectures. As an artist preoccupied with landscape as a spiritual category, the Flemish Renaissance painter provides a fitting model for Breton's interest in landscapes of the mind.[26] At the beginning of the shot, a boat furrowing along the river, leaving a white trail in its wake, generates the movement we traditionally associate with cinema. But as the landscape, held in a long shot, regains its majestic calm, it becomes tableau-like in its stillness. Commenting on this arresting last image, the director states: 'I wanted to show that at the end, if your eyes are used to looking at things, everything becomes a painting.'[27]

ART AS (DIVINE) REVELATION: *LE FILS DE JOSEPH*

Art as a source of revelation and transmission is equally central to Eugène Green's *Le Fils de Joseph*, a modern fable of adolescence and parenthood. American-born Green is a latecomer to cinema, having taken to the camera in the early 2000s after having made a name for himself as an expert in Baroque theatre. He is also a playwright, stage director and writer of fiction and non-fiction, including two essays on cinema, *Présences: Essai sur la nature du cinéma* and *Poétique du cinématographe*.[28] Shaped by his work in theatre and music, many of his films draw explicitly on the other arts: *Le Pont des arts* (*The Bridge of Arts*, 2004), for instance, traces the life of a singer who specialises in Baroque music; *La Religieuse portugaise* (*The Portuguese Nun*, 2009) revolves around the shooting of a film based on a seventeenth-century epistolary fiction; and *La Sapienza* (2015) follows an architect's journey to Italy to complete a book on one of the masters of Baroque architecture, Francesco Borromini. With their pared-down style, flattened dialogues and stylised performance, Green's films can be situated in the anti-naturalist tradition of Robert Bresson, whom he openly acknowledges as an influence. Beyond his signature predilection for fixed-camera shots, long takes and close-ups of actors looking directly at the camera, what makes his works instantly recognisable is the diction of the actors, whom he requires to pronounce all final consonants in French words (*faire la liaison*). Tying in with the director's wider anti-psychological stance, the non-naturalistic dialogues, enhanced by the marked pronunciation, are, above all, a means to access the characters' interiority. For, in Green's spiritual, not to say mystical, conception of the medium, the essence of cinema is to 'render visible what remains hidden in the world'.[29] In *Poétique du cinématographe*, he explains: 'The cinematograph, by its essential nature, is an art of the icon and its functioning is based on the notion of a real presence in the fragments of the world of which the film is composed.'[30] He adds: 'When the inner energy of beings, but also that of objects and materials, becomes apprehensible, the cinematograph reaches its essential functioning.'[31]

If Green's theoretical writings evince a Christian metaphysics influenced by Jansenism and the mysticism of Meister Eckhart,[32] his sixth feature, *Le Fils de Joseph*, is loosely inspired by the Old and New Testaments. Divided into five chapters, the film revisits episodes of the Bible – evoked in titles such as 'Le Sacrifice d'Abraham' [Abraham's Sacrifice] or 'Le Veau d'or' [The Golden Calf] – from a contemporary point of view. Enmeshing a wry parody of the Parisian intelligentsia with the allegorical story of a spiritual rebirth, the filmic narrative revolves around troubled teenager Vincent's (Victor Ezenfils) plan to murder his biological father, the egotistical editor Oscar Pormenor (Mathieu Amalric). Yet, in a peripeteia typical of Green's classically inflected plots, he finds a spiritual father and new companion for his mother, Marie (Natacha Régnier), in Pormenor's estranged brother Joseph (Fabrizio Rongione).

Assimilated into a humorous tale about power, love and forgiveness, the biblical intertext is overlaid with Baroque pictorial, literary and musical references, which, as in Pascale Breton's *Suite armoricaine*, mediate the protagonist's emotional journey. Green structures his filmic narrative around two contrasting representations of the father–son relationship: Caravaggio's *Sacrifice of Isaac* (c. 1603), a dramatic visualisation of the moment in the Old Testament when Abraham is about to sacrifice his only son, and Georges de La Tour's *Christ with Saint Joseph in the Carpenter's Shop* (c. 1642), a work indebted to Caravaggio and his followers in its skilful use of chiaroscuro. Some nine minutes into the film, a large-scale reproduction of the Caravaggio painting adorning Vincent's room – making mockery of any desire for verisimilitude in the filmic *mise en scène* – gives visibility to the adolescent's rage at not knowing his father's identity and his ensuing self-image as a victim. We are instantly struck by the physical resemblance between the boy in the painting and the actor embodying Vincent, hinting at a shared plight between the biblical character and the twenty-first-century teenager. As a painter who, in the words of Yves Bonnefoy, 'represents only to attest to suffering',[33] Caravaggio conveys an intensity of emotion that is carefully concealed in Victor Ezenfils's pared-down performance. The painting's affective charge changes when, having discovered that his father is a cynical businessman who is indifferent to the needs of even his close family, Vincent is consumed by revenge. Face to face with the Caravaggio, his eyes glide from father to son, back to the father, and from there to the angel who commands Abraham to 'not lay a hand on the boy',[34] before coming to rest on the brandished knife: in a reversal of the biblical myth and stark defiance of its message, the painting becomes an incentive for parricide. In the chapter 'Le Sacrifice d'Isaac', the youth is about to slay his father when a divine intervention, evoked by the apparition of a luminous halo on the wall (recalling the light symbolising divine grace in the backdrop of the painting), summons him to halt. Green does not quite go as far as to stage a *tableau vivant* of the painting here, but the composition of the father brutally held to the ground, his face filled with terror like that of Isaac in the painting, while his son crouches over him with a knife ready to strike, emulates that of Caravaggio, suggesting a migration – on both a formal and a thematic level – from the painting to the moving image.

Whereas the Caravaggio painting mediates a conflictual relation to the father figure, in striking similarity to Pascale Breton's film, it is in contemplation of a La Tour that the adolescent is able to reconsider difficult parental bonds. Here, also, a seminal moment of awareness is triggered in the museum space, in this instance the Louvre, which Vincent is visiting in the company of his new-found friend, Joseph (who came to his aid as he was fleeing the site of his assault). Like the art lecturer Françoise in *Suite Armoricaine*, the middle-aged man teaches the adolescent how to read a painting. The camera embraces their point of view as they look at Baroque-era painter Philippe de Champaigne's *The Dead Christ* (c. 1654), their eyes wandering from the stigmata in Christ's feet to the wound in his side, tellingly resembling, according to Benoît Chantre, 'the genitals of a woman who has just given birth'.[35] In an adjacent room, the pair stop before La Tour's *Christ with Saint Joseph in the Carpenter's Shop*, an intimate depiction of Saint Joseph at work, watched by the child Jesus, illuminated by a candle in his hand. Filmed first in its entirety, then in close-up, the painting triggers a discussion about the relationship between the two figures in the picture. Vincent at first corrects his friend when the latter refers to Joseph as the father of Jesus, but takes to

Figure 10.3 Spiritual paternity: Georges de La Tour's *Christ with Saint Joseph in the Carpenter's Shop* (Eugène Green, *Le Fils de Joseph*, 2016).

heart his explanation that 'it was through his son that he became a father'. Fatherhood, he comes to understand through the painting, is not limited to biological relationships, encompassing just as importantly a spiritual sense of kinship. Paternity is bestowed on Joseph not through connection by blood, but through his willingness to adopt and care for the son of Mary.

Initiated in the Louvre, Vincent's spiritual rebirth through art is fittingly accomplished in the Chapel of the Virgin of Saint Roch – a late Baroque church in Paris – where the two men attend a musical rehearsal. The golden glow of candles and softly contrasted light and shadow endow the scene with a painterly quality, reminiscent of the chiaroscuro in La Tour's *Christ with Saint Joseph in the Carpenter's Shop*. Towered over by a sculptural group representing the Nativity, an actress recites Baroque poet Honorat de Bueil de Racan's *Epitaph pour son fils*, followed by a musical interpretation of Domenico Mazzocchi's *Lamentum matris Euryali*, two lamentations on the death of a son. Green renders the recitals in their full duration, alternating between shots of the performers and the audience, with a particular focus on Vincent, whose face is visibly moved by the rehearsal. Though unable to understand the Latin words, 'he directly receives their emotion through the music and the energy of the performers'.[36] The artistic experience, we are made to understand, marks a conversion for the adolescent, helping him overcome his anger at not knowing his father's identity. Like Ion in *Suite armoricaine*, Vincent belatedly understands his mother's love for him, and, in turn, is able to reach out to her. 'Beyond the aesthetic experience', the director comments, 'the meaning of these two works strikes Vincent', awakening in him 'a light, a generosity'.[37]

The new understanding of filiation afforded by the artworks opens the path to the recomposed, secular 'holy family' formed by Marie, Joseph and Vincent. The film comes closest to a modern adaptation of the Bible in the last chapter 'La Fuite en Egypte' [The Flight to Egypt], when the trio are hunted down by Pormenor, who is unaware that his attacker is none other than his biological son. Green playfully restages painterly representations of the final episode of the Nativity in his *mise en scène* of Marie – dressed in virginal blue – riding on a borrowed donkey, led by her son and flanked by Joseph, except that in his reimagined scene the fugitives are arrested by a police patrol. Questioned about their relationship to Vincent, both Marie and Joseph affirm their parenthood. The film ends with shots of the couple walking along the shore, enlaced, while the adolescent stands back, a radiant smile on his face – a new family is born.

What, then, do these two films, so strikingly similar in their themes and intermedial poetics, tell us about the function of the other arts in cinema? How do they negotiate artistic iconographies, traditions and techniques? And to what extent do the artworks they reference and reframe resonate with the filmmakers' own artistic quests? Used as conduits to processes of inner awakening, in *Suite armoricaine* and *Le Fils de Joseph*, as we have seen, artworks accompany the characters' spiritual journey, helping them find their place in the world and forge meaningful relationships with family members and their broader environment. Whether it be in Pascal Breton's sensitive landscapes, which map the protagonist's interiority, or in Eugène Green's harnessing of painting, poetry and music as a source of revelation, both directors share a belief in the epiphanic powers of art. In the lineage of Proust – invoked by Breton – both suggest that a deeper understanding of the self and the world can be obtained by means of artistic experience, rather than merely through intellectual endeavour. As Green comments:

> [i]t is important, in my opinion, that people apprehend the world through art in a direct way, without the intervention of the intellect, and that aesthetic experience makes them see another reality, reveals to them another truth than the one they believe they know.[38]

Through their invocation of the other arts, *Suite armoricaine* and *Le Fils de Joseph* open breaches where ideas and emotions become apprehensible in a non-verbal, sensory mode. Given the two filmmakers' concern with giving expression to what cannot be fully grasped in words, it is perhaps unsurprising that both put Baroque painting at the centre of their artistic interrogations. For, as one of the most subtle analysts of the Baroque, Yves Bonnefoy, points out, Baroque art, far from being obsessed with futile appearances, stages above all a journey into interiority: 'Despite all the visible that it deploys, the baroque only relates to the inner experience of grace.'[39] The purpose of Baroque art, the critic and poet argues, is no longer knowledge, as it was for the Renaissance, but 'the construction of a *place* for presence to oneself'.[40] From Caravaggio's anguished depiction of human suffering to Poussin's 'mental painting',[41] in both films Baroque works trace the characters' interior landscapes at different stages of their personal development. As a painter concerned with 'captur[ing] the tactile reality of form, but in order to conjure up the image of humanity confronted with destiny',[42] to quote Jacques Thuillier, Georges de La Tour occupies a privileged place in their inner journey. What is more, on a formal level too, both films effect a series of migrations from painting to moving image, most notably in their espousal of painterly compositions, use of chiaroscuro and intermittent moments of stillness. But, though painting is central to their project, it is by no means the only art form invoked by the two directors, who, as we have seen, also harness the arts of literature, music and the theatre in their artistic quests. 'Magnified' by the cinema, these other arts are imbued with what Badiou calls a 'distinctive emotional power': '[t]here's a power of revelation of the arts, a power of subjugation of the arts in cinema that truly makes it the seventh art.'[43]

Notes

1. André Bazin, 'In Defense of Mixed Cinema', in *What is Cinema?*, ed. and trans. by Hugh Gray, 2 vols (London: University of California Press, 1967–71), vol. 1, pp. 53–75.
2. Bazin predicted a general hybridisation between media for the year 2050, when 'the (literary?) critic [. . .] would find not a novel out of which a play and a film had been "made," but rather a single work reflected through three art forms, an artistic pyramid with three sides'. 'Adaptation, or the cinema as digest', in James Naremore (ed.), *Film Adaptation* (New Brunswick: Rutgers University Press, 2000), pp. 19–27 (p. 26).
3. '"Cinema has given me so much": An interview with Alain Badiou by Antoine de Baecque', in Alain Badiou, *Cinema*, texts selected and introduced by Antoine de Baecque; trans. by Susan Spitzer (Oxford: Polity Press, 2013).
4. Badiou, *Cinema*, pp. 1–20 (p. 7).
5. See, *inter alia*, Pascal Bonitzer, *Décadrages: Peinture et cinéma* (Paris: Éditions de l'Étoile, 1985); Jacques Aumont, *L'Œil interminable* (Paris: Éditions de la Différence, 2007); Angela Dalle Vacche, *Cinema and Painting: How Art is Used in Film* (Austin: University of Texas Press, 1996); Raymond Bellour, *Between-the-Images*, ed. by Lionel Bovier, trans. by Allyn Hardyck (Dijon: Les Presses du réel, 2012); Giuliana Bruno, *Public Intimacy: Architecture and the Visual Arts* (Cambridge, MA: MIT Press, 2007); Jean Cléder, *Entre littérature et cinéma: Les Affinités électives* (Paris: Armand Colin, 2012); and Steven Jacobs, *Framing Pictures: Film and the*

Visual Arts (Edinburgh: Edinburgh University Press, 2012).
6. Bazin, 'In Defense of Mixed Cinema', p. 74.
7. Borrowed from Jacques Aumont, this term will be elucidated further in the first section of the chapter.
8. Fabrice Gaignault, 'Entretien avec Pascale Breton', booklet accompanying *Suite armoricaine* DVD, Blaq Out, 2016, p. 6. All translations are mine, unless otherwise indicated.
9. Giuliana Bruno, *Atlas of Emotion: Journeys in Art, Architecture and Film* (London: Verso, 2007), p. 2.
10. See Éric Thouvenel, 'Des réponses flottent dans notre intelligence sous forme d'image', booklet accompanying *Suite armoricaine* DVD, p. 15.
11. Cf. Philippe Dubois, 'The written screen: JLG and writing as the accursed share', in Michael Temple, James S. Williams and Michael Witt (eds), *For Ever Godard* (London: Black Dog, 2004), pp. 232–47.
12. Gaignault, 'Entretien avec Pascale Breton', p. 5.
13. The newspaper *Sud Ouest* calls it 'a Proustian film carried by the grace of Valérie Dréville' (*Suite armoricaine* DVD, back cover). Breton also alludes to another modernist writer, William Faulkner, through the shot of a bust adorning the university librarian's office (where it is irreverently used as a scarf holder), as well as in her note of intent for the film where she cites Faulkner's 'the past is never dead' (booklet, *Suite armoricaine* DVD, p. 4).
14. Marcel Proust, *In Search of Lost Time*, ed. by Christopher Prendergast, 6 vols (London: Allen Lane, 2002), VI, p. 224.
15. E. Panofsky, '"Et in Arcadia ego": Poussin and the elegiac tradition', in Erwin Panofsky, *Meaning in the Visual Arts: Papers in and on Art History* (Garden City, NY: Doubleday, 1955), p. 314.
16. The term 'interior landscape' is borrowed from Bruno, *Atlas of Emotion*, p. 2.
17. Gaignault, 'Entretien avec Pascale Breton', p. 9.
18. Gaignault, 'Entretien avec Pascale Breton', p. 6.
19. Bazin, 'Painting and cinema', in *What is Cinema?*, vol. 1, pp. 164–9 (p. 166).
20. Jacques Thuillier, *Georges de La Tour*, trans. by Fabia Claris (Paris: Flammarion, 2002), p. 210.
21. Badiou, *Cinema*, p. 92.
22. Ágnes Pethő, *Cinema and Intermediality: The Passion for the In-between* (Newcastle: Cambridge Scholars, 2011), p. 48.
23. Aumont, *L'Œil interminable*, p. 16.
24. Jacques Aumont, *Matière d'images* (Paris: Images modernes, 2005), p. 56 (emphasis in original).
25. 'Rencontre avec Pascale Breton', Boutique POTEMKINE (23 September 2016). Available at <https://vimeo.com/186493916> (last accessed 5 August 2020).
26. Reindert L. Falkenburg reads *Landscape with Charon's Bark* as an example of Patinir's landscapes as 'meditational images of the pilgrimage of life'. See his *Joachim Patinir: Landscape as an Image of the Pilgrimage of Life* (Amsterdam and Philadelphia: John Benjamins, 1988), p. 105.

27. Manuel Betancourt, 'ND/NF Interview: Pascale Breton' (22 March 2016), *Film Comment*. Available at <https://www.filmcomment.com/blog/interview-pascale-breton-suite-armoricaine/> (last accessed 5 August 2020).
28. Eugène Green, *Présences: Essai sur la nature du cinéma* (Paris: Desclée de Brouwer, 2003); *Poétique du cinématographe* (Paris: Acte Sud, 2009).
29. Green, *Poétique du cinématographe*, p. 91.
30. Green, *Poétique du cinématographe*, p. 49.
31. Green, *Poétique du cinématographe*, p. 80.
32. See Fabien Gris, 'Eugène Green: Un pont intempestif entre les arts', *Revue critique de fixxion française contemporaine*, 7 (2013), pp. 60–72 (p. 66).
33. Yves Bonnefoy, 'Un des siècles du culte des images', in *Rome, 1630* (Paris: Flammarion, 2000), pp. 219–62 (p. 246).
34. Genesis 22: 12.
35. Benoît Chantre, 'Eugène Green, Le Fils de Joseph', *Art Press*, 435 (2016), p. 92.
36. 'Entretien avec Eugène Green', interview by Hugues Perrot. Press release, *Le Fils de Joseph*, p. 8. Available at <https://medias.unifrance.org/medias/235/100/156907/presse/le-fils-de-joseph-dossier-de-presse-francais.pdf> (last accessed 5 August 2020).
37. 'Rencontre avec Eugène Green pour son film *Le Fils de Joseph*', Boutique POTEMKINE (21 October 2016). Available at <https://vimeo.com/190150987> (last accessed 5 August 2020).
38. 'Entretien avec Eugène Green', p. 9.
39. Bonnefoy, *Rome, 1630*, p. 44.
40. Bonnefoy, *Rome, 1630*, p. 52 (emphasis in original).
41. Bonnefoy, *Rome, 1630*, p. 8.
42. Thuillier, *Georges de La Tour*, p. 240.
43. Badiou, *Cinema*, p. 7.

Part 4

Intermedial Creation

CHAPTER 11

What Does a Dance Filmmaker See?
Adam Roberts

As a filmmaker I have been constantly puzzled by what I see, what is represented, projected onto a wall or screen, in front of the eyes of others. What is that shadow play up there? What relationship can that image have to the things and people that I worked with in the odd ritual called 'the shoot' (such a worryingly lethal allusion)?

And those that submit to such ritual killing, what of them? Is what I do to them redeemed by a later act of resurrection? Am I an embalmer, a maker of mummies? Can I assure them of an afterlife in my alchemical edit suite?

I choose to work with dancers because that puts me into very direct contact with moving bodies. Their interest in the issue of ephemerality is also intriguing to me, because in contrast to actors who harbour the idea that they must inhabit the lives of others, dancers are very aware of the poignant tragedy of the passing out of existence of every moment. Dancers can choose to record their work, if only in their bodies (as 'muscle memory'), because they have to be able to recreate the dance whenever necessary. Video helps, but muscles are preferred. To a dancer, the wordless knowledge stored in the body is often all they need.[1]

The promise of my arriving with a film camera (not video!) is always exciting to dancers, because they are drawn to the preciousness of expensive and scarce film. But more than that, they acquire, when seen through the lens and made present in a layer of photochemical emulsion, a monumental quality that they know matches in some mysterious way their sense of themselves in the world. To be a dancer is to possess not only an eye that looks out, but also an eye that is accustomed to look in. They must know how what they do will seem to others. This technique or knowledge is developed by a process of daily practice in groups ('class') and by repetition. The goal is to acquire an exquisite awareness of bodily position and a superb kinaesthetic sense.

I will discuss films that, in very different ways, look at dances and dancers, and which have brought me to think about what dance film does and why I like it.

Hands (1995)

Hands is a short film I made with a small TV screen in mind.[2] I have written elsewhere about how it is structured, and about the practicalities of its making,[3] but I have not written about how it presents the body of the dancer, and what informed the image-making.

To describe the film briefly: the camera begins on a textured wall, but it soon tracks sideways to reveal a room beyond, whose walls are also heavily textured and designed as a 'negative' space, in the manner of a Rachel Whiteread casting. A fireplace, for example, extrudes into the space. A figure is discovered next, already in motion, eyes cast down, performing a choreography for hands. Music plays from the start, and sync sound mixes in to underline the physicality of the gestures.

Once the camera has found the hands of the figure, it stops and never moves again, except for the focusing, which pulls back and forth, generally to follow the moving hands. After a while, even the movement of the hands is stilled and the camera holds on while the music plays out.

Carved objects called *stelae* have, since Antiquity, marked places of burial or served as memorials. They can carry text in outline of a life, or feature a relief portrait of a face, or sometimes show a seated figure gesturing for the benefit of passers-by or those paying their respects.

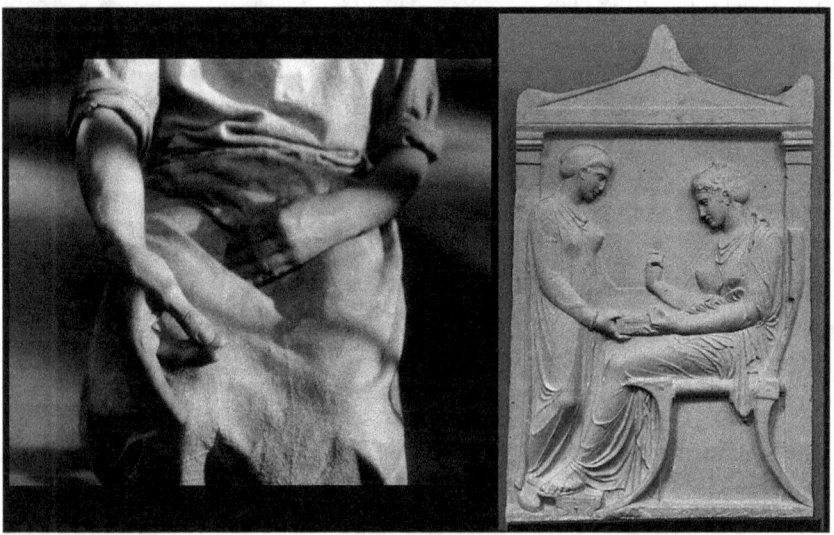

Figure 11.1 Still: *Hands* (Adam Roberts, 1995), image courtesy of BFI and BBC; and plaster cast in the Ashmolean Museum of the Hegeso stele 410–400 BC, photograph Adam Roberts 2017.

I have always relished the experience of my approach to such objects. As I move forward, the figure appears, in better and greater detail. I might now pause to attempt to decipher an inscription. My eyes may follow the text and scrutinise the frozen gesture. As I investigate, it is as if I am discovering a sequence, a series of clues, a choreography of sorts. This paradigm of approaching, of coming near, implicated in a sequence, applies to *Hands* as much as to *blue/yellow* (which I will discuss below). I would say that these points define how I regard film generally. Film is a chance to come into proximity, to make steps towards and through the object.

As I look at a *stele*, I am taken into the life of the departed by means of a series of gestures connected across time. These gestures, whether represented as bodies gesturing or invoked by means of narrative inscription, are intended to bring into my mind – to make present – the departed. The *stele* is not standing for that person but serves as an invocation, recreating that person in my mind.

I am struck that *stelae* are a special variety of sculpture, not the statues of the gallery. These are stone figures who have recovered their voices through the mediation of carvers who have put words back into the mouths of the departed, giving them identity and an ability to communicate. It is as if their gestures are subtitled. I fancy I can almost hear a voice. Statues are, by contrast, always mute, their bodies saying all they can ever say.

But perhaps *stelae* are, after all, mere statues, just as silent, their words cryptic or so specific to an individual who is so long gone that these objects are now, at best, decorative. In general, the gestures of statues defy a sense of past and future: they are adrift in a sea of time whose location is uncertain. And yet they inhabit space, brilliantly. Their gesture in this moment seems perfected for all time. Statues need no words or, as Michel Serres says, statues are 'perpetuated in a permanent and definitive stability [. . .] the statue remains in silence'.[4]

The sculpture therefore slips out of time. A filmmaker, used to looking at movement as merely a series of frozen moments, which, when played back in sequence, provide an illusion of time passing, cannot believe in permanent stability, nor in silence. Sound cannot be freeze-framed as can a film strip. It is easy for a filmmaker to be sceptical with regard to time, as she works always outside of time, poring over moments, oscillating on viewing devices between *now* and *then* as if there were no difference between past, present and future, nor even a natural order. Moments are equivalent, all alike.

Dance filmmaking is a procedure in which the bodies of dancers are like statues. It is as if they are a series of paused moments. Consequently, they are silent, without words. My relationship with those bodies is the pursuit of the curve or stretch or reach of the body; I am in search of its capacities or its potential, as if I were moving among an infinitude of related similar positions, as if potentially related stances lead away like reflections in an infinity mirror. The moment of this posture, of this exact pose, of this exact frame is related to an infinite number of frames, stretching ahead and behind. From this comes the viability of film. It is the implied presence of an infinity of alternatives that vivifies, or perhaps embalms or mummifies these figures, wrapping them in swathes of other selves. If they were to speak, as characters in a drama must, then the alternative versions would cease to exist, and the moment would become specific, dragged into becoming unique. The speaking figure ceases to be spatial.

I do not see anything remotely causal about the chain: object, camera, screen. Instead, I see a single instance or moment of implication of dancer and camera, which jam the door open onto a realm of infinite possibility, revealed as a glowing expression of that infinitude on screen. Yet fables about document, about socio-historical context, about realness, about alienation and about reproduction are persuasive and intrude upon the infinitude I detect.

The Band Wagon (1953)

I am transfixed by the scene in Vincente Minnelli's *The Band Wagon* (1953) in which Fred Astaire and Cyd Charisse stroll through Central Park at night. To start with, they walk gracefully enough, but they are not dancing: we know that because their steps are out of time with one another. Indeed, Astaire makes small corrections to keep it that way. Suddenly, Charisse makes a step that has nothing to do with the utility of movement, of walking in the park. It is a small gesture, but Astaire is prompted to join in with her rhythm. What follows is undeniably dance.

I am fascinated by this moment, this moving from not-dance to dance. How does Minnelli mark the moment? For one thing, we know (in plot terms) that these characters are professional dancers. Moreover, they have just walked through a group of dancers (the scene purports to be after-dark couples dancing in the open air) but, studiously, have taken no notice of them. Will they or won't they join in? I watch the scene again and again. The moment when the dancing starts is always elusive, but when the time comes, there is no mistaking it. Talk is at an end. Silence, the opposite of 'talk', reigns. No one talks while dancing; that is a hallmark of dance.

Choreographers talk of making dance 'on' the body; I wonder what Minnelli is making his films 'on'? And what lies outside the frame? Watching Astaire and Charisse dance, I reflect on my not asking what they might be thinking. And I watch them without expecting an outcome, as if they might well go on dancing for ever. I am held in this unfolding moment. There is no before, no after.

The perfection of the forms and the gestures of Minnelli's dance scene I can take for granted. In other words, they are as perfect as is a sculpture: we are not privy to the errors made in the crafting of this work; we see only the final form. This is a film that shows us only a perfect version of itself.

Indeed, the perfect shot was specified in contractual terms: Astaire's had a clause that demanded only head-to-toe framings, that there be few, if any, edits and no close-ups. The Astaire dolly was built to his specification, to move the camera to reduce cuts, and at a certain height off the ground, so dictating the angle of elevation of the camera view. No such thing as outtakes for a DVD release in this rarefied idiom! Any number of takes were guaranteed so that there might be no blemish.

I suspect that only a dancer would object to close-up framings. To a dancer, a close-up cuts up the body and dissociates parts. To a filmmaker, a close-up provides the potential for a reassembly of parts. She revels in cutting up bodies, bodies that are made armless, headless or truncated. The Venus de Milo, in this way of thinking, would not be lovelier if she had all her parts. Film is, after all, an art (after Susan Sontag) that focuses attention or improves the facility for attention.[5] Framing serves to validate, to emphasise the mass and substance of the bodies whose parts are shown in close shots. To resist is surely to deny an essential human instinct to take a closer look?

To film the human figure is, in a manner of speaking, to unveil repeatedly a body, in a complex ceremony, a celebration of the moment of discovery. Film assists seeing, rather than merely looking. I take 'looking' to be lazy, stupid, indolent and casual. I take 'seeing' as smart, knowing, detailed and considered.

Not Portraiture

I link filmmaking to still life, not to portraiture. Portraiture insists on narrative. It is deliberate and posed. It wants to underline the social. Still life dwells on the paradox of living things depicted post mortem – in fact it revels in the post-mortem scene, often showing off the artist's ability to present a dead thing, already in a state of decay, in as lifelike a way as possible. Still life arranges the sequence of our looking and makes space for our process of apprehension. That is, it shows us first the thing then the means of its representation. Still life is never insistent because it can only arrive quietly. Still life excludes the speech and life of people, suggesting instead the absence of a spectator. It is as if to say: here are some things that were flung there, without awareness or intention. Consequently, the content of a still-life scene takes a while to take in.

Film does not like to think it is a matter of accident. It thinks it is deliberate and deals in momentary poses. But that is not right, because film is like a witness who cannot possibly know what will happen next. The very moment in front of the lens is a perpetual surprise (even if I have seen the film before) and cannot be repeated. And looking back at a piece of film, it is clear that there is always much more than was anticipated, much more than could be listed or logged even by the best continuity/script person. Only by stopping the film and looking carefully can the full content of any shot be taken in.

Stelae are often presented in a frame or niche – the architectural term is *aedicula*. This is a structure that presents, composes, hopefully reverences. In my film *Hands*, the film frame, no less than the lap in which the hands rest or above which they move, serves as an *aedicula*. Dancers are like figures on a frieze; their postures are a sequence of recognisable moments. Dance in this way is like a memorial, caught in the stone of moving film instead of being framed by an inscription. For in my *stele* the figure itself makes a sequence of gestures – an ageless performance, endlessly repeatable, in an invocation of a life once lived: that is, not the life of the dancer, but the life of the stuff that we see, that of a filmed figure in motion, connecting back to the substance that cannot otherwise be brought into the presence of the audience.

THE GLADE

It is a cause of great surprise for dancers to see themselves on screen. I suspect they find the situation, the crude images, intrude on their sense of what they do. Their experience of dancing, they have told me, is to be nowhere in particular, other than in their bodies or in relation to other bodies. They are not natives of any particular place; they make their own space. They can dance anywhere. They extend, and by so doing, define a context. They know there is nothing beyond that.

Theirs is to be a dwelling place, whose ground is trodden down and readied. Some dancers clean the floor before and after they work: they domesticate their space. This is to create an enclosure with no need of an external world other than the anticipated audience. An external world, if it exists at all, is brought into being only by virtue of the dance gestures and the choreography.

Yet in my watching the dancer undertaking this readying of ground, a lesson about film emerges. If they are nowhere in particular, where are they? My decision has generally been to place the dancers metaphorically into a glade, into a clearing in the forest where light creates and defines what we see and know. Human actions make this place possible. Of course, outside of the light, outside the frame, there is nowhere. By the same token, the making of this space brings into being that which lies outside the confines of the light, and it is this realm outside the light that infuses the figures in the light with poignant delight. Their activities now matter, and the boundless potential of what they could be springs into being.

My conversations with dancers have often involved discussion and anxiety about how film represents the body, how it will capture the nuance and structure of a performance, how it might be edited so as to amplify the gestures, so as to arrest the attention of the audience. But this conversation fails to take notice of the fact that inside the light of this glade every gesture is drawn not only for itself, but in the context of an increasing multitude of alternatives not chosen. Beyond this clearing lies the infinitude of everything that they could have been.

I have tried to evoke glade or forest clearing explicitly in two films, *blue/yellow* and *Pieces of the Quiet Dance*.[6]

The presence of light makes visible, makes tangible. The trodden area is all that there is (the light divided from the darkness). Steps define and conjure. We understand the physics and laws of *that* place because of what we see done there. In the case of *blue/yellow*, the light was beyond, in the dancer's space.

Figure 11.2 Still: *blue/yellow* (Adam Roberts, 1995), image courtesy of Warner Classics.

Figure 11.3 Still: *Pieces of the Quiet Dance* (Adam Roberts, 2006), copyright Adam Roberts.

The choreography was specifically limited to a narrow orbit, and indeed ends with the dancer (Sylvie Guillem) pacing as if she were caged and planning an escape. Even so, we know quite well that there is nowhere to escape to!

In *Pieces of the Quiet Dance*, the dance is composed out of a set of permutations and patterned steps. The pacing is arduous, the measuring and counting requires hard work. Only at the end of sections can there be rest, and this is when I bring up the forest glade, superimposed in editing. It is a reward for the work done: the place has been made.

Blue/yellow was also inspired by the idea of passing by – of noticing and approaching a *stele* or statue, as if hoping to take it all in. The camera was mounted on an arm that permitted lateral movement and a quality of *hovering*. To begin with, what we look for (a figure glimpsed through a door) is far away. Approaching permits a clearer view and a chance to reflect. For me, it is the change from dim-and-distant to closer-and-brighter that provides the perpetual delight of any film. This is to say, it is to go from not knowing to knowing. It is the fruit of an encounter with figures who are busy marking out turf and insisting on their place in the light.

The dancers I have filmed show themselves as tillers of the soil, builders of walls, weavers of baskets, makers of pots. Those hands, arms and bodies make things and have practised skills. Unlike an actor, a dancer is never afraid of repose because repose is the fulfilment of work. A dancer has no possessions. Instead, their bodies are the storehouses of every possibility. They connect the sunlit simplicity of the glade with the infinite potential of what is outside the clearing. And, in this way, the work I do becomes a matter of kneading, squeezing, shaping and extruding. To me, the thing produced is a container for all other possibilities, even if it does not look much that way.

Notes

1. For a really very good exploration and qualification of this notion, see Susan Leigh Foster, *Choreographing Empathy: Kinesthesia in Performance* (London: Routledge, 2010).
2. www.adamroberts.info/adam-roberts-dance-films.html (last accessed 26 September 2020). The film was commissioned for BBC2 and the Arts Council, for a strand called *Dance for the Camera*.
3. Adam Roberts, 'Notes on filming dance', *The International Journal of Screendance*, 2 (2012), pp. 107–13.
4. Michel Serres, *Statues: The Second Book of Foundations*, trans. by Randolph Burks (London: Bloomsbury, 2015), p. 194.
5. Cf. Susan Sontag, 'The aesthetics of silence', in *Styles of Radical Will* (New York: Farrar, Straus and Giroux, 1967).
6. www.adamroberts.info/adam-roberts-dance-films.html (last accessed 28 March 2018).

CHAPTER 12

Performance, Moving Image, Installation: The Making of Body of War *and* Faith

Isabel Rocamora

I am a moving image artist working at the intersection of contemporary art and cinema. My practice evolves from the body. I first set out to counter the logic in the narrative traditions of theatre, literature and film with the hope of inviting, through the abstract shapes of physical movement, an aesthetic experience beyond shared linguistic and intellectual realms. My aim was to open up our sense of lived space, time and the world by reimagining the perceptual and representational forms that surround us. The first experiment, which I made as a student, was a film titled *Fragmented Transparencies* (1992), in which, immersed in hologram backdrops borrowed from Jim MacIntyre, two female figures perform corporeal calligraphies to Pierre Boulez's serial score *Pli selon Pli* (based on improvisations on three sonnets by Mallarmé). Using the body suspended in space, between 1994 and 2004 I focused, through collaborations (primarily with Sophy Griffiths and Camila Valenzuela) and as a solo artist, on live 'anti-gravity' performance works.[1] Unbound by gravitational pull, the suspended human seemed to me naked, disconnected from worldly appearance, simply being. My attention now shifted from the abstracted formalism of some previous works to the observation of human states of consciousness, exploring themes of personal identity, solitude, memory and transcendence.

These explorations often took shape in site-specific interventions, where, for several days, weeks or even months, I/we inhabited urban dwellings, disused churches, and industrial and cultural sites. What I found compelling, time and again, was the freedom with which I and my collaborators, imbued with a site's residual history, responded to its architectural forms. As Sophy and I negotiated the columns and arches of the cloister of Casa de Caridad in Barcelona (*Dialogue between Nun and Arch*, 1998), and Camila and I carved through the air surrounded by large-scale sculpture casts in London's Victoria and Albert Museum (*The Rapture of Matter*, 2003), it felt as if we were one with the place. I believe that what made these approximations to residual histories and interior states of being possible was the use of expanded temporality. I

Figure 12.1 Isabel Rocamora in 'Attunement', urban performance intervention. Part of *A Space in Place*, Colchester Arts Centre. Image by Muff Architecture-Art, 2001.

had been deeply moved by the openness evoked in the slowness and stillness of Japanese butoh 'dance', as taught by master Daisuke Yoshimoto. Departing from similar principles, I developed (with my collaborators) a series of expansion techniques for the aerial body. Slowing our movement right down to achieve a sense of continuum through space heightened at once the presence of the suspended human and the attentiveness of its spectator. Drawn by this magnetic relation and the introspection it afforded, I wanted to bring the performer optically closer to the viewer, so I began to integrate digital moving images into my performances. This took various forms: site-specific or on-stage projection, live-relay projection mapping onto the figure, and interactive video editing through the moving body.

As the ethical predicament of the world became a central concern in my practice, aesthetic treatment of that world necessarily shifted from the (often) allegorical registers of performance towards the social and historically recognisable scenarios made possible by the moving image. *Mise en scènes* were nonetheless to remain non-narrative, non-dramatic (in the classical sense), non-literal. When I look at the world through the lens, what opens up for me (before socio-cultural signification) is its phenomenal presence, its simply being there. It is this strictly non-visible perception – the experience of accumulated time that emanates from a site's so-called unconscious – that

I aimed to capture in *Residual* (2005). Installed site-specifically in St John's Crypt, Bristol, *Residual* used a diptych format and prolonged cross-dissolves to interweave still-life traces of the city's abandoned sites (water architectures, port infrastructures, underground tunnels) in a temporal remapping of their historical relations. Observing the bare environment devoid of subject and event helped me envisage an image where human beings, their actions and the settings in which these take place could be shown outside realistic representation (that which matches our external seeing of the world), inviting a more direct apprehension of social and ontological problems as they manifest before us.

Like most artists, my practice unfolds cumulatively, with one creative journey organically informing another. The question of whether, or indeed how, my moving images are intermedial makes me consider ways in which these images often draw from principles grounding my performance work, as well as the fertile transformations to and deviations from those principles that film and video installation invites in the production and exhibition process. Were I to list the core elements that shape my creative process – my palette, so to speak – these would be: human gesture, place, temporality and presence. In my recent films these elements attend to questions of selfhood and relational responsibility.

Body of War (2010) and *Faith* (2015) have a common aim: to destabilise ideas of social unchangeability by interrogating the complex bond people hold to history in legacies of trauma.[2] Reading *War and Cinema* (1989), where Paul Virilio draws some fascinating connections between the technologies of war and film (such as the development of technicolour to document aerial strikes during World War II), I could not resist contemplating the missing subject. While wars are largely fought at a distance, they are still planned, executed and suffered by humans. From this perspective, for me, the face-to-face encounter remains the iconic bellic event. Focused on the most accepted form of organised violence, the Army, *Body of War* examines, on a single screen, the process of the militarisation of the human, asking how a person can be convinced to take another's life.

I return to the question of human transgression with *Faith*, yet this time in a social context. I first visited Israel and the Occupied Palestinian Territories in 2012 for the exhibition of *Body of War* at the Herzliya Museum of Contemporary Art in a show titled 'Delimitations'. As I stood in Jerusalem's Old City and closed my eyes, I became immersed in a cacophony of sounds that, at varying distances and volumes, interweaved the prayers of the distinct communities into an auditory unity. On reopening my eyes, I was struck by the walls, checkpoints and flags that, in a spirit of surveillance, today separate the Jewish quarter from the Christian, Christian Armenian and Muslim areas.

Prompted by the irony between the manifold manifestations of belief and the palpable tension reigning in the air, I returned to Jerusalem in 2015 to produce *Faith*. Across three screens, *Faith* simultaneously observes the morning worship of an Orthodox Jew, a Greek Orthodox Christian and a Sunni Muslim. My aim is not only to make evident resonances and distinctions between the three Abrahamic traditions, but to bring into relief the fundamental difference grounding the equal value of individual lives.

I earlier evoked the potential of the photographic image to capture the world as we see it. The question I face when transposing experiences and ideas to the screen in forms that bypass the tellings of realistic narrative and documentary is: how to construct the action while allowing place and subject to present themselves autonomously? In other words, how to conceive of *mise en scène* and performance while maintaining a fundamental connection with the subjects and the places they inhabit? I first address these questions in *Body of War* and *Faith* by casting non-actors from military, ex-military and religious communities: Nick Maison, Robert Gajewski, James Hobson and Krzysztof Szczenpankski (today competing professionals of the Israeli military hand-to-hand combat form Krav Magà), on the one hand, and Michael Cohen (pertaining to the Breslav tradition), Issa Taljieh (Father at the Church of Nativity in Bethlehem and one of the only Palestinian priests in the Greek Orthodox order) and Feras Kazaz (Quran reader at Al Aqsa Mosque), on the other hand. In the case of *Body of War*, I also layer live action with voice testimonies from serving and retired soldiers: Nigel Ilsley (British Army, recently returned from Iraq) and Misha Solorov (Serbian conscription soldier who fought in the Bosnia conflict). I then place live-action subjects in locations historically resonant with the action (Normandy and the Judean Desert).[3] While these choices help to ground the films' events in the shared world, through preserving a certain distance between subject, action and site, my intention is to create spaces where ethical dilemmas can present themselves without the need for situational dialogue or authorial commentary. It is, for me, in human gesture that approximations and clashes between the social and the personal are made most immediately evident.

I think of human gesture on two levels: the private and the public. In the first instance, gesture is the deepest expression of the self, as it shows itself: an expression that, while emerging from the most intimate realm, is also physical because it takes place in space. Unlike forms of movement or dance that perform willing incursions into our shared environment by drawing abstract or expressionist shapes that ultimately create a self-referential language (think of Merce Cunningham or Pina Bausch), the personal gestures I am referring to serve to expose our most hidden individuality without announcing itself to the world. Then there is functional gesture, the bold enactment of collective

Figure 12.2 Film still of *Body of War* (Isabel Rocamora, 2010). Courtesy of the artist and Galeria Senda.

codes, which includes everyday sign language, ritual practices and organised combat. In many of Jeff Wall's photographs (such as *Milk*, 1984, and *Knife Throw*, 2008) the human stands out from its context by adopting a stillness that invites us to view it externally, as a sign. Conversely, in the performance works of Socìetas Raffaello Sanzio (I am thinking of *Oresteia*, 1995, and *Tragedia Endogonidia*, 2002–4) bodies deconfigure through expressions or excretions of primordiality that transgress social norm in disturbing, because illegible, ways. While Wall's gesture figures through mimicry, that of the Socìetas unfigures by errancy. I, on the other hand, observe the sign (collective gesture) in order to expose the human (personal gesture), aiming to contrast performative action with ontological presence. In this sense, what drives *Body of War* and *Faith* is the desire to facilitate instances where, in a near state of solitude, the subject transcends the social structures it gesturally upholds (through combat and prayer) in a phenomenal self-showing that revises the social relation by foregrounding the self-definition and accountability of the individual.

In *Body of War* four soldiers repeatedly perform one sequence of hand-to-hand combat. Their forceful movement quietens as the fight is dissected into slower and slower iterations, disclosing, from the brutal act of bellic confrontation, auratic instances of human intimacy. Reversing training methodology, which usually starts with slow rehearsals and builds to accelerated trials, the main sequence expands the furious ninety-second opening action performed by Nick and Robert into a serene exchange that, lasting seven minutes, is now delivered in actual *ralenti* by Krzysztof and James. My initial focus was on capturing the impulse and impact of the act of violence as it becomes visible in the oscillating power relation between the two men, as each aims to debilitate his opponent with kicks and punches, bayonet slashes and rifle strikes. When, during rehearsals, we slowed down the action in order to map its trajectory, I was astonished to find that underneath the brutal continuum of attacks and deflections lay gestures that, perceived in isolation, offered unexpected openings. Momentarily transfiguring into iconographies of care, a military waist lock became an embrace; a bite to the jugular an amorous kiss; a lowering restraint a *pietà*. Such images reminded me of Emmanuel Levinas's philosophy of the voluptuous, which, in *Time and the Other* (1947) and *Totality and Infinity* (1969), posits human touch as the ultimate confirmation of the unknowability of the Other, that at once prevents my acting upon them – taming them or taking their life – and reveals my aloneness. This is, I believe, what Levinas means when he evocatively states that 'the caress does not know what it seeks'.[4] From this perspective, the intimate gestures (the hug, the hold, the kiss) of the soldiers mid-combat invite an acknowledgement of the Other's singular humanity that reverts each to his solitude. In these moments, the legibility of the socialised gesture dissolves, giving way to a presence that I perceive as fundamental.

While recognising the validity of social discourses in modern and cultural critiques of the subject, I have come to understand the notion of fundamental presence in affinity with Martin Heidegger's definition of human being. What I find compelling in *Being and Time* (1927) and *Introduction to Metaphysics* (1935) is their distillation of the human down to its (undetermined) simply being there in the world, or indeed absence from it. A phenomenon is, in Heidegger's words, that which shows itself in and for itself, and, in the case of the human subject, this radiant self-showing serves to assert its humanity before it becomes imbricated in social, political, ritualistic or indeed performative practices. I earlier stated that by making evident the ritualistic nature of religious and combat re-enactments, *Body of War* aims to offset the action sufficiently from its performer so that the subject may become independently perceptible. It is about creating intervals where that subject discards its mimetic shield to show itself simply there, in advance of its narrative. In *Faith*, the performative nature of ritual is complicated by the figures' states of contemplation that, while providing a productive sense of commonality (even communion), for me also projects the presence of those figures out of the immanent plane into the spiritual (transcendental) one. For this reason, the final moments of the film aim to bring the subjects back to the shared world, where ethical change is possible.

Following an extended sequence of recitations, confessions and prostrations, gestured by the folding and raising of arms, the joining and offering of palms and the contracting of bodies, Issa, Feras and Michael conclude their practices. In their own time, each shifts their focus outward, standing firmly side by side, eye to eye with the lens, doing nothing, simply being, in a sudden auditory emptiness punctuated only by the wind and the chirping of distant birds. The living stillness of this moment invites a release that is once more an opening. Heidegger describes the opening of the human as a horizontal projection of the self, as it understands itself (that it exists) in perspective and manifests its existing to the world – an event he describes as 'standing presence'.[5] There is, for me, something of this in the standing figures of Michael, Issa and Feras, who, having been immersed in their acts of prayer for twenty sustained minutes, now stand before us, gazing directly at us. If an essential characteristic of the cinematographic is its ability to draw our attention to expression that is near imperceptible, its selective framing, play with distances (optics and focal lengths), spatial movement and durational impact can also make us feel that we are in the company of the onscreen subject. From this perspective, the priority of *Faith* was to present the value of individual humanity by appealing to the viewer's being-with the subject on screen in dual recognition of their self-defining difference. My task was to translate this intention into self-evident sound images.

The creative process was guided by two priorities: firstly, that each subject should be granted their own visual frame and uninterrupted time in which to inhabit it; secondly, that, forming a triptych, the projection screens should be installed, side by side, offset from the wall and each other, creating a continuum of world (the Judean desert) wherein subjects remain distinct, and in relation to which the viewer may position herself spatially, on a one-to-one-scale with the onscreen subject. Simultaneous action meant the overlap of vociferous prayer. One way to orchestrate sound was to play with optical distance, moving now closer to, now further away from each subject over time while cautiously echoing the frontality that characterises the (often triptych) religious icon in Christian pictorial traditions – a means of intermedially acknowledging my own cultural gaze. For this, director of photography Laurent Machuel built a counter-weight system that, suspending the camera off a tracking platform, afforded intimacy and perspective on the action, at once achieving a controlled handheld aesthetic.

In live performance, we, as spectators, can become witnesses by being-in-the-presence of the performer, who, either on stage or environmentally, shares our spatio-temporal existing. While this is not the case in filmic experience, I believe that moving images can, perhaps especially in the installation context, invite their own forms of attestation. The role of the witness is to provide certitude that an event has taken place. For me, this also implies a responsibility to reflect not only on what I have seen, but on how it affects me

Figure 12.3 Exhibition view of *Faith* (Isabel Rocamora, 2015) as installed for *Troubled Histories, Ecstatic Solitudes* at the Koffler Gallery, Toronto, 2015. Still courtesy of the artist and Galeria Senda.

and thereafter informs my relation to the world. I have stated that my *mise en scènes* attempt to steer away from pedagogical commentary by creating spaces where the subject asserts itself in a so-called naked state – recall the detained image of the two embraced men on the landing strip in *Body of War*. I aim to take this further in *Faith* by inviting an actual face-to-face between the three standing figures and the standing viewer. The way that the confident gazes of Michael, Issa and Feras cross offscreen, bouncing, via the intermediary of the viewer, from one subject to the other, elicits multiple encounters that appeal to that viewer as witness – in what Levinas might call a 'moral summons'.[6] This dynamic between existential assertion and ethical recognition is made uniquely possible in the relation between the spatialised projections and the mobile seeing characteristic of gallery exhibition.

These reflections bring me to appreciate further how, in my moving images, performance, installation and the cinematic dialogue collide and interweave. Such intermedial processes pose questions of form, structure and register that are helpful for rethinking audio-visual testimony and its witnessing. The driving question for me remains how a work might, in its encounter with the viewer, invite resistance to under-challenged forms of violence and injustice, in the hope of reimagining better ways of living together.

Notes

1. In a first instance under *Momentary Fusion* (1994–2000), a performance company for which I was co-artistic director with Sophy Griffiths, and which we co-choreographed and I stage-directed; in a second instance as independent artist, director and choreographer (2000–4).
2. *Body of War* premiered at Galería Senda, Barcelona, on 10 May 2011; *Faith* premiered at the Koffler Gallery, Toronto, on 17 September 2015.
3. I refer to the following: in *Body of War*, the World War II bunker-strewn beaches of Néville-sur-Mer; in *Faith*, the Qum'ran Valley (where the Jewish Dead Sea scrolls were first discovered in 1946), Wadi Qelt (place of the early Christian retreat caves, then monasteries) and Nebi Musa (pilgrimage site where Muslims believe Prophet Moses is buried).
4. Emmanuel Levinas, *Time and the Other* (Pennsylvania: Duquesne University Press, 2008), p. 89.
5. Martin Heidegger, *Introduction to Metaphysics* (New Haven, CT: Yale University Press, 1956), p. 61.
6. Emmanuel Levinas, *Totality and Infinity* (Pennsylvania: Duquesne University Press, 2011), p. 196.

CHAPTER 13

Muybridge's Disobedient Horses: Non-stop Stop-motion
Anna Vasof

Sometimes I wonder how we would understand cinematic illusion today if we could change a parameter in one of Eadweard Muybridge's (1830–1904) pre-cinematic experiments. Muybridge was a pioneer in photographic studies of motion and in motion-picture projection. He used multiple photo cameras, capturing the movement of a galloping horse in sixteen successive positions, and became one of the leading figures of photo-realistic sequences of motion stills. Later, he animated these images by using self-invented pre-cinematic devices. His experiment is the example most commonly used to demonstrate how the illusion of cinematic movement is underpinned by still images.

But what if Muybridge, instead of using one horse captured in sixteen stills, had used sixteen different horses captured in sixteen stills? Could he also have turned those stills into an animated sequence? I do not know the answer because I did not carry out this particular experiment, but I conducted several others in order to find out what creates continuity in a sequence. My experiments took me to alternative ways of creating moving images that differ from those devised by Muybridge. Taking inspiration from, but also reframing, Muybridge, my ongoing *Non-stop Stop-motion* project investigates where we can find the essence of cinematic illusion when we look into everyday life, and what happens when we use everyday situations, objects, spaces and actions as cinematographic mechanisms. The object, space or action that forms the basis of the cinematic illusion and the illusion itself often appear in my videos simultaneously. In this way, the illusions and the mechanisms used to produce them enter into a dialogue, but they can also contradict one another. Containing irony and metaphor, *Non-stop Stop-motion* is a self-referencing method of telling stories about personal and social conflict. At the crossroads between video, performance and photography, my creative approach challenges traditional artistic axioms by reframing cinema's relationship with other media, as well as with everyday life.

Invisible Stop-motion

I started working and experimenting with moving images in 2004. I always use digital technology because it is much more accessible. I have never had any contact with analogue film projectors. I do not have the intermittent sound of a filmstrip passing in front of a light source in my ears. Everything for me has always happened inside closed devices that capture images with sensors and transform them into digits, which are then transformed again through processors into moving images made out of pixels. This process can teach me a lot about electronics, but does not really help me to understand fundamentally how we perceive movement in a sequence of frames. So, for many years, I believed that if I just moved a sequence of frames quickly in front of my eyes, I would be able to see moving image illusions. However, in 2011, when I actually first took a filmstrip and moved it quickly in front of my eyes, I realised that I was not able to see anything. This was a shocking moment. How was it possible that I had worked for so long with moving images and could not understand something so basic? I then observed an analogue projector to understand how this device is able to move a filmstrip to create the illusion. I saw some gears that were very quickly interrupting the continuity of the filmstrip movement and realised that the whole principle was based on these interruptions. A sequence should move intermittently and not continuously. The stills should be connected through their figurative continuity in the sequence and at the same time be projected in front of our eyes separately. However, these millions of interruptions are invisible, especially when the sequences are captured or displayed with digital devices. To understand better, I needed to think about stop-motion films, such as those by Jan Švankmajer, Yuri Norstein or the Brothers Quay, where the interruptions are somehow visible. I gathered that every video and film is a kind of an invisible stop-motion film and every moving image illusion contains a kind of non-stop stop-motion effect.

Cinematographic Mechanisms

I then started wondering whether some everyday settings, situations and movements in my surroundings could also interrupt continuous movements, function as cinematographic mechanisms and create moving image illusions. I started to make lists of various possibilities that included, for example, walking down the stairs, breaking or exploding something intermittently, opening and closing a door, and using a banknote counter or a domino effect. I selected and tried out some of these possibilities, documenting them in the form of short films, which I call *Non-stop Stop-motion* films.

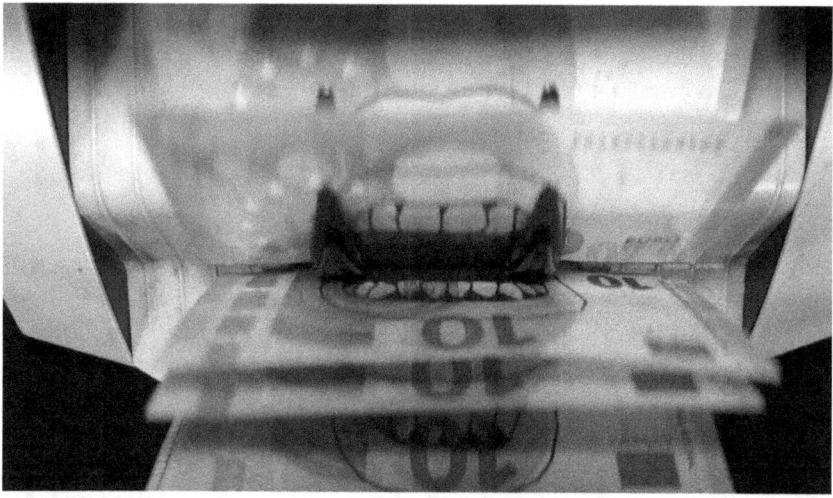

Figure 13.1 Still from the film *Banknotes* (Anna Vasof, 2018).

In Chapter 2 of the *Non-stop Stop-motion* series, entitled *Banknotes,* a banknote counter counts twenty banknotes in a loop.[1] A sequence of an opening and closing mouth is drawn on the banknotes. When the counting takes place, we see the banknotes falling one after the other and, at the same time, the illusion of an aggressive mouth opens and closes. The banknotes are very strong images and their presence puts the animated movement into second place. The illusion, however, appears almost as if it were natural and, in fact, several viewers asked me if the mouth was already somehow on the notes and whether I had performed some kind of magic to reveal this information.

It was very easy to transform the banknote counter into a cinematographic device because its mechanics are very similar to that of a film projector. However, in most of my experiments, the objects, the spaces or the actions need to be modified or hacked in order to be able to display moving image illusions. For example, in my film *Domino* (2014), which was the first work that could be described as a *Non-stop Stop-motion* film, I used a domino fall as a cinematographic mechanism. I had to plan and build a very precise domino path, which would also allow a camera to follow the action. I observed that the average rate of a domino fall is twenty-eight bricks per second, which is very close to the typical video frame rate (25 frames per second). In this film, domino bricks are replaced by framed pictures, which show a corridor in different moments. When the first picture falls, the second is revealed, when the second falls, the third is revealed and so on, until all the framed pictures have fallen and the illusion of movement down the corridor ends. The sound of the fall supports the illusion and is interpreted as human steps along the corridor. In *Domino*, the viewer can first watch the process of setting up the mechanism that produces the film and the filming action, then witness the fall as the video camera records the action, which then gives the impression of someone running down a corridor.

HYPERFRAMES

When I determine the object, action or space that might function as a cinematographic mechanism, I usually also need to define the different stages of movement that will be displayed. Sometimes, as with the banknotes in the banknote counter, the subject is nearly inseparable from the device. Sometimes the subject is related only to its own physical properties, as, for example, anything that can fall as a domino brick. These objects have the same role as the frames in a filmstrip: they are the units of illusion. However, if I use the word 'frames' to describe these units, I then start to confuse them with the frames that the camera actually records when documenting the process. On the other hand, the idea of the movement described in a sequence is much older than the invention of the camera. The first known cinematic sequence is over 5,000 years old. A ceramic bowl, found in Iran, was decorated with a series of images portraying a goat jumping towards a tree and eating its leaves. I need a word to describe how these units of images or objects form a new sequence of movement through their figurative continuity and also have the same role as a frame in a sequence. These units can also be understood to exist separately from known cinematic devices such as cameras or projectors. I decided to use the term 'hyperframe' in order to underline this wider interpretation. I was thinking of using the word 'still', but this word relates to a frozen extraction of a movement. It is a really good word to describe each of the images that Muybridge captured. He froze single phases of the movement. I do exactly the opposite: I compose forms that have not previously existed.

In my film *Walking in Circles* (2005), different people perform the eight stills of Muybridge's walking man: that is, a series of eight photos made in 1887 showing the phases of two steps. Thirty-two volunteers are separated into groups of eight and stand freeze-framed in a circle, each performing a different moment of Muybridge's walking sequence. In the centre of the circle, a mechanism with a camera rotates by increments and films the performers. Even though all thirty-two participants have very different body shapes and do not move at all, when the machine reaches a specific speed they appear to be one figure walking in circles. Theoretically, if every person on the planet performed this Muybridge sequence, we could unify them through this eight-still sequence and create the contemporary walking human portrait.

Narrative

In *Non-stop Stop-motion* films, the content of the story is usually affected by the materiality of the hyperframes. As regards content, my film *Machine* (2015) explores how a machine can function only through its own destruction. In order to achieve this effect, ceramic plates with gears painted on them were used as hyperframes. They were arranged in a stack and were sequentially smashed with a hammer and filmed with a camera from above. When the smashing speed reached a certain velocity, the gears 'moved' and the machine 'functioned'. Only five plates were used, but the gears rotated smoothly. This is possible because every cog rotates only one tooth, but the eye sees the gears completing an entire round. This optical illusion is possible only with symmetrical cogs.

Fluttering (2016) is further example of a *Non-stop Stop-motion* film, this time inspired by another pioneer of the moving image, Étienne-Jules Marey (1830–1904). Marey invented a photographic device that could record several phases of movement in one photo. Using these pictures, he studied horses, birds, dogs, sheep and several other animal movements, such as in his 1880 single-photo capture which shows several flying phases of a bird. In my film, the hyperframes are 'wings', each made of two feathers, hanging from strings one above the other. The camera was mounted on my left hand and recorded the sequence in an upward motion, stopping each time when the right hand cut the wings with scissors. When this action reaches a certain speed, the

Figure 13.2 Still from the film *Machine* (Anna Vasof, 2015).

viewer can simultaneously watch both the cutting of the wings and the wings flying.

In these two examples, the action that causes the illusion and the illusion itself not only enter into a dialogue, but also contradict each other by telling stories containing metaphors for social conflicts. Initially, the cinematographic mechanisms, which in this case are performative actions, are in contrast with the illusions that they display. The medium, the cinematographic mechanism and the hyperframes not only remain visible, but also take on the role of protagonists.

DOCUMENTATION

After building the cinematographic mechanism and creating the hyperframe sequence, I start activating the illusion and documenting the illusion with a video camera. There are three reasons behind my approach: firstly, it helps to show the perspective of the viewer. For example, in the first part of my film *Traveling*, we see a window of a moving train reflecting the face of a traveller, and in the second part, we see no train and everything takes place under an umbrella. However, it is very difficult to understand from which location the first part of the film was observed. If we see the camera which was filming the illusion, then the viewer's point of view is clear.

Secondly, I like to document the display of cinematic illusions because they become much more visible due to the fact that the cameras film intermittently. This is easy to understand when observing a zoetrope[2] with our own eyes or through a filming camera's viewfinder. When we observe this interrupted movement through the camera's viewfinder, the cinematic illusion becomes clear, because the camera also records non-continuously: for example, it records twenty-five frames per second.

Finally, and most importantly, the work shows clearly how the cinematic illusion has been produced. The process not only has a didactic role, as is usual in the making of films, but new meaning is created when the subject comes either into direct dialogue or into conflict with the narrative of the illusion.

NON-LINEAR PROCESS

The activation of the illusion can be successful at first attempt or it might require repetition and corrections to all previous steps. This makes a *Non-stop Stop-motion* film production a non-linear process with a lot of toings and froings. Sometimes, during editing, I realise that the illusion would work better if I changed hyperframes or even if I redefined the whole mechanism.

When the mechanism takes the form of an action, I need also to train myself to perform it: for example, to become faster or smoother in my movements. The process is reminiscent of the preparation required for a traditional performance piece. However, in this case, I do not use my body to perform an expression; I activate an illusion, I become a cinematographic mechanism. I try to keep the film editing to a minimum in order for the *Non-stop Stop-motion* animations to appear as natural as possible. However, sometimes I manipulate the speed of the video.

THE SPEED OF THE ILLUSION

My films *Domino, Self-Portrait* (2016), *Time Travel, Ping Pong with Myself, Humanoid, Before Writing, Moving Nuts* (all 2017) and *Banknotes* (2018) use objects or situations as cinematographic mechanisms that can display live illusions visible to the human eye. All these mechanisms have the advantage that they can create camera-less films and also be presented as installations or live performances. Sometimes there are mechanisms where the speed does not correspond to that of a visible cinematic illusion. For example, the action of smashing something sequentially is a mechanism that is based on human movement. These actions unfold at a slower rate than the corresponding speed of an illusion.

In order to be able to use slower movements as cinematographic mechanisms, I decided to determine the minimum number of frames per second that the human eye requires in order for the mind to create the illusion of continuous movement in the sequence. I call it 'illusional speed'. A *Non-stop Stop-motion* action carried out by a human body will almost always be slower than the illusional speed. My films *Machine, Walking in Circles, Travel to the Window* (2015), *Dancing with You* (2017), *Escaping* (2016), *Traveling* (2016), *Fluttering* and *Walking under my Foot* (2016) could reveal an illusion only when the speed was digitally enhanced after filming. This interference was something that was destroying the purity of the main idea. Through my attempts to figure out the illusional speed, I found out that each film actually had a different illusional speed. In order to watch the illusion in the film *Machine*, seventeen hyperframes per second were required. For the film *Walking in Circles* only eight hyperframes per second were needed. This difference in speed happens because the walking is a lot more obvious and expected than the rotation of a cog. That is why I believe that when comparing expected movements with unexpected movements, less illusional speed is required for the expected ones. In other words, the illusional speed depends on the topic of the narrative. The minimum speed required to observe an illusion could also be a completely subjective measurement, related to each individual person's perception. As the LINCS (Literacy Information and Communication System) theory claims, the speed of word recognition is related to how familiar people are with the word's shape. Twenty-five frames per second is a standard minimum that cameras record or projectors project. It is a kind of safe speed by which most moving illusions can be displayed. However, the interruptions of the continuous movement of the sequence remain invisible, and as a result, the principle itself is unseen.

Perhaps, in the future, subjective projectors might exist. These machines would possibly be able to recognise known or unknown illusions for each viewer and display different frame rates according to individual recognition of different topics. The subjective projectors would allow everyone to see the little interruptions of the sequence and the illusion would not be disturbed. This apparatus would keep the basic principle of the moving image illusions always visible.

Something else I observed, when I was speeding up the videos in order to see the illusions, was that I was able to see two different speeds simultaneously. I could see the illusion in a natural speed and the action that it is activating in fast motion. This reminded me of Tim Macmillan's 'time-slice', better known as 'bullet time' from the film *The Matrix* (Lana and Lilly Wachowski, 1999), where the camera appears to move around the actors in a natural speed and the actor in slow motion. This effect detaches the time and space of a camera (or viewer) from that of its visible subject. In *Non-stop Stop-motion* films the two visible speeds detach the cinematic illusion from the cinematographic mechanism that displays it. This detachment invites the viewer to choose what to see: the cinematographic mechanism in the form of the real spaces, objects and movements, or the illusions that they display. It works like the famous rabbit–duck illusion, in which some see a rabbit and others see a duck. After some time, most people are able to see both images simultaneously.

THE MEDIUM

Even if most of my research questions refer to cinematic illusions, I often exhibit self-constructed objects, give public performances and document processes, and a lot of my results are similar to those of short animations. It becomes very difficult to define a medium when moving between several artistic practices and especially when my projects are not presented in cinemas as films. Combining video, performance and a fine art approach, my work is closer to expanded cinema, which allows greater experimentation and a porosity between artistic practices. By turning everyday movements, spaces and objects into cinematographic devices and by crossing over into other artistic domains, I want to make the processes behind the moving image video visible and reveal their workings. In comparison with all other known cinematic devices (analogue or digital), such as cameras, projectors, flipbooks and so on, the medium of video is able to display only very limited amounts of moving-image illusions. This limitation becomes in itself a method that helps the discovery of new narratives. Even if the principle behind the illusion has existed since chronophotography and is taken for granted, each of my films produces its own unique illusion. Unlike in the illusory spectacles of a magician, the secret behind the magic trick in *Non-stop Stop-motion* films is revealed, thereby making the cinematic illusions even more magical.

Notes

1. For a selection of my films see <http://www.filmandarts-network.hss.ed.ac.uk/podcast/filmclips/> (last accessed 6 August 2020).
2. A zoetrope is a simple analogue device that, even if it moves continuously, allows interrupted visibility through its holes, thereby creating cinematic illusion.

CHAPTER 14

A Dialogue with Claude Cahun: Between Writing, Photography and Film in Magic Mirror *and* Confessions to the Mirror

Sarah Pucill

This text will examine the dialogue that my films *Magic Mirror* (2013) and *Confessions to the Mirror* (2016) create between the photographs and writing of Claude Cahun and my own practice as a filmmaker. What unites my 16 mm work from the past three decades is a concern – born out of experimental film practices – for the primacy of the image, and for it to speak without the guidance of text. My filmmaking began in 1989 with projecting images on to objects, creating Surrealist juxtapositions through in-camera photomontage in the films *You Be Mother* (1990) and *Milk and Glass* (1993). This language of superimposition evolved in later work in different forms, which included split frames in mirrors, performing with photographs, animation mixed with live action, and film projection mixed with live action. The films have been mostly shot in an intimate space, and many of these works incorporate a *mise en abyme* reflexivity. Part of the intimate language arises from the fact that the camera and artwork are not separated – both are handled by the filmmaker. A particular quality of my cinematic language is the creation of ambiguity in what the viewer sees on screen, where spatial orientation is rendered uncertain through the indeterminacy between photograph, performance and film projection. Visual disturbance between what is body and what is reflection or paper is explored with an unpredictability of what physically moves. Independently moving objects alternate with movements of the body, and still and moving image projection intermix with live action. In *Stages of Mourning* (2004), I filmed myself performing to camera with large and small photographs, a 16 mm film projection on a wall, and seated at a desk with an image of my late partner, Sandra Lahire (1950–2001), displayed on a computer screen. I then restage earlier photographs of myself with my absent lover, juxtaposed with the originals of myself when she was alive. My next film, *Taking My Skin* (2006), explores the mirroring and inhabitation of a close female other, as I film my mother, who at the same time films me. A spoken dialogue between us narrates the experience of both filming and being filmed, as well as my mother's pregnancy with me and my bereavement of my lover. The question of how to locate self or other, as image or as voice, and of which experiences are separate and connected, is enmeshed with a desire for closeness and separation between a mother and daughter who physically hold each other's image in a mirror as they speak. Tropes of self-splitting in visual reflections and projections, and the creation of unclear boundaries between subjects and between a body and its representation, anticipate the thematic concerns and filmic language in my two films inspired by the French Surrealist artist Claude Cahun (1894–1954). It is the disturbance caused by the bleeding of a feminist and queer subjectivity in Cahun's photographs that drew me to her work and has held me captive since. Her gaze in frozen black and white was an invitation or call to arms to join in some way the imaginative world and struggle she shared with her partner, Marcel Moore (1892–1972).

Cahun made small black and white self-portrait photographs, in which she masquerades as fictional and actual others, including her father, her uncle, Bluebeard's wife, a Buddha and an angel. These photographs, which have been a long-standing influence on my filmmaking, were made in collaboration with Moore. Cahun was a member of the Surrealist group, and whilst she is best known for her photographic work, she was also a writer of essays and creative texts and performed in avant-garde theatre.[1] The indeterminancy of her self-portraits that are simultaneously portraits of others is commonly discussed in relation to their destabilisation of subjectivity; however, much less discussed is the transgression of the boundaries between photographic genres in her work. For example, the photographs entitled *auto-portraits* lie between portrait and self-portrait, as they are also masquerades of someone else. Other photographs, her miniature still lives or *objets trouvés*, suggest a surrogate self, stretching the categories between self-portrait and still life. And in many of her photographs, Cahun appears too far in the distance of a landscape for the image to be read ordinarily as a self-portrait.

Described as a 'Surrealist anti-autobiography',[2] Cahun's major Surrealist text, *Aveux non avenus* (1930), which I explore in *Magic Mirror*, brings together different types of text, such as personal letters, diary writing and poems, which are presented alongside a series of ten photogravures drawn by Moore. *Aveux non avenus* is a creative examination of a self that is fictional and portable, dissected and split. This division between voice and image, and the concomitant genres of autobiography and self-portraiture as assumed offerings of truth, lies at the heart of the book. *Aveux non avenus* translates as 'Confessions Unmade': a gesture to tell a truth that is withheld. The writing offers a way to think the self not as autonomous, self-knowing or unchanging, but as fluid, interconnecting, intersubjective and metamorphosing. My films respond to Cahun's critique of the aspiration for and pretence of a true expression of oneself in self-portraiture or autobiography by creating a dialogue that reaches for collaborative authorship in the plural (including Marcel Moore and others[3]) across different time frames and media.

Both *Magic Mirror* and *Confessions to the Mirror* re-enact photographs by Cahun in the form of *tableaux vivants*. Overlaying these reinterpreted tableaux are voices reading two of Cahun's major texts: *Aveux non avenus* in *Magic Mirror* and *Confidences au miroir* (1945–52) in *Confessions to the Mirror*. Shot on 16 mm in an interior domestic space, the films employ an experimental film language that in parts shows the location of filming and the performance of making up faces. The props and set are handmade or improvised to mimic the artwork in the photographs. The interpretation of the photographs as living tableaux creates a relationship between the photographic and written œuvres of Cahun. I selected most of the photographs because of their connection to Cahun's writing and, in other instances, because of their relationship to my previous films. The text was selected because of its connection with Cahun's photographs or my films, and to highlight what I felt was of most interest or importance in the respective manuscripts written by Cahun. My own body of work and that of Cahun are connected by shared tropes and themes that include: Surrealist-inspired language of juxtaposed contradiction; split and multiple female figures through projections and reflective surfaces; and intersubjectivity between a lesbian collaborative couple.

The films interweave multiple representations of a metamorphosing self, inspired by Cahun's photographs. Each photograph is a new masquerade, and sometimes two performers inhabit the same costume in the photograph. Different voices read lines from Cahun's text translated into English, sometimes together, sometimes alternately and sometimes alone. Whilst there is fluidity between the voices and faces, a separation is enunciated in the non-synchronisation of voice that always speaks over the image. The disconnect between one's outer image and what is felt underneath the image surface is a recurring theme in Cahun's œuvre, as well as in my own. It is highlighted in both *Magic Mirror* and *Confessions to the Mirror* through the text and images selected and through the absence of synched voice. Through Cahun's text and photographs, my films interrogate the relentless emphasis on a woman's image in Western culture. I also draw inspiration from the idea of femininity as a masquerading image, theorised by Cahun's contemporary, the psychoanalyst and early translator of Freud, Joan Riviere, who states:

> Womanliness therefore could be assumed and worn as a mask, both to hide the possession of masculinity and to avert the reprisals expected if she was found to possess it – much as a thief will turn out his pockets and ask to be searched to prove that he has not the stolen goods.[4]

Many of Cahun's most striking and well-known images show her wearing a mask of make-up, and in others an actual mask covers the eyes. For Cahun, this mask is not literal, the skin being the most effective of masks. She writes 'the carnal mask and the verbal mask are worn in all seasons', and explains that she prefers the non-commercial strategies of masking (through flesh and word).[5] In *Magic Mirror* a quotation from Cahun is combined with a surrogate Cahun putting on a mask from an image where many masks hang off a large black cloak that covers her body. In this moment that reimagines the photograph, we hear Cahun's words 'Why do I unravel the moment I close my eyes?'[6] When she closes her eyes, her self-image disappears and her voice speaks of the split between inside and outside. I read from Cahun's text, here, that the image a woman might construct for herself begins when she can no longer be seen; when the imagination takes over, the image is created or voiced.

The *tableaux vivants* in the film connect Cahun's text and photographs, which often express the same idea, though in a different medium. Through this connection, points of convergence in Cahun's œuvre become apparent. In many examples, such as the masked image mentioned above, a space is opened up between the *tableau vivant* and the related text, that allows us to interpret both the text and the photograph further. This montaging of text and photographs from the same author (albeit with Moore's contribution) combines research into Cahun's œuvre with a creative interpretation of it through cinematic language.

Magic Mirror encompasses the earlier part of Cahun and Moore's life, which was spent in Paris. The photographs from this period are mostly self-portraits shot indoors, including some of Cahun's best-known photographs. A couple of the restaged images in the film show Cahun and Moore standing separately but positioned in the exact same space, in front of a mirror looking back at the camera and at their own reflection. This reveals an intersubjectivity that underscores much of my own practice, as well as that of Cahun and Moore. Cahun moves through the mirror to inhabit the space behind it with Moore, a Surrealist trope that also figures in an early film of mine, *Cast* (2000).[7] Many of the *tableaux vivants* add a mirror or reflective water that either is not present or is suggested only in the original, thus making more explicit an interconnectivity that can cut through time.

The Cartesian examination of consciousness, where we are both subject and object of our body, underlies much of the writing in *Aveux non avenus*. In *Magic Mirror*, the photographic and drawn images of body parts are taken from the photogravures in Cahun's book.[8] I recreate these images as two-dimensional animation and accompany them with early fairground music and voices speaking from Cahun's writing. The film explores magical effects,

Figure 14.1 Cahun and Moore in the mirror, film still, *Magic Mirror* (Sarah Pucill, 2013).

utilising the Bolex 16 mm camera technique of duplication, where one half of the frame is exposed, the film is rewound and the other half exposed. This process can create the illusion of the same person appearing on both sides of the frame at the same time. It is employed in two key scenes where the performer splits between left and right of the frame, both of which restage photographs that mimic Cahun's duplication technique in her works *Que me veux-tu? (auto-portrait double)* (1928)[9] and *Auto-portrait as Elle in Barbe Bleue* (c. 1929). In my *tableau vivant* of *Que me veux-tu?*, two identical bald heads face and look at each other, and in my *tableau vivant* of Cahun performing Elle in *Barbe Bleue*,[10] the reimagined figure has two upper torsos that split apart as she bends to the right and again to the left.

A later scene in the film explores Cahun's rewriting of the Narcissus myth from a female perspective. Cahun's text casts a positive light on the relationship between Narcissus and the artist figure, as the vision Narcissus sees

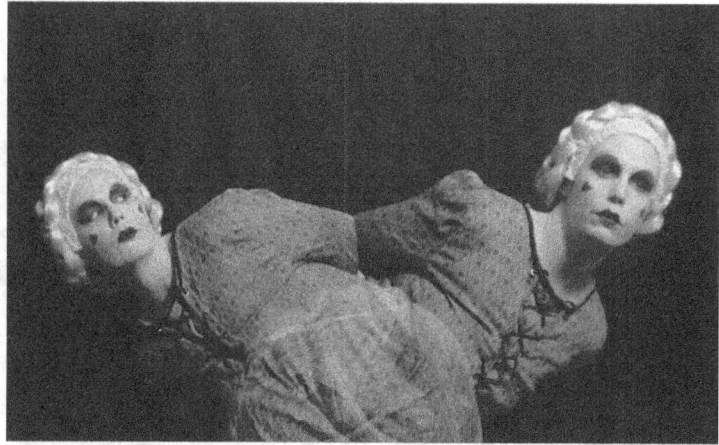

Figure 14.2 Bluebeard's wife, film still, *Magic Mirror* (Sarah Pucill, 2013).

reflected in the water is a vision of a better world. A voice (Helen MacGregor) reads from *Aveux non avenus*:

> Our mirrors are almost perfect. We still suffer from their vertical position. The beautiful child was able to draw the infinite from his reflection while we remain, always the same, unable to go further. But what makes Narcissus despair is not being able to drink himself . . . He sees enough of his ideal to be disgusted by the rest of the world.[11]

If *Magic Mirror* is inspired by Cahun's and Moore's earlier life, *Confessions to the Mirror* takes its title and spoken text from Cahun's posthumously-published memoir *Confidences au miroir*, written after the war and shortly before her death. The text for the film was selected for its connection to the photographs, and to cover the salient events in Cahun's life that appear in the memoir: narratives from her childhood, Cahun and Moore's resistance during the Nazi occupation and imprisonment on the island of Jersey, and post-war reflections on the loss of family and friends. In many *tableaux vivants* restaged photographs are collaged with the text, whilst in others the text functions as a starting point for the images.

Ágnes Pethő's writing on *tableaux vivants* in film as 'the most debated intermedial image type'[12] is useful to elucidate how the reimagined photographs create a tension between media, where uncertainty and indeterminacy are brought to the fore. Pethő describes the importance of a *tableau vivant* as figuring a complex intermedial relation derived from the memory of the painting that is represented in film.[13] In *Magic Mirror* and *Confessions to the Mirror*, the 'ghost' of the original photograph overlays the re-enactment performed in film. It is this ghost image that creates a sense of undecipherability

Figure 14.3 Narcissus, film still, *Confessions to the Mirror* (Sarah Pucill, 2016).

between the earlier black and white photograph and its mimicry as a filmed performance held still. By directly incorporating Cahun's text into the film and referencing the photographs, the film co-joins different time periods, art forms and authors. The referenced image is endowed with sound, the original performer becomes a surrogate, the black and white becomes colour and the still image moves. The reworking of photographs in film undoes certainties that might be fictions, such as the linearity of time, or the separation between self and author, or between media and material. The film becomes a vessel to create a dialogue between Cahun's work and my own.

What is it to inhabit another person, transforming a small black and white photograph into a performance that breathes life into the work, be it through feathers waving or the performer breathing? There is something in the making material from the immaterial. Obscured detail in the small black and white photographs needs to be imagined in order to be materialised. The materiality of being present emerges in the inhabitation of pose as a performance that restages what is seen in the photograph. In the act of fabricating sets, props and costumes, the making material excites the imagination and the lived moment breathes life into the recalled photograph. The gesture of inhabiting the physical body of Cahun (and sometimes Moore) is a summoning of that which was material for the couple. Playing roles that shift between performer and filmmaker, I ventriloquise Cahun's voice and image. This role-play satisfies a fantasy to cross time, to lose oneself in the inhabitation of another, and to embrace an artist who was struggling with issues that strongly resonate in our contemporary context: nationalism, far-right politics, patriarchy, racism, homophobia. It speaks to those artists who continue to make work from the margins. But maybe, most importantly, the work I have done in *Magic Mirror* and *Confessions to the Mirror* extends what Cahun was doing. My filmic adaptations resituate the original photographs by adding movement, colour and sound. Lines taken from Cahun's writing are put in dialogue with her visual work, acquiring a new meaning within the context of my own filmmaking. The films navigate a space between that which is interpreted and that which is recreated. They embody a dialogue between artists of different times: Cahun speaks to me through her writing and photographs, and in turn I respond in cinematic language. Authorship and time periods both conjoin and separate.

Notes

1. Claude Cahun performed as Le Diable, Le Monsieur and Bluebeard's Wife in the avant-garde theatre company 'Le Plateau', directed by Albert Birot between 1930 and 1939. See Louise Downie (ed.), *Don't Kiss Me: The Art of Claude Cahun and Marcel Moore* (London: Tate, Hersey Heritage Trust, 2006).
2. Tirza T. Latimer, '"Le Masque verbal": Le travestisme textuel de Claude Cahun', in *Claude Cahun* (Paris: Jeu de Paumes, 2011), p. 81.
3. The collaborators working on the film, including the performers.
4. Joan Riviere, 'On womanliness as masquerade', *International Journal of Psychoanalysis*, 9 (1929), pp. 303–13 (p. 306).
5. Jennifer L. Shaw, *Exist Otherwise: The Life and Works of Claude Cahun* (London: Reaktion Books, 2018), p. 78.
6. Translated by Rachel Gomme from Claude Cahun, *Aveux non avenus* (1930), in *Claude Cahun Écrits*, ed. by François Leperlier (Paris: Jean Michel Place, 2002).
7. *Cast* (2000) incorporates a very similar scene of a lesbian passing through a mirror that smashes and was inspired by the aforementioned photographs of Cahun and Moore.
8. Each chapter in *Aveux non avenus* begins with a photogravure designed by Cahun but drawn by Moore. In the film, these collages are reconstructed from imitative photographic photomontage. The image is simplified, but each is rephotographed, printed as a photomontage and then animated.
9. The title translates as 'What do you want from me?'
10. Cahun performed as Bluebeard's wife (Elle) in the experimental theatre company 'Le Plateau', directed by Pierre Albert-Birot.
11. Translated by Rachel Gomme from Cahun, *Aveux non avenus*, in *Claude Cahun Écrits*.
12. Ágnes Pethő, *Cinema and Intermediality: The Passion for the In-Between* (Newcastle: Cambridge Scholars, 2011), p. 44.
13. Pethő, *Cinema and Intermediality*, p. 44.

Index

Adamson, Natalie, 106
Akerman, Chantal, 62–5
   La Captive, 62–3
Althusser, Louis, 107, 109
Amalric, Mathieu, 158
Antonioni, Michelangelo, 24–34
   Lo Sguardo di Michelangelo, 25–32, 33–4
Aristotle, 107
Arnheim, Rudolf, 32
Artaud, Antonin, 110
Art and Artists, 88, 95; *see also* Nicolson, Annabel
art history, 73, 75, 83
art schools, 74, 89, 93; *see also* Le Grice, Malcolm
Artforum, 74, 77
Ascott, Roy, 93
Askevold, David, 96
Astaire, Fred, 170
Aumont, Jacques, 150, 156

Bacon, Francis, 53, 61–2; *see also* blur
Badiou, Alain, 150, 155, 162
Baroque art, 105–6, 151–5, 157–62
Barthes, Roland, 41, 46
   'The Third Meaning', 137–8
Bataille, Georges, 145–6
Batchen, Geoffrey, 41
Baudelaire, Charles, 131
Bauhaus, 108
Bausch, Pina, 179
Bazin, André, 2, 46, 150, 155
Bellour, Raymond, 1, 2, 143, 150
Bergman, Ingmar, 59
   Persona, 59
Bergman, Ingrid, 30
Betts, Ernest, 81
Blakeston, Oswell, 75, 76, 81–2; *see also* POOL Group
blur, 52–3, 54–5, 59–60

Böcklin, Arnold, 157
Bois, Yve-Alain, 146
Bond, Ralph, 82
Bonitzer, Pascal, 150
Bonnefoy, Yves, 161–2
Börlin, Jean, 83
Borromini, Francesco, 158
Boulez, Pierre, 176
Brakhage, Stan, 105, 108, 110–11, 114–15
Bresson, Robert, 158
Breton, Pascale, 151–7
   and Georges de La Tour, 155
   Illumination, 151–2
   and Marcel Proust, 153
   Suite armoricaine, 151–7
Brooks, Rosetta, 98
Bruhn, Jørgen, 151
Bruno, Giuliana, 150, 152
Bryher (Annie Winifred Ellerman), 81
Buñuel, Luis, 31
Burden, Chris, 14
Bürger, Peter, 75

Cahiers du cinéma, 145
Cahun, Claude, 7, 195–201
Canudo, Ricciotto, 2, 75, 80
Caravaggio, 56, 151, 158–9, 162
   Sacrifice of Isaac, 158
Cassavetes, John, 31
Castaing-Taylor, Lucien, 60
Cavell, Stanley, 56–9
Cendrars, Blaise, 80
Ceylan, Nuri Bilge, 49
Champaigne, Philippe de, 159
Charisse, Cyd, 170
chronophotography, 61, 64, 121–2, 132, 193; *see also* Marey, Étienne-Jules
cinema
   and the avant-garde, 5, 54, 73–5, 89–91, 107, 108, 115–16

and dance, 6, 167–75
and digital technology, 12, 38–9, 61
and literature, 81–3, 151, 153
and painting, 5, 52–9, 63–4, 66–7, 74, 152, 153, 154–7, 158–60, 162
and performance, 4, 11–22, 92–3, 176–8, 182–4, 194–201
and photography, 6, 13, 38–9, 44–9, 52, 194–201
and sculpture, 23–34, 99; *see also* Michelangelo
origins of, 13, 16, 121–33
silent era, 54, 58–9, 63
Cléder, Jean, 150
Close Up, 75–6; *see also* POOL Group
Cocteau, Jean, 27, 31–2
conceptual art, 90–1, 94, 95, 98, 100–1
Conrad, Tony, 137
Coplans, John, 77; *see also* Artforum
Cork, Richard, 90, 98, 99
Cunningham, Merce, 179
Curtis, David, 73

Dada, 74, 79, 80, 82
Dalle Vacche, Angela, 150
Degas, Edgar, 126
Deleuze, Gilles, 55
  The Logic of Sensation, 61–2; *see also* Bacon, Francis
Demenÿ, Georges, 64, 132–3; *see also* chronophotography
Descartes, René, 110
Desnos, Robert, 79
Desormière, Roger, 83
Dibbets, Jan, 88, 90
Dickson, William, 18
Documents, 145
Donald, James, 76, 79
Dréville, Valérie, 152
Dubois, Philippe, 137
Duchamp, Marcel, 2
Dulac, Germaine, 1–2, 53
Dusinberre, Deke, 75–6
Dye, David, 90, 91, 97–101
  Confine, 97
  exhibits at *Filmaktion*, 100
  Unsigning for Eight Projectors, 97

Eckersall, Peter, 12
Eggeling, Viking, 2
Eisenstein, Sergei, 31, 137

Epstein, Jean, 2, 52–3, 57
  Coeur fidèle, 57–9
expanded cinema, 12, 75
Ezenfils, Victor, 158, 159

Faraday, Michael, 125–7
  and origins of cinema, 126
Faure, Jacques-Élie, 80
Field, Simon, 99
Film Culture, 105
film studies, 73–84
  and literary criticism, 81, 82–3
Fischinger, Oskar, 74
Fluxus, 80
Fondane, Benjamin, 80
Forcellino, Antonio, 27
Foster, Stephen, 79
Framework, 74, 75
Frampton, Hollis, 77
Fried, Michael, 55–7
Friedberg, Anne, 76
Freud, Sigmund, 26
Futurism, 80

Gance, Abel, 54
Garrity, Jane, 82
Gaudreault, André, 1
Gell, Alfred, 131
Gibson, James, 92
Gidal, Peter, 73, 89, 98
Gilman, Claire, 78
Gjelsvik, Anne, 151
Godard, Jean-Luc, 152
  Le Mépris, 30
  Sauve qui peut (la vie), 60–1
Goddard, Linda, 106
Goll, Yvan, 80
Gordon, Douglas
  Zidane, a Portrait of the 21st Century, 65–6
Gowing, Lawrence, 111–13
Goya, Francisco, 65
Graham, Dan, 88–9, 90, 92–6
  2 Consciousness Projections, 93
  Two Correlated Rotations, 92, 94, 96
Grandrieux, Philippe, 60
Grant, Dwinell, 74
Green, Eugène, 157–62
  Le Fils de Joseph, 158–61
Greenberg, Clement, 94
Griffiths, Sophy, 176
Gross, Kenneth, 34
Guggenheim, Solomon R., 75
Guillem, Sylvie, 174

Hall, David
60 TV Sets, 99
haptic image, 3–4, 29, 30–1, 56, 129
Harrison, Charles, 90, 94, 95
H.D. (Hilda Doolittle), 81
Hedges, Inez, 79
Heidegger, Martin, 181–2
Hein, Birgit, 73
heliography, 123–4
Herder, Johann Gottfried, 29
Herring, Robert, 81, 82; *see also* POOL Group
Higgins, Dick, 107
Hildebrand, Adolf von, 29
Hilliard, John, 88, 89, 90, 96–7, 98
Ten Runs Past a Fixed Point, 96
Höch, Hannah, 82

Iimura, Takahiko, 15
impure cinema, 2, 150–51
installation, 5, 91, 97, 98–100, 132–3, 138, 140, 142–4, 183
Institute of Contemporary Arts (ICA), 88, 90, 97, 99, 100
intermediality
 and interdisciplinarity, 83–4
 definitions of, 2–4, 80, 107
 origins of, 11, 121–33
Italian cinema, 78

Jacobs, Ken, 95
Jacobs, Steven, 150
Jenkins, Henry, 1
Jerslev, Anne, 2, 151

Kardia, Peter, 93
Kar-Wai, Wong, 136
Kiarostami, Abbas, 49
Kott, Alexander, 40
Test, 40, 42, 43, 46
Kracauer, Siegfried, 44, 53, 78
Kraszna-Krausz, Andor, 82
Krauss, Rosalind, 41, 107, 146
Krauss, Sigi, 98
Kren, Kurt, 14, 15, 137
Kubelka, Peter, 137
Kuenzli, Rudolf, 79
Kühne, Wilhelm, 22

La Tour, Georges de, 155–60
Christ with Saint Joseph in the Carpenter's Shop, 158–60
The Newborn Child, 155

Laing, R. D., 95
Langoët, Kaou, 152
Latham, John 94, 98
Latour, Bruno, 43, 47
Lawder, Standish, 73–4, 75, 78–9, 83
The Cubist Cinema, 74
Le Grice, Malcolm, 74, 83, 89, 93, 95, 100; *see also* art schools
Le Prince, Louis, 18
Lee, S. Charles, 15
Leenhart, Roger, 129
Léger, Fernand, 2, 79–80
Lettrist cinema, 14
Levinas, Emmanuel, 181, 183
L'Herbier, Marcel, 54–5, 57–8
El Dorado, 54–5
Lippard, Lucy, 94
Lisson Gallery, 90, 92, 96, 99, 100
London Film-makers' Co-operative, 89–91
Long, Richard, 90, 96
Löwensohn, Elina, 152
Lumière, Auguste and Louis, 16, 19, 122–3, 139
Lye, Len, 81
Lynch, David, 61
Lost Highway, 62
Lyotard, Jean-François, 49

McCabe, Susan, 82, 83
McCall, Anthony, 98
Machuel, Laurent, 182
Macpherson, Kenneth, 81, 82; *see also* POOL Group
Mallarmé, Stéphane, 176
Malraux, André, 32
Man Ray, 2, 76, 77, 79
Mannoni, Laurent, 122
Manovich, Lev, 45
Manvell, Roger, 74
Mao, Douglas, 76
Marcus, Laura, 76
Marey, Étienne-Jules, 22, 61, 121–2, 189; *see also* origins of cinema
Marion, Philippe, 1
Marker, Chris, 136
Marx, Karl, 109
The Matrix (Lana and Lilly Wachowski), 192
Mazzocchi, Domenico, 160
Medalla, David, 98
melodrama, 42–3, 55, 57–8
Metamorphoses (Ovid), 33
Metz, Christian, 137

Metzger, Gustav, 98
Michelangelo, 24–32
 in films of Antonioni, 25–32
 Moses, 24–6, 27, 28–34
 The Titan (Oertel), 24, 27
Michelis, Christian, 73
Michelson, Annette, 77–8
Miggitsch, Susanne, 140–3, 144–5
Minnelli, Vincente, 170–1
Missiroli, Roberto, 28
Moholy-Nagy, László, 2, 23, 27, 74, 77
Mroué, Rabih, 20–2
Mulvey, Laura, 14–15, 56
Musaoglu, Elchin, 38
 Nabat, 40, 42–3, 46
Muybridge, Eadweard, 13, 16–17, 18, 20, 137, 185–6

Nagib, Lúcia, 2, 151
Nicolson, Annabel, 5, 88–90, 91–5, 96–7, 101
 'Artist as Filmmaker', 88–9, 101
 Precarious Vision, 92–93
 Slides, 89, 94
Niépce, Nicéphore, 123–4
Norstein, Yuri, 186

October, 77–9
Oertel, Curt, 24, 27; *see also* Michelangelo

painting, 40, 41, 48, 62, 90
 in film, 52–9, 111–16, 152–62
Pajot, Louis-Léon, 122
Panofsky, Erwin, 153
Paravel, Véréna, 60
Parreno, Philippe
 Zidane, a Portrait of the 21st Century, 65–6
Patinir, Joachim, 157
Pethő, Ágnes, 2, 3, 4, 151, 199
photogénie, 52–3; *see also* Epstein, Jean
photography, 32–3, 46–7
 origins of, 123
 and painting, 40–1, 52, 60; *see also* cinema *and* heliography
Photoshop, 54, 83
Picabia, Francis, 75, 77, 83
Picasso, Pablo, 81
Pierce, Leighton, 60
Plateau, Joseph, 121
Pleynet, Marcelin, 107–9
Pollock, Griselda, 115
Ponti, Carlo, 124–5
 Megaletoscopio, 6, 124

POOL Group, 81–2
Poussin, Nicolas, 153–4, 156, 162
Proust, Marcel, 63, 151, 153, 156
Pucill, Sarah
 Confessions to the Mirror, 196, 199, 201
 Magic Mirror, 195, 197, 199, 201
Pygmalion, 33–4

Quay, Stephen and Timothy, 186

Raban, William, 89, 96, 100
Racan, Honorat de Bueil de, 160
Rancière, Jacques, 150
Régnier, Natacha, 158
Renaissance art, 152, 154, 162
Renan, Sheldon, 73
Reynaud, Émile, 128–32
 animation, 128
Richardson, Dorothy, 82; *see also* POOL Group
Richter, Hans, 2, 60, 74
Riefenstahl, Leni, 27
Roberts, Adam
 blue/yellow, 169, 173, 174
 Hands, 168–70, 172
 Pieces of the Quiet Dance, 173, 174
Rocamora, Isabel
 Body of War, 178, 179, 181, 183
 Faith, 178, 179, 180, 181–3
 Fragmented Transparencies, 176
 Residual, 178
Rodowick, D. N., 1
Rondepierre, Eric, 140–1
Rongione, Fabrizio, 158
Rose, Barbara, 77
Rotha, Paul, 74
Ruttmann, Walter, 2
 Berlin, Symphony of a Great City, 77

Satie, Erik, 83
Schimmel, Paul, 12
Sedgwick, Edie, 60
Sengmüller, Gebhard, 138–40
 Slide Movie, 139
Serra, Richard, 77
Seymour, Anne, 90
Sharits, Paul, 104–16
 and Johannes Vermeer, 105, 111–16
 'Notes on Films', 105, 107, 110
 N:O:T:H:I:N:G, 105–8, 110–16
silent era; *see* cinema
Sinden, Tony
 60 TV Sets, 99

Sissako, Abderrahmane, 38, 45;
    Timbuktu, 38, 39–40, 43, 44
Skladanowsky, Max and Emil, 16–20
Smithson, Robert, 14
Snow, Michael, 77
    Wavelength, 136
Societas Raffaello Sanzio, 180
Sokurov, Alexander, 49
Sontag, Susan, 171
Soviet cinema, 77–8
Springer, Anton, 32
Staël, Nicolas de, 66
Stampfer, Simon, 121
    Toy Merry-Go-Round with Four Horsemen, 130
Sternberg, Josef von, 54
stop-motion, 105, 140, 186
Streitberger, Alexander, 38
stroboscope, 121–2
structural film, 75, 96–7
Studio International, 74
Surrealism, 79, 194
Švankmajer, Jan, 186
Symbolism, 80

Tarsia, Andrea, 96, 97
Taylor, Richard, 78
Truffaut, François, 136
Tscherkassky, Peter, 138–40
    Motion Picture, 139
Tsivian, Yuri, 78
Turvey, Malcolm, 78

Ulmann, Sylvie Pierre, 145, 146

Valenzeula, Camila, 176
Van Gelder, Hilde, 38
Vasari, Giorgio, 27
Vasof, Anna
    Domino, 187
    Machine, 189
    Non-stop Stop-motion, 185–92
Velázquez, Diego, 65
Vermeer, Johannes, 63–4, 105, 110, 112–13
    Lady Standing at the Virginals, 111, 113–14;
    see also Sharits, Paul
Vertov, Dziga, 77, 78
    Man with a Movie Camera, 136; *see also*
    Soviet cinema
Viennese Aktionists, 14
Virilio, Paul, 178

Walkowitz, Rebecca, 76
Wall, Jeff, 180
Warburg, Aby, 123, 156
Warhol, Andy, 14, 59, 136
    Poor Little Rich Girl, 59–60
Welsby, Chris, 89, 96
Whiteread, Rachel, 168
Wiener, Norbert, 93
Wiest, Rolf, 73
Wollen, Peter, 77, 94
Woolf, Virginia, 81

Zhangke, Jia, 49

EU representative:
Easy Access System Europe
Mustamäe tee 50, 10621 Tallinn, Estonia
Gpsr.requests@easproject.com

www.ingramcontent.com/pod-product-compliance
Lightning Source LLC
Chambersburg PA
CBHW071841230426
43671CB00012B/2030